How Consumer Culture
Controls Our Kids

How Consumer Culture Controls Our Kids

Cashing in on Conformity

Jennifer Hill

Childhood in America
Sharna Olfman, Series Editor

 PRAEGER ™

An Imprint of ABC-CLIO, LLC
Santa Barbara, California • Denver, Colorado

Library of Congress Cataloging-in-Publication Data

Hill, Jennifer Ann, author.
   How consumer culture controls our kids : cashing in on conformity / Jennifer Hill.
      pages cm.—(Childhood in america)
   Includes bibliographical references and index.
      ISBN 978-1-4408-3482-0 (alk. paper)—ISBN 978-1-4408-3483-7 (ebook)   1. Child consumers—United States.   2. Consumption (Economics)—Social aspects—United States.   3. Child development—United States.   I. Title.
      HF5415.332.C45H55 2016
      306.3083′0973—dc23   2015024628

ISBN: 978-1-4408-3482-0
EISBN: 978-1-4408-3483-7

20 19 18 17 16   2 3 4 5

This book is also available on the World Wide Web as an eBook.
Visit www.abc-clio.com for details.

Praeger
An Imprint of ABC-CLIO, LLC

ABC-CLIO, LLC
130 Cremona Drive, P.O. Box 1911
Santa Barbara, California 93116-1911

This book is printed on acid-free paper ∞

Manufactured in the United States of America

Contents

Series Foreword

The rich diversity of cultures created by humankind is a testament to our ability to develop and adapt in diverse ways. But no matter how varied different cultures may be, children are not endlessly malleable; they all share basic psychological and physical needs that must be met to ensure healthy development. The "Childhood in America" series examines the extent to which U.S. culture meets children's irreducible needs. Without question, many children growing up in the United States lead privileged lives. They have been spared the ravages of war, poverty, malnourishment, sexism, and racism. However, despite our nation's resources, not all children share these privileges. Additionally, values that are central to U.S. culture, such as self-reliance, individualism, privacy of family life, and consumerism, have created a climate in which parenting has become intolerably labor intensive, and children are being taxed beyond their capacity for healthy adaptation. Record levels of psychiatric disturbance, violence, poverty, apathy, and despair among our children speak to our current cultural crisis.

Although our elected officials profess their commitment to "family values," policies that support family life are woefully lacking and inferior to those in other industrialized nations. U.S. families are burdened by inadequate parental leave, a health care system that does not provide universal coverage for children, a minimum wage that is not a living wage, "welfare to work" policies that require parents to leave their children for long stretches of time, unregulated and inadequately subsidized daycare, an unregulated entertainment industry that exposes children to sex and violence, and an exhausted public education system that delivers inferior education to poor children and frequently ignores individual differences in learning styles and profiles of intelligence. As a result, many families are taxed to the breaking point. In addition, our fascination with technological innovation is creating a family lifestyle that is dominated by screen rather than human interaction.

The "Childhood in America" series seeks out leading childhood experts from across the disciplines to promote dialogue, research, and understanding regarding how best to raise and educate psychologically healthy children to ensure that they will acquire the wisdom, heart, and courage needed to make choices for the betterment of society.

Sharna Olfman, PhD, Series Editor

1

Culture Jamming and Other Ventures

[The] average kid only spends 30 minutes a day outside, an amount that shrinks yearly. In this brave new world of Facebook and YouTube, Twitter and Google, iPod and Wii, kids are tuned into technology, and kindergartners start school with 5,000 hours of TV under their belts. Typical tweens put in a 40-hour week—a virtual full-time job—watching screens: TV, laptop, cell phone, and so on. They can name dozens of corporate logos and celebrities on site. . . . But they cannot name three animals that live in their neighborhood, or three plants.[1]

—M. Weilbacher

My interest in consumerism began, unexpectedly, in 1998. I was sitting with my husband sifting through his collection of old magazines, but not just ordinary magazines. They were called *Adbusters: Journal for the Mental Environment*. I could not put them down as I flipped through the pages and saw one advertisement parody after another, mocking and critiquing how corporations play with our emotions to get us to buy. And I was curious about the meaning of the "mental environment." As a psychology student, I was well aware of the workings of the subconscious and conscious thought processes but had not really considered that, collectively, our mind-set was up for grabs to the highest corporate bidder. *Adbusters* held the belief that corporations were dominating the airwaves, print news, and all forms of digital communication as a means of getting across a particular message; namely, material satisfaction is equated with happiness. According to its founder, Kalle Lasn, the magazine was devoted to a deconstruction of consumer culture in order to expose its hypocrisy, falsities, and deceit. In particular, one advertisement labeled "Pucci," in which a dog's head was attached to a human body in an expensive-looking suit, really grabbed me. The line accompanying the visual said: "Tight Collars, Short Leashes." I had not given a lot of thought to the power that brand names held over all of us, playing on our desires to be accepted and seen as status holders.

There were many other spoof ads, including a series designed to shock and question what was really behind the Calvin Klein motif, for example. *Adbusters* had a particular dislike for the ways in which young girls and women are made to believe their bodies are inadequate unless they purchase a particular product. The Calvin Klein Corporation was very good at manipulating women's emotions through advertisements that exhibited strong sexual overtones. Even worse, Klein was sexualizing young girls to the point that his advertisements had the look of child pornography and were being scrutinized by the Justice Department for that reason.[2] *Adbusters*'s counter charge, among other things, was to change Calvin Klein to "Calvin Swine" with an image of a scantily clad young girl wearing her Calvin Kline underwear while throwing up in the toilet. The advertising campaign by R. J. Reynolds to sell cigarettes to young people by using a cartoon figure whose name was "Joe Camel" was extremely successful and one that *Adbusters* also challenged. They depicted the Joe Camel figure in a hospital gown with an IV attachment and called it "Joe Chemo." I was immediately drawn to and motivated to join Lasn's "culture jam," the effort to resist mainstream consumer culture dominated by powerful corporations whose sole motive was to further enhance their profit margin. Lasn defined his manifesto as follows:

We call ourselves culture jammers. We're a loose global network of media activists who see ourselves as the advanced shock troops of the most significant social movement of the next 20 years. Our aim is to topple existing power structure and forge major adjustments to the way we will live in the 21st century. . . . Above all, [culture jamming] will change the way we interact with the mass media and the way in which meaning is produced in our society.[3]

Thus began my 15-year examination of how consumer culture impacts us *all*. Why do we buy and what does it fulfill? Are we in control of our own decisions, or do advertisers control us so we will believe their pitch? And what of children—do family and community protect them from the sway of advertisements? Do children have an innate desire to acquire commodities as consumer culture would have us believe? When my nephew was three years old, he believed that a mouse was a computer appendage long before he recognized it to be an animal. Somehow, his world, even at such a young age, was immersed in technology, the bridge to consumption of a kind we have never before seen. Indeed, the exponential rise of technology use is inextricably linked to life as a consumer. Technology has made advertising, shopping, and social networking that much easier, to the extent that our kids cannot imagine life without it. Like it or not, they are hooked. Is technology really the problem, or is it being blamed the way television once was for causing so many evils in the world? And since technology appears to be with us to stay, is there any hope that rebellion is possible, that culture jamming could work? Is there a chance that our kids would choose to *not* conform and forge a path of resistance?

* * *

I wanted to immerse myself in the *Adbusters* culture by choosing to complete my master's degree placement at the magazine's headquarters in Vancouver. The building was full of images about corporate culture to remind us about and shock us into seeing the true nature of advertising—a campaign to keep us endlessly running a treadmill of consumption. For example, the staff displayed a life-size American flag in which the 50 stars were replaced with corporate logos. *Adbusters* also promoted a "Buy Nothing Day," a 24-hour moratorium on shopping annually, in part to help us realize how hooked we really are into a buy-and-consume modality. It was surprisingly harder to implement than it sounds. I slowly started to realize how convincing corporate culture had been. I had never considered that I was being duped or taken in. I felt immune to all of that, priding myself on being somewhat of a rebel. It was all so smooth—advertising and corporate messaging—so smooth that most of us have no idea what is influencing our behavior. It was also mind-numbing to be surrounded by commercial messaging from morning to night with no obvious objection. Having grown up within a family that was immersed in the corporate world, I wondered if some of this might have been an exaggeration, that North Americans were not that naïve. After all, government seemed to be reasonably in charge or was it? Lasn boldly professed that America was no longer a country but had become one big whopping brand. I had to delve into this more deeply and find out for myself the extent to which culture jamming was a worthwhile investment and venture.

It was during my master's degree studies in 2002 that I decided to interview elementary school teachers to get their viewpoint on how consumer culture was impacting children.[4] The teachers all had at least 10 years of experience in schools with children between kindergarten and grade six. They all relayed how dramatically childhood seemed to have shifted, that for example, kids had become self-conscious about their appearance in a way they had never seen before. It was not unusual to see a five-year-old coming to school dressed provocatively or for the kids to all have logos on their backpacks, lunch boxes, shoes, and articles of clothing. Furthermore, all the teachers expressed consternation over a reduction in children's ability to learn basic academic skills, particularly in the ability to work with instruction, to be taught. As one of the teachers put it, "They don't know how to think." She attributed this, in part, to children's obsession with technology, whether it was the television, the computer, video games, and so on. This same teacher concluded that "someone else is doing the thinking for them and indirectly telling them what to buy, what to wear, what toys to play with." The teachers also felt that because children are constantly stimulated with fast-moving visual images and media exposure, their capacity to concentrate in the classroom had diminished. They noticed that basic social skills such as regard for others, including peers and teachers, were seen to be in decline. Specifically, "the ability to get along and socialize has deteriorated over time. I saw a huge inability to get along and play that I found rather frightening." Additionally, all of these teachers were consistently emphatic that both verbal and physical aggression among boys and girls was on the rise as a direct result of consumerism. They felt that the benchmark to what is acceptable in children's minds, about what they think is the norm, had gone down and that they were imitating behavior seen on television and in movies. For example, one of the teachers, who had 30 years of experience, noted that there was a significant change among girls, particularly in the area of sexual behavior. She said, "I see six- and seven-year-olds strutting physically, showing off their clothes, wearing little halter tops and physically trying to present themselves as adult women." There was a consensus that corporations were trying to get kids to grow up fast so as to partake in a full-fledged consumer lifestyle. And, the teachers suggested that some of the children's psychological disorders had a direct link to consumer culture; for example, the prevalence of Ritalin had increased dramatically, mainly to treat attention-deficit disorder (ADD) and was really being prescribed, in their opinion, to treat a societal sickness. They noted that children were constantly stimulated with fast-moving visual images through media exposure and that the capacity to concentrate was linked directly to this phenomenon. "They are glued to these media. They're being trained to respond to these visual flashes. My impression is that the kids . . . want to be entertained, visually and auditorily."

Due to the fact that children assume a passive role while engaging in television watching, two of the teachers attributed this phenomenon to a decrease in play, outdoor activities, and social interaction. One of the teachers also felt that children had become passive listeners as a result of television: "Their brains do not have the conditioning to be reflective or critical listeners." The teachers added that television suppresses children's natural impulses in the area of play. Children appeared to be struggling with cooperative play, even requiring being taught how to play, a form of behavior that is generally agreed to be innate in children. The teachers also felt that the forces of consumerism had molded children's play as corporations dictate, depending on the latest marketing campaign.

*   *   *

After I completed the interviews, I began to ponder seriously the totality of the effects of consumer culture on child development and felt that my work had only just begun. When I decided to pursue a PhD in 2007, I felt strongly that the only area that interested me and held my concern would be a further pursuit of the topic of consumer culture and children. I was not totally clear about what type of research to engage in, but I knew that I wanted to include children in the study, I wanted to hear directly from them what they felt were the effects of consumerism on themselves and their peers. Did they understand the power of corporate culture and its immediate impact on the self? Were they able to articulate the intricacies of life as a consumer, the highs and the lows? After careful deliberation, we (my dissertation advisor and I) decided that the best course of action would be to interview young people, those who were 18 or 19 years old, and ask them to reflect on their childhoods. The result was a study conducted in 2012 as part of my PhD dissertation and that forms the basis of this book. Throughout Chapter Seven, I will cite the participants of the 2012 study as a means of connecting the results with the literature and theory that best explain how consumer culture controls our kids. Many of the questions in the interview guide dealt with the phenomenon of conformity, how corporations benefit when our kids conform to corporate standards of health, beauty, intelligence, and what it means to be popular and cool.

A BRIEF REVIEW OF THE LITERATURE

The data over the past 25 years have shown and continue to show, that enhancing consumerism in children, tweens and teens causes harm.[5]
—Juli Kramer

After having read these words, I wanted to pursue empirical literature on the many facets of consumer culture and children.[6] During the period of my dissertation research, the literature I reviewed confirmed that consumer culture dominates almost every aspect of life whether it is honoring special occasions through gift-giving or simply the way shopping has become a form of entertainment, as *the* favored pastime. And in the past few decades, in particular, consumerism has more and more invaded the lives of children like no other time in history.[7] Indeed, consumer research on children conducted from the 1990s onward strongly suggests that they are being harmed by corporations, especially in the United States and Canada, where the intensity of consumerism is high. Children have come to be regarded as a lucrative market for corporate commodities and are thus targeted in every imaginable way to ensure a steady stream of profit continues. The mechanism by which corporations access youth is through all forms of media, including television, computers, phones, DVDs, iPods, movies, magazines, and advertising of all kinds. I also confirmed through evidence supplied by many scholars that consumerism is generally harmful to both the psychological *and* physical health of children.[8] Additionally, decades of research on the negative impact of television and other forms of media raised concerns for children's overall well-being.[9]

The process of consuming has become increasingly significant in understanding how the lives of youth are culturally, psychologically, and socially constructed. Their everyday life is dominated by the ubiquitous and ephemeral nature of consumerism to the degree that children in the West have never known differently. Wherever children go— whether it be at home, at a friend's, at school, at church, at the mall, or on the school bus—consumer culture has an "answer" to every challenging problem and is a tempting escape from "mundane" everyday existence. It promises an endless array of stimulating activities and tempting goods to please whatever it is that one may desire. There are no limits, no hope of satiation. Additionally, marketers manufacture or generate desires that are not necessarily conceived of by any of us, that is, until repetitive messaging convinces us otherwise. Perhaps the most insidious aspect of consumer culture is the creation of these manufactured or false wants. Why? Because it fuels an unfulfilled desire to endlessly crave as though caught in Dante's Inferno for an eternity. With no internal compass to guide their desires, children begin to doubt themselves, to feel a loss of emotional security, to distrust their own feelings and, eventually, to seek the dangling carrots.[10]

Between 1990 and 1998, advertising to children increased dramatically—by a factor of 20.[11] It is not surprising then that young people's lives are enmeshed with a buy-and-consume modality and that they appear to be losing the capacity for authentic forms of spontaneity or creativity.[12] So much of children's play is scripted whether it is through toys, books, or videos; as a result, children's imaginations are restricted and perhaps even underutilized. By the time they reach adolescence, children have experienced years of corporate structuring about how to think, act, and even fantasize. Children now seek to define themselves through the acquisition of actual goods, particularly those that are branded.[13] Increasingly, they are exposed to violent and sexually explicit media, sexist programming that marginalizes young girls, and advertisements for junk food, tobacco, and alcohol.[14] In 2004, the American Psychological Association's (APA) *Task Force on Advertising and Children* strongly recommended an advertising ban for children under the age of eight based on years of research.[15] Children between the ages of eight to twelve are only just starting to become aware of the impact of media and its significance.[16] Yet, despite the APA's credibility, corporations continue to remain unencumbered in their advertising pursuits of children. The elephant in the room is annihilated through the power of media to repetitively and relentlessly persuade. Consumer culture is so much the norm that most of us can hardly define it.

Millions of children now integrate consumer culture in their lives as a means of expressing "individuality" when in reality they strive to mimic those who have mastered the "art" of consumerism, including celebrities, pop music stars, their parents, and even some of their peers. Indeed, it appears that rather than pursue their own ambitions, they are locked into repeating and replicating those of their idols, conforming to the very norms they often protest about and claim to be free of.[17] The current decline in children's creativity and the tendency toward cultural conformity may ultimately have profound implications for the survival of forms of democratic processes.[18] And not least of all, youth seem to have developed a blind acceptance of the neoliberal ideology of "free-market" capitalism and the efficacy of consumer culture. In time, it became obvious how lucrative it was for corporations to get us to conform to their standards, that conformity was the key to ensure raging profit.

2012 RESEARCH STUDY—DECONSTRUCTING CONSUMERISM: FROM THE VOICES OF YOUNG PEOPLE

Despite the pervasiveness of consumer culture in the lives of children, there is a paucity of research in this area, especially studies that solicit directly from children about their experiences, past and present. This is both astonishing and confounding, considering that millions of children are being exposed to corporate advertising from the time of birth in what has proven to be the "largest single psychological project ever undertaken by the human race," according to psychologists Allen Kanner and Mary Gomes.[19] And this in spite of the fact that the massive campaign called consumer culture impacts all: rich, poor, black, white, immigrant, or native resident. In particular, do children have a sense that they must conform to the dictates of corporations or do they conform willingly in order to adopt "cool?" Cool is a key element to motivate children to participate in consumer culture and is played upon in a big way by corporate sponsors. It was not known whether young people were aware of the specific forces that were imposed upon them as children to adopt popular consumer norms as a mode of being. I knew it was plausible that having grown up in a consumer-oriented society from birth, that by the time they are 18 or 19 years old, young people may be incapable of detecting and analyzing the effects of consumerism on either themselves or their peers. They might not have acquired the detachment necessary to make an objective analysis. It was also possible that young people were aware, to some degree, that their lives had been influenced by consumer culture in profound ways and could share insight as to the personal ways (psychologically, culturally, and sociologically) in which they were and are affected. I felt it was important to uncover not only whether children have gained insight into their predicament, but whether or not they developed strategies to offset the negative effects of consumer culture. Understanding how young people experience consumer culture is fundamental to appreciating what it means to be growing up in modernity. A young person's perceived affinity with and strategic targeting by marketers make them a particularly fruitful lens through which to examine the nexus of consumption, conformity/resistance, and individualization.

I was highly motivated by economist Juliet Schor's seminal work in 2004 in which she identified several negative effects that consumer culture imposes on children between the ages of eight and twelve.[20] Schor studied approximately 300 children and their families in the area of media use, consumer values, involvement in consumer culture, physical and psychological well-being, and parental relationships. Her results indicated that there is a *causal* relationship between high consumer involvement and depression, anxiety, low self-esteem, and psychosomatic complaints. Put simply, the more a child is immersed in consumer culture, the greater the possibility of specific and predictable forms of harm. In another study, researchers Moniek Buijzen and Patti Valkenburg[21] used Schor's survey instrument with additional items specific to materialism and found that children who frequently watch television advertisements held stronger materialistic values than peers who watched less often. Overall, they found a direct relationship between advertising exposure and materialism, an indirect relationship between advertising exposure and parent–child conflict, and an indirect relationship between advertising exposure and unhappiness.

Furthermore, psychologists Tim Kasser and Richard Ryan have conducted numerous studies that link consumer culture involvement with the harmful effects of overvaluing materialism.[22]

Through the research it became possible to hear about and understand young people's perceptions, ideas, impressions, and possible concerns regarding their childhood as it relates to consumer culture. Hence, the study involved both a current and retrospective analysis based on the perceptions of the research participants. Though clearly important, conspicuously absent from the existing literature was a focus on understanding the intricacies of the psychological and social understanding of consumer culture on children that goes beyond an exploration of mere brand association as seen in Richard Elliot and Clare Leonard's,[23] and Liz Frost's[24] study. Additionally, the studies on materialism, while revealing important elements about the downside of accumulated wealth, cover only one facet of consumer culture—acquisition of material goods—and not such important aspects as conformity/resistance, for example. All of these studies help to establish the facts of the matter, but they do not get below the surface and dig deeply for the meaning and understanding of these facts for children. The significance of the study involves two aspects that, together, try to get beyond the facts and move toward a more complete understanding of the meaning of consumerism for children from the perspective of young people: first, by documenting the experiences of children as consumers and, second, by analyzing that experience through the traditions of critical theory. (This will be elaborated upon in Chapter Six.) The study also provides discussion on the ramifications of individual conformity and potential forms of resistance, or lack thereof, within the wider cultural level.

It is my hope that the information garnered from the study improves societal awareness and leads to a rethinking of the cocoon of consumerism that children currently function within. The study may also provide some insight into the nature, importance, and urgency of understanding media-induced conformity. Ironically, the continuing high media involvement of children, an important aspect of consumer culture, has been largely ignored by many academic disciplines—most notably, psychology[25] and sociology.[26] Children are said to be merely keeping up with the times of modern life and under no real threat by consumer culture—a position David Buckingham, professor of education, asserts in *After the Death of Childhood*.[27] Children and adolescents, despite having access to sophisticated technology, are largely voiceless and possibly misunderstood when it comes to deconstructing the impact of consumer culture.[28] The study afforded a chance to clarify their position.

OVERVIEW OF THE BOOK

This book explores the intricacies of the psycho-cultural and social underpinnings associated with consumerism and youth as well as speculates about the greater societal impact on human well-being. To tackle the conundrum of consumer culture and children, we will need to thread our way through a number of topics that take us in many directions. The book is divided into eight chapters and an appendix. Chapter Two provides details as to the impact of consumerism with respect to children and a number of the current issues at stake. Between 2000 and 2010, a number of prominent scholars began to voice their concerns about the mounting negative effects of consumer culture on children and adolescents. In particular, 2004 was a watershed year for it was at that point in time that Schor published *Born to Buy*[29] and psychologist Susan Linn released *Consuming Kids*.[30] Both of these books detailed serious concerns about how children's development was being compromised by consumer culture involvement. Kasser and Kanner also published in 2004 one of the first anthologies that covered the psychological effects of consumer culture on children.[31] In addition, it was in this same year that Joel Bakan, law professor, released his book *The Corporation: The Pathological Pursuit of Profit and Power*.[32] Bakan's findings confirmed that corporations were running roughshod over consumers, including children, with very little interference from government or special interest groups. Between 2000 and 2006, Helga Dittmar, a social psychologist, conducted a number of studies on the cost of consumerism for children and the downside of the so-called material good life.[33] In 2003, two other important texts were published: *Einstein Never Used Flashcards*, written by three developmental psychologists,[34] which highlighted the importance of creative play unfettered by mass-produced paraphernalia; and *Branded*, written by journalist Alissa Quart, in which she described how teenagers are targets for everything branded from clothing to plastic surgery.[35] Psychologist Sharna Olfman sponsored, as editor, two important anthologies in 2005 and 2009, respectively: *Childhood Lost*[36] and *The Sexualization of Childhood*.[37] Both books were important in providing a detailed analysis on childhood in America from the perspective of professionals from a wide range of fields. In 2008, *The Lolita Effect* by M. Gigi Durham, professor of journalism and mass communication, exposed disturbing details about how young girls are being sexualized in U.S. culture and how normalized this process has become.[38] Chapter Two summarizes the findings of numerous studies, all pointing to the ways in which children are suffering under the auspices of "free choice" that so characterizes the zeitgeist of consumer culture.

Chapter Three speaks to the issues of identity, that is, how children living in consumer cultures regard themselves. Do they suffer from low self-esteem as a result of being surrounded by "body-beautiful" media messages that forever point out our physical deficits? Do children use their possessions to reinforce a form of identity? Is identity in consumer cultures reduced to appearances and superficiality?

Chapter Four provides the reader with the opportunity to enter into the debate: Is consumer culture good or bad for children? Both the pro and con sides are explored with specific arguments so as to better understand the context within which the debate rests. Are children faced with the issues of empowerment (pro) or manipulation (con) with respect to media and advertising? Do children demonstrate agency as a consumer (pro), or are they dupes (con)? Can children act independently of their parents when making consumer decisions (pro), or is parental involvement critical to their development (con)? These types of questions (and more) will be answered, leaving the reader to decide.

The main purpose of Chapter Five is to demonstrate the ways and means of enforcing conformity and to describe methods of persuasion that are commonly used by corporations through advertising. Several studies on conformity taken from psychology and sociology are reviewed to reveal how we can easily be led to think and behave in ways contrary to our own liking. Chapter Five also reviews what it means to be creative, and what types of environments promote creative play to provide comparison and contrast to the face of conformity.

Chapter Six covers the theoretical underpinnings of my research study with particular focus on the theories of Theodor Adorno that dealt with culture and consumption.[39] Adorno was part of a group called the Frankfurt School scholars (Max Horkheimer and Herbert Marcuse among others), who criticized Western culture because they believed that every aspect of that culture had become a commodity. In *Dialectic of Enlightenment*, Horkheimer and Adorno coined the term "culture industry" to capture how culture in the United States was being mass-produced, having become stale and predictable.[40] Adorno, in particular, was polemic about the repetitive and standardized characteristics of U.S. culture in its attempts to gratify the illusion of individual cultural taste.[41] The "culture industry" thesis that he developed offers a complex and sophisticated model with which to critique how the commodification of culture influences our perceptions of and actions in the world.

Marcuse, like Adorno, observed and wrote about the analogy between American-style democracy and totalitarian states in *One-Dimensional Man*.[42] He believed that those who controlled the economic and communication infrastructures essentially gained control of most of society. Marcuse viewed consumer culture as repressive because its primary task was to create false needs.

The work of Stuart Ewen is also covered in Chapter Six, with focus on his book *Captains of Consciousness*.[43] He provides a chronology of the development of consumer culture and deconstructs the harbinger of "branding"—lifestyle as a commodity form. Indeed, Ewen believes that industry aspires to attain widespread social dependency on the commodity market to ensure corporations accrue profits.

Benjamin Barber's thesis on the effects of consumer culture is reviewed in Chapter Six as well. According to Barber (2007), the commodity form is no longer associated with the specific content of a product or service—it is the brand itself which is being marketed. He goes on to note that brands are now mistaken for identities.[44] Sheldon Wolin (2008) picks up where Barber left off, stating that U.S. democracy has become an "inverted totalitarian" state. Wolin attributes the erosion of democracy to the power of the corporation and its elitist group of shareholders, those who were able to capture the power of the government in a silent coup d'état.[45]

All six of the theorists reviewed in Chapter Six take issue with the fact that liberal democratic societies have relinquished power to corporations to such a degree that the sovereignty of its citizenry has greatly diminished. They all assert that the modern-day corporation has undoubtedly become the most powerful of institutions and that consumer culture has facilitated this coup. And while adults presumably have the capacity to reject consumerism, children, especially young children, do not. With the theories presented in Chapter Six, we can begin to look at and understand the workings of consumer culture and why it may detract from individual enlightenment or autonomy.

Chapter Seven summarizes the methodology employed in the study as well as the results: impressions and beliefs that the participants identified to be associated with the process of consumption and all other related experiences linked to consumer culture. The study utilized qualitative interviewing methods by focusing on the experiences of young people who have faced the ubiquitous presence of consumer culture since birth. The purpose of the study was to describe the experience of being a child and young person in a consumer culture and then interpret the meaning of those findings within the critical framework of the wider social, political-economic, and cultural context. The end goal of the study was *not* to explore the ways and means of how consumer culture is harming children—this has in large part already been established. Rather, the aim of the study was to determine how young people have *experienced* consumer culture throughout their lives and their perceptions. Thus, the primary research question: "How do young people understand and experience consumer culture over the course of their lifetime?" The results section of the book is organized around three themes that emerged through analysis: Inside the Culture Industry, Identity, and Media.

Chapter Eight presents an overview or interpretation of the study's results and how they relate back to the theory and literature delineated in Chapters Two, Three, Four, and Five. The book concludes in Chapter Eight with the position that the developing brain has become the new territory for corporate infiltration, meaning that media has now penetrated to the core of our thought processes, molding how we think, behave, and view the world. Hence, this explains *Adbusters*'s attempts to protect the mental environment and fight back for public space while simultaneously resisting the "privatization of consciousness" as Jerry Mander coined it.[46] Because we all share in the mental environment collectively, why should any one person or corporation have more influence than the rest of us combined? How do we protect ourselves and our children from mental "pollution" when it is so ubiquitous and all-consuming? Is it possible that our kids can be brainwashed to believe in the American dream, that materialism is equated with happiness? Chapter Eight sidesteps a solution-oriented list of recommendations for parents and other concerned citizens. Many have already done an excellent job in this area.[47] Whatever form resistance takes, it seems obvious there is the need for civil society to confront the corporate onslaught in which profiting from childhood is the symptom of a greater disease—the privatization and commodification of culture. We could literally consume ourselves to death, depleting the natural resources beyond recognition. Activist and writer Bill McKibben noted that in the last 50 years, we have consumed "more stuff than all of humanity in all the millennia before."[48] Manufacturing desires has become such a powerful industry that few recognize the manipulation and mendacity even in the obvious case of childhood.

2

The Children's Culture Industry

MEDIA USE AND CONSUMERISM

Corporations have inculcated children's culture with the belief that consuming commodities is the predominant path to happiness and fulfillment. Advertisers spend billions of dollars a year encouraging, persuading, and manipulating children into a consumer lifestyle. Access to children is achieved through the media in which advertisers exploit insecurities; create extraneous wants; and foster unyielding desire, instant satisfaction, and dissatisfaction in rapid succession to ensure a cycle of perpetual consumption. Indeed, much of consumption has little to do with the fulfillment of basic needs; rather, it has evolved into a desire for dispensable and rapidly obsolete goods. Without doubt, the media is one of the prime sources shaping our children's brains, minds, and emotions. I argue throughout this chapter that consumption is now an intrinsic part of children's everyday lives and identity formation. In fact, the extent of children's immersion in consumer culture is unprecedented, regardless of culture and geographical location, though the extent of consumerism is particularly salient in the Western world. For example, while only 6 percent of the world's population, the United States consumes 57 percent of the world's advertising. The average American will see or hear more than seven million advertisements in his or her lifetime.[1] Children experience a steady stream of invasive marketing messages throughout their day, an assault of "mental pollution" on their developing brains.[2]

Consumerism has become a powerful and evocative symbol of modern capitalism, and it is strongly associated with democratic processes. Today, materialism and consumption have never been so prevalent, affording opportunities of self-expression,[3] as well as cause for great concern in regards to children's health and well-being.[4] After modest increases from 1960 to the mid-1980s, commodity consumption per child in the 1990s seemed to know no bounds. By 2004, it was at $670 billion (money spent on or by children in the United States)[5] and in 2000, the teen market alone was worth $155 billion in direct expenditures.[6] Statistics from 2002 reveal that those under 13 years old spent over $40 billion in comparison to $17 billion less than a decade previously.[7] Consumption plays a major role in day-to-day living and leisure through the endless availability of media technology in the form of television, computers, digital accessories, and a wide array of goods. Children living in consumer societies are exposed to an ever-growing number of products and services produced by corporate entities that include the largest of business conglomerates. It comes as no surprise that children comprise the largest consumer economy in the world.[8] Specifically, ages two to fourteen have sway over $500 billion in household purchasing each year. In 2003, 33 million U.S. teens spent an average of $103 a week.[9] It appears that shopping has become *the* number one pastime for most American children.[10]

Since about 1990, children have increasingly behaved much like adult consumers in that their lives are closely linked to media access and the consumption of goods. According to Schor, by age 10, children are making an average of 5.2 shopping trips per week, on par with that of adults.[11] Children are more and more defined and evaluated by their spending capacity. Living in a culture of consumption (or any culture for that matter) is to be exposed to enormous pressures to conform to the beliefs and values of that culture. Part of the allure of consumer culture is due to the way commodities have evolved to be symbols of caring and affection.[12] Indeed, parents have come to believe that money and gifts are symbolic expressions of their love for their children. Additionally, commodities are used to express who we are and who we want to be. As corporations search for new markets and maximum sales, they are crowding children by leaving them little unmediated space within which to develop their own identities. Driven by a relentless effort to promote consumerism, regardless of the effect on the child, companies are guilty of what activist Enola Aird[13] refers to as "marketing authoritarianism." Childhood, it seems, has been all but co-opted by marketing conglomerates.

In contemporary marketing, children are portrayed as "naturally" desirous beings with an innate drive to consume.[14] To a child growing up, immersion in a culture of images appears to be the most natural thing in the world. Indeed, children are taught to operate and accept consumerism as ordinary.[15] For example, on-demand digital technology has become second nature to millions of children. American youth spend more time per week with media than they do with their parents, with friends, or in school.[16] To be exact, by 2010, children were spending 7:38 hours per day with media, up from 6:21 in 2005. When multitasking is factored in, this figure jumps to a whopping 10:45 hours per day—considerably more than a full-time work week.[17] Infants and babies are no exception to children's engagement with media. The figures for children younger than the age of two are lower but still substantial. For this cohort, the average daily use of television is 34 minutes and for DVDs is 13 minutes per day. A little more than half watch TV every day, with 19 percent having a television in their bedroom.[18] One of the outcomes is that adult caregivers struggle in their ability to capture the attention of children and guide them accordingly. The absence of parenting has huge ramifications for a child's well-being.

Just how ubiquitous is consumer culture? According to sociologist Todd Gitlin, television, DVD players, and radio use does not vary significantly among white, black, and Hispanic children; along gender lines; or with socioeconomic status.[19] Furthermore, poor families are not insulated by their poverty from the consequences of consumer marketing. Indeed, most research shows that low-income families spend proportionately *more* on their children than wealthier families.[20] Moreover, there appears to be no direct correlation between parents' income and children's media possessions. Children in families whose parental earnings are under $500,000 all own pretty much the same media-based technology.[21] Thus, the ubiquity of corporate operations and media has, to a large extent, infiltrated beyond differences of class, ethnicity, and gender. This is not to say that there is no variation in children's consumer behaviors across cultures, socioeconomic status, and race. Kaiser Family Foundation surveys (2003, 2005) estimate that 99 percent of U.S. families with children own televisions, 97 percent own video or DVD players, more than 80 percent own a video game, and 86 percent own a computer.[22] The 2003 Kaiser Family Foundation study on newborns to six-year-olds and media use found that on a typical day 73 percent of children watch television, 48 percent watch a video or DVD, 18 percent use a computer, and 9 percent play video games.[23] It would appear that technologies of all forms have become the backdrop against which the lives of children and adults are set. For adults even, there seems to be no escape, let alone for children.

THE SHIFTING SAND OF CHILDHOOD

It can be argued that many children are being deprived of a full childhood or series of experiences which distinctly differentiates them from that of the adult world and meets their developmental needs. One of the more significant outcomes of consumer culture has been the steady erosion of childhood, whether measured in terms of health trends, consumer behaviors, or accessibility to adult culture. There are many academics who are concerned about the fact that childhood is fading out altogether.[24] Developmental psychology posits that children and adults are intellectually, physically, emotionally, and psychologically different and that children are incapable of making the same sort of judgments that adults do. Children are, arguably, distinct from adults and should therefore be shielded from adult responsibilities and harmful influences.[25] Yet, if we just look at television as an example, it is relatively easy for children to watch whatever they want, adults' or children's programming alike. Even 20 years ago, psychologist Stephen Kline argued that television was not only a significant socializing agent for children; it was also "the undisputed leader in the production of children's culture."[26] The culture of childhood has an important play component that is impoverished and undernourished by preprogrammed play and passive time associated with television, computers, and other electronic media.[27] Furthermore, play has become professionalized and tainted with adult cues, imagination, and expectations—no longer reflecting the creative mind of a child. Kline also argued that television advertising and programming has commercialized childhood to such an extent that media logos now substitute for the very symbols of childhood.[28] Further to this, cultural critic Neil Postman opined in his controversial book *The Disappearance of Childhood* that children are treated as adults and assumed to be capable of absorbing adult information.[29] Indeed, there is no aspect of adult life, including perversity, promiscuity, dishonor, or aggression, that seems outside the realm of today's children.[30] It has become obvious that most television programming is not governed by theories on child development; it is driven by profit-seeking conglomerates with few governmental regulations.

MARKETING STRATEGIES AND THEIR EFFECTS

The typical North American child is now immersed in the world of consumerism to a degree that dwarfs historical experience. In 1983, $100 million was spent in television advertising directed at children, and by 2004 that figure had jumped to $15 billion.[31] Marketers used to direct their campaigns at mothers as a way of reaching the consumer child; they no longer tread so carefully, bypassing parents altogether and targeting children directly.[32] They no longer attempt to assuage mothers that their products will improve their child's well-being; rather, they exploit children's likes, dislikes, interests, and activities, commodifying their experiences. Big Tobacco specifically targeted children by using animated cartoon figures to sell cigarettes. By championing children's "intelligence" and "sophistication" as a positive rationale, marketers are able to justify the onslaught of child-targeted advertisements. We now know that young children, including babies and toddlers, are highly susceptible to many forms of suggestion, including marketing.[33] The stakes are high, as children between two and fourteen years old now influence purchases of $700 billion annually in the United States, including $40 billion of their own money and $340 billion each in direct and indirect expenditures.[34] Marketers are now actively pursuing children's "loyalty" on big-ticket items like cars and boats, all-terrain vehicles, and other home equipment. As James McNeal, psychologist and market researcher who was instrumental in spurring the commercial child market over the past 25 years, noted, "advertisers are lining up to pay a premium for access to their most valuable *targets*" (italics added).[35]

Even toddlers are in on the game. Marketing strategies have increasingly focused on the very young, that is, zero to three years of age; this group of children has now become the first segment in "cradle-to-grave" marketing.[36] These children are at the most impressionable stage of life and are particularly vulnerable to the marketers' influence. As media analyst Douglas Rushkoff comments:

Today the most intensely targeted demographic is the baby—the future consumer. . . . By seeding their products and images early, the marketers can do more than just develop brand recognition; they can literally cultivate a demographic's sensibilities as they are formed. . . . This indicates a long-term coercive strategy.[37]

Babies and toddlers have come to represent potential adult consumers. The corporation that succeeds in securing a child consumer can count on $100,000 over the course of the child's lifetime, all through brand loyalty.[38] Younger children are more open and gullible to believing an advertising message is the truth. In the early phases of consumer marketing, babies were considered off limits to advertisers because of ethical concerns. Now, that is a thing of the past: "cradle-to-grave" marketing represents billions of dollars a year drawn from a pool of 52 million children in the United States alone.[39] "Cradle to grave" refers to the practice of marketing to children with the hope that they will become lifetime loyal customers of a particular corporation's product or logo. Remarkably, by the time they are three years old, many children are able to identify and ask for specific brands— the responsibility almost always falls in the lap of the parents.

One of the more successful marketing campaigns is the "baby genius virus," a zeitgeist that reinforces the belief that technology makes you smarter and better. There is no research of any kind that has substantiated these claims (i.e., the "Mozart effect" in which advertisers claimed listening to Mozart's music would make babies and toddlers smarter though no empirical evidence supported this position). On the contrary, babies may be suffering from "problem-solving deficit disorder" resulting from overstimulation by screen technology.[40] As a result, they begin to experience a kind of sensory overload and may be incapable of focusing to their full capacity. Twenty-nine percent of babies younger than 12 months of age are watching screens daily and 23 percent have televisions in their bedroom.[41] Fisher Price, in partnership with Apple, has designed a "Newborn-to-Toddler Apptivity™ Seat for iPad® Device." The Apptivity Seat is set up as a bouncy seat for infants, securing them directly in front of an iPad.[42] Never before in the history of humankind have babies been so passive in their exploration of the world around them. They have more and more become attuned to watching media rather than engaging with their environment and other human beings.[43] By 2000, babies and toddlers were watching preschool shows in record numbers of which *Teletubbies* was prominent, a program touted as appealing to this age group. Though parents did not always approve of television, they were more easily persuaded when education was said to be conflated with entertainment. Even megacorporations like Wal-Mart are in the baby/toddler business, retailing large quantities of books, complete with accessories. Disney has been sending out "educational" kits to daycare centers and preschools as a means of claiming market share.[44] Despite this, research demonstrated that young children were not learning anything that the producers of *Teletubbies* intended. In fact, there is very little evidence that children gain any educational benefit from television under the age of two. On the contrary, background television was found to diminish the length of children's play time and their capacity to stay focused during play.[45]

CONSTRUCTING THE TWEEN

The social phenomenon of the "tween" is one of the more striking examples of how consumerism has shaped children's culture, values, and identities. The tween category refers to children from eight to twelve years of age. The tween rapidly became a definable, knowable *commercial* persona and stage of youth starting in the 1990s.[46] Nowhere is age compression (children getting "older" at younger ages) marketing more evident than in the tween age range.[47] These children, in particular, are being enticed and encouraged into adopting an identity older than their developmental age. It is worth noting that in North America, 25 million children in the eight-to-twelve age bracket form the most powerful consumer group since the baby boom and are spending billions annually.[48] In addition, the four-to-twelve age group annually influences $565 billion of their parents' purchases.[49] Thus, it comes as no surprise that marketers are clamoring for tweens' attention. As an example, the McDonald's Corporation launched its "Big Kids Meal," complete with its McWorld advertising campaign in an attempt to capture the tween market. Other examples of age compression include advertisements designed to attract children to cigarette smoking and drinking of alcohol. In 1998, two such advertisements, Joe Camel and the Budweiser frogs, were the most popular children's commercials of the year.[50] As more countries (including Canada and the United States) imposed bans on tobacco advertising, the industry found ways to promote their brands surreptitiously, especially with young people. Such "indirect advertising" methods include sponsoring sporting events and teams; promoting rock concerts; and placing their brand logos on t-shirts and other merchandise popular with children. Another tactic has been to give away free cigarettes and brand merchandise in areas where young people gather, such as rock concerts, clubs, and shopping malls.[51]

Advertisers have capitalized on the insecurities of preadolescence—a vast need to be cool and desire to break free from the confines of parents—when catering to tweens. Marketers are hiring child psychologists and other experts to maximize their understanding of the characteristics and nuances of the tween market. The tween phenomenon is more closely associated with girls than boys and rather successfully—female youth are now one of the most lucrative consumer niches.[52] Tweens watch more television than any other age group, which may explain why approximately 40 television programs aimed for a tween audience have since been produced.[53] Television showcases "hip" stars that embody all qualities toward which tweens aspire, such as independence and popularity. For example, marketers have created tween toy lines such as the *Bratz* doll, which exemplifies girl power and attitude. Further, the dolls are sexualized with their heavily made-up faces, revealing clothing, and skinny bodies. The tween persona has been characterized to feel empowered by separating themselves from adults and partaking in a world free of their rules. Indeed, marketing research reveals that children over the age of 11 no longer think of themselves as children, and neither do the Toy Manufacturers of America. Their target demographic changed from zero to fourteen to zero to ten years old.[54] By coining a term like "tween" and creating a persona to emulate tween characteristics, the industry helped to transform what it means to be a child. Chronological age is less of a standard with which childhood is defined.

GAUGING CHILDREN'S HEALTH

Trends on children's health, including their physical and psychological functioning, are important indicators of cultural impact. Close examination of children's health in North America reveals much about the way media, including advertising and all forms of technology, affects children in this region. Key health problems plague today's children, including obesity, poor nutrition, diabetes, smoking, drinking, and emotional and behavior problems, including suicide. While it would be speculative to suggest that consumer culture is *the* root cause, there is enough evidence to link media exposure with poor health habits and conditions. Of significance, the United Nations' first report on the well-being of children in countries considered to have "advanced economies" placed the United States second from the bottom. Six dimensions used to measure quality of life were applied: material well-being, health and safety, education, peer and family relationships, behaviors and risks, and young people's own subjective sense of well-being. The only country that scored worse than the United States overall was Britain, with Scandinavian countries (The Netherlands, Sweden, Denmark, and Finland) scoring the highest.[55]

In Canada, 31.5 percent of children were overweight or obese as of 2012.[56] In the United States, obesity rates for children have more than doubled, and they have quadrupled for teens since 1980.[57] As of 2012, 18 percent of children aged six to eleven were overweight in the United States.[58] Research demonstrates that overweight and obese girls are significantly more likely to grow breasts earlier because body fat can produce sex hormones (estrogen). Some girls are entering puberty as early as age seven and eight, earlier than even a decade ago. Early maturation in girls is associated with lower self-esteem and less favorable body image, as well as greater rates of eating problems, depression, and suicide attempts.[59] At the most concrete level, physical effects, including obesity and its concomitant, Type II diabetes, may be strongly tied to the high number of food advertisements viewed by children, including breakfast cereals, confectionery, savory snacks, and soft drinks, with fast-food restaurants taking up an increasing proportion of the advertisements.[60] Dietary patterns established in early childhood play a critical role in the prevention of childhood diseases such as obesity and Type II diabetes, both of which can persist into adulthood.[61] Furthermore, poor diet in childhood can lead to heart disease and cancer in adulthood; an estimated 65 percent of chronic diseases are diet related and, thus, preventable.[62] Studies have shown significant associations between hours of television viewing and the prevalence of both high cholesterol and obesity in children.[63] Children see one food commercial about every five minutes on Saturday morning television programs.[64] One study found that a 30-second food commercial impacts children's brand choices, even at the age of two; repeated exposure is that much more salient.[65]

Promotion of fast food containing high proportions of fat, sugar, and salt is rampant in food advertisements for children.[66] For example, in 2002, McDonald's spent over $1.3 billion on advertising in the United States, followed by Burger King's $650 million; PepsiCo spent more than $1.1 billion, only marginally outspending Coca-Cola.[67] The food industry is estimated to spend up to $33 billion a year in advertising, and increasingly, those dollars are targeted at children.[68] Research shows that foods heavily advertised on television are rated highly by children.[69] It is interesting to note that about a third of the food advertisements during children's television are for candy and snacks, and none of these advertisements are for fruits and vegetables.[70] In the United States, the Federal Trade Commission has recently proposed new guidelines that may influence the food industry to moderate how it advertises to children. As an example, regulators have flagged *Toucan Sam*, the brightly colored *Froot Loops* cereal character, as a questionable marketing tactic.[71] Like the United States, Canada relies on the food industry to self-regulate in the area of food marketing to children. In 2008, the Canadian Children's Food and Beverage Advertising Initiative (CAI) was established. This initiative, comprising 17 food and beverage manufacturers, pledged to allocate 50 percent of their advertisements directed at children toward "healthier dietary choices."[72] Monique Kent, professor at the school of Health Sciences with the University of Ottawa, and colleagues conducted an analysis in 2011 to determine whether the CAI was doing what it proposed. The results showed that the CAI food/beverage promotions were *higher* in fats, sugar, and sodium than non-CAI. Further, the CAI promotions were considered *less healthy* than those of non-CAI corporations.[73] Not surprisingly, the CAI initiative is clearly not in the best interests of children and is a good example of how the food industry (and other industries) cannot be relied upon to regulate themselves, even with public health at stake.

Despite encouraging children to eat foods that can lead to obesity, marketers also place great emphasis on looking physically attractive, the result of which can contribute to the prevalence of eating disorders. Remarkably, patterns of disordered eating are now occurring in preschool-aged children. Indeed, a study published in the *British Journal of Psychiatry* noted that eating disorders are occurring in about three in every 100,000 children in the United Kingdom and Ireland, some of whom are as young as five years old.[74] Furthermore, girls as young as seven are well aware of dieting as a means of attaining an "ideal" weight; desire for thinness can begin as early as six years old.[75] We now know that greater use of media for females, specifically fashion magazines, television, and music videos, is significantly correlated with higher levels of body dissatisfaction and higher scores on eating disorder measures.[76] About 53 percent of 13-year-old girls report dissatisfaction with their bodies—that number increases to 78 percent by the time they are 17 years of age.[77] Additionally, bombardment of thin body ideals from media may lead children to overestimate the prevalence of such body types, thus placing undue pressure to conform. Even if conforming is detrimental to one's health, the desire to fit in and match the unattainable is powerful, as evidenced by the fact that 65 percent of women and girls will acquire an eating disorder in their lifetime.[78] Ultra-thin and anorexic models are held up as the norm despite the fact that their clothing size dropped from an average of six to two, then to zero in 2005. Eventually, the fashion industry reluctantly banned underweight models whose body mass indexes were too low.[79] While seemingly less vulnerable, preadolescent and adolescent boys can also experience significant body dissatisfaction, negatively comparing to "socially ideal" male images.[80]

Despite intensive campaigns to eliminate smoking among youth, it still remains a problem. Specifically, by the time U.S. children are in the eighth grade, approximately 7 percent are smokers and that number almost quadruples by the twelfth grade.[81] Health Canada reported in 2010 that the number of youth who identify themselves as daily smokers is on the rise in certain age groups; furthermore, their surveys showed that young smokers were more likely to use drugs than their nonsmoking counterparts.[82] It is concerning to note that nine out of ten adult smokers started their habit by the age of 18.[83] Once a tobacco company "recruits" a new child smoker, the company is essentially guaranteed a lifelong customer.

Approximately 10 percent of 12-year-olds say they have used alcohol at least once. By age 13, that number doubles, and by age 15, approximately 50 percent have had at least one drink.[84] Forty percent of alcoholics were drinking excessively between the ages of 15 and 19.[85]

Rates of emotional and behavior problems among children ages four to fifteen soared between 1979 and 1996.[86] For example, childhood and adolescent depression can be persistent and cause significant impairment; depressive disorders occur in approximately 2 percent of primary school–aged children and between 4 to 8 percent of adolescents.[87] The average age for the onset of depression is now 14.5 compared to 29.5 in 1960.[88] According to Jean Twenge, a psychologist who studies generational patterns, 21 percent of teens between the ages of 15 and 17 have already experienced major depression.[89] To put it in perspective, only 1 to 2 percent of Americans born before 1915 experienced a major depressive episode during their lifetime.[90] Twenge is clear about the fact that these changes are too large and verified by too many studies to be explained solely by reporting bias. The evidence bears out: the number of children on mood-altering drugs tripled between 1987 and 1996. "Normal" children, those free of psychiatric disorders, reported higher levels of anxiety than child psychiatric patients in the 1950s. All this despite North Americans becoming massively more affluent. As Twenge concluded, "*when you were born* has more influence on your anxiety levels than family environment" (italics added).[91] In comparing teens from the 1950s to a 1989 cohort, researchers found that the latter group felt more alienated, had greater difficulty developing and maintaining close personal relationships, had more somatic symptoms and bodily concerns, felt more vulnerability, and were more self-critical.[92] Suicide rates for children 10 to 14 years old almost tripled between 1968 and 1985[93] and have doubled from 1979 to 1992.[94] As for adolescents, suicide rates have quadrupled since 1950.[95] In a 2013 survey by the Centers for Disease Control and Prevention, 17 percent of high school students admitted they had seriously contemplated suicide.[96] Suicide is the third leading cause of death for teens aged 15 to 19 years old.[97] The hike in suicide rates parallels the increase in standard of living over the past number of decades, suggesting that materialism does not offset well-being. Further, as Asian countries adopt Western lifestyles and beliefs, their rates of depression begin to rise accordingly.[98]

Research suggests that the problems children struggle with in consumer cultures may have something to do with too much indulgence. Remarkably, children of privilege or affluent cultures, like that of the United States and Canada, are no better off emotionally and psychologically than their less financially advantaged counterparts. In fact, America's newly identified at-risk group is preteens and teens from affluent, well-educated families. Research on this cohort revealed their lack of spontaneity, creativity, enthusiasm, and, oddly, the capacity for contentment. Affluent adolescents seem to lack a fundamental sense of identity, instead having what psychologists call a "false self" that correlates with a number of emotional problems, most notably depression.[99] Despite such evidence, marketers promote the belief that increased wealth is essential to happiness mainly because of the increased capacity to acquire commodities and all the "benefits" that ensue. It is also telling that in the developing world, the more "Americanized" the populations become, the higher the rate of mental illness.[100] Exporting toxic cultures, despite rises in industrialization, compromises well-being.

THE POTENCY OF TELEVISION AND ADVERTISING MEMES

> Indeed, if the basis of advertising is to make us feel good and it has surrendered any objective basis for this feeling, in what way is it different from religion? Why not also tea leaves, Ouija boards, black cats, dice, sounds that go bump in the night? Why not God?[101]
>
> —Sut Jhally

While today's children are avid users of video games and computers, television continues to capture the largest portion of their time (this includes "on-demand" television via Netflix or YouTube[102]). Television has been and continues to be a powerful delivery system of consumer culture. It remains one of the most prominent media through which advertisers communicate to children, and this is happening at younger and younger ages. A recent study cited that 40 percent of three-month-old babies are watching television.[103] The exposure of American children and adolescents to television continues to exceed the time they spend in the classroom: 15,000 hours versus 12,000 hours by the time they graduate from high school.[104] Almost three years will have been spent watching television by the time children are adults. This figure does not include time spent watching DVDs or playing video games. To put it further in perspective, based on surveys of the type of television children watch, the average child sees about 12,000 violent acts, 14,000 sexual references and innuendos, and 20,000 advertisements *annually*.[105] The American Academy of Pediatrics (AAP) puts it at a minimum of 40,000 advertisements annually.[106] Regardless, the total number of advertisements that children are exposed to on television, by the time they reach adulthood, is in the hundreds of thousands. Additionally, Internet advertising on children's websites is significant and represents an easy venue with which to capture their attention. Not surprisingly, in 2001 only 2 percent of children's websites were found to be free of advertisements and this number has probably lessened today.[107] As with television, children are having difficulty determining what is advertising versus program content since they so often appear simultaneously on the screen.[108]

The AAP recommends that children under two years watch *no* television at all.[109] Research indicates that children as young as one year of age are responsive to the positive and negative emotions exhibited on television programs, even with their limited capacity to moderate emotions.[110] Furthermore, babies between the ages of 12 and 24 months show little aptitude to learn from television, certainly not enough to justify programs tailor-made for this age group.[111] For example, despite the warnings by the AAP, Baby First is a corporation that specifically targets television viewing for infants and toddlers. Their website boasts that "electronic media can enrich the connection between parents and their baby and give them new opportunities for exploring and playing together." Pediatricians such as Dr. Dmitri A. Christakis caution against this trend: "Nothing is better than human interactions. Babies' activities should be structured around physical interactions, like the engagement with blocks, reading, and singing. The technologization of childhood is a new phenomenon."[112]

Advertising, marketing, and related activities are now the tasks of multi-billion-dollar industries aimed at promoting the sale of goods and services produced. Advertising is considered a necessary part of capitalism but has become recklessly out of control with only about 100 companies that do most of the advertising. Further, advertisers drive much of the programming created by the media.[113] The time devoted to advertisements per hour of television viewing has doubled in the last two decades; this means that a one-hour prime time show has about 18 minutes of advertisements scattered throughout.[114]

Twenty-five years ago, advertising to young children was largely discouraged because it was believed they were incapable of viewing it critically or with a discriminating eye. A comprehensive review of the literature over the past twenty-five years reveals that by age five, most children are able to discriminate between advertising and programming.[115] A deeper understanding of the persuasive intent of advertisements, however, occurs by about age eight, and it is also at this age that children begin to recognize advertisements are not always truthful. Children's conceptual understanding of brands or the more abstract features is not mastered until they reach approximately twelve years of age.[116] Although children have been found to remember television advertisements, their intent is not fully comprehended, even by many 10-year-olds.[117] While advertising is not the entire story behind children's consumer expenditures, it plays a critical role in understanding their relationship with consumer culture. Advertising has become a tour de force that the majority of children cannot reckon with—notably, between 1990 and 1998, advertising to children increased twentyfold.[118] The lines between commercials and program content are so regularly blurred that corporate advertisers get away with continuous promotion of their products. Consider how product placement in movies and television allows companies to reach those using digital video recorders, which by design can bypass advertisements. Indeed, advertisers spent about $1 billion on product placement in 2006, and by 2010 it was $5.6 billion.[119] Further, many reality television shows have essentially become hour-long advertisements, including *American Idol*, *Celebrity Apprentice*, *The Biggest Loser*, and *America's Next Top Model*. Marketers have even used the "educational" angle of advertising as a cover by framing their sales pitch in terms of learning.[120]

Evidence is growing that strong emotions, such as fear, induced by media viewing are sometimes severe and long-lasting. A survey of more than 2,000 elementary and middle-school children revealed that heavy television viewing was associated with self-reported symptoms of anxiety, depression, and posttraumatic stress; watching more than six hours of television a day put children at greater risk for scoring in the clinical range of trauma symptoms.[121] Also, heavy exposure to television violence as a child predicted increased physical aggression in adulthood.[122] On the other hand, viewing prosocial programming appears to enhance children's positive interpersonal behaviors such as altruism.[123] It should be noted that while computer and interactive game use is being marketed for children as young as six months of age, the effects of such technology are unknown. Still, according to the Kaiser Family Foundation, 61 percent of children under the age of two are exposed to screen media on a typical day.[124] A recent study found that children in middle childhood who exceeded the recommended two hours per day of screen time (television, computer, video games combined) were one and a half to two times more likely to have attention problems in the classroom.[125] It should also be noted that children's desire to play with technology over engagement in the outdoors leads to a more isolated, passive and inactive existence.[126]

One of the indirect negative effects of advertising to children is the stimulation of wants, leading to frequent demands on parents—what has been coined the "nag factor."[127] Not only do children influence purchases that directly affect them such as groceries, clothing, and games; they also impact purchases of bigger items, including cars, holiday destinations, and electronics. Parents give their children's preferences serious consideration when making major purchases.[128] A child's familiarity with commercial television, in particular, appears to be a reliable and significant predictor of nagging.[129] Aggressive marketing strategies seek to maximize the chance that parents will relent to persistent nagging. This tactic is particularly concerning when applied to toddlers who are only just beginning to form a critical capacity for self-control and regulation of emotion.[130] It comes as no surprise that children's nagging has the capacity to erode positive rapport with their parents—yet another negative offshoot of consumerism.[131]

Lastly, advertising is a powerful way to spread the "memes" of consumer culture, the buzzwords or cultural sound bites associated with a life motivated by consumption. The term "meme," first coined by biologist Richard Dawkins, is in essence a cultural artifact that replicates like a gene and spreads as it gains momentum and popularity. To be more specific, memes are defined by scholar Howard Bloom as "words, slogans, poems, pop songs, religions, ideologies, opinions, rallying cries and pleas for peace. . . . They slip from molecule to molecule in the brain and from mind to mind."[132] Memes can be very potent, occupying our mental space with ferocious tenacity. Advertising, if done well, uses memes that are particularly salient to hook the viewer in ways that benefit the advertiser. For example, "all-American" products such as soft drinks, fast food, and various articles of clothing like Levi's jeans have been conflated with the American dream that is said to embody affluence, freedom, and individualism. These ongoing campaigns are, according to professor Lynne Ciochetto, "the most successful achievements of the American media industries of the twentieth century."[133] Memes can also invade at a subconscious level and induce behaviors that would otherwise lie dormant—"good" advertising guarantees this occurrence. Children are like sponges in that they absorb memes readily with repeated exposure, lacking the cognitive skills to filter the salubrious from the harmful. Corporations invest considerable dollars to determine the memes that have the greatest punch, those most likely to saturate the psychological and physical environment.

USURPING PLAY

> Play, the most important modality of childhood learning, is thus colonized by marketing objectives making the imagination the organ of corporate desire. The consumption ethos has become the vortex of children's culture.[134]
> —Stephen Kline

Play comes naturally to children, as a means of self-expression, to gain a sense of control over their world.[135] Play is also critical to the development of the intellect and creative expression.[136] Children's play is not only about how they create their culture but also about how they learn. Additionally, *unfettered* play is one of the prime modalities in which children develop and form a sense of identity.[137] In other words, children should be allowed to engage in a type of play that allows for free expression, which is not tied to the use of a particular toy or piece of technology. More specifically, children under the age of seven should be encouraged in playful activities that do not involve a computer.[138] When children are flooded with stimuli from television, computers, or video games, they have fewer opportunities with which to initiate action or to influence the world they inhabit and less chance to exercise creativity. The lure for sophisticated electronic technology has made it increasingly difficult to provide children an environment that fosters creativity or original thinking through play.[139] As children are assaulted by a stream of media messages, accompanied by a flood of accessories, including toys, books, videos, and clothing, the time and space available for their own ideas and images is compromised. The implicit message is that children's creativity is simply not adequate—they are seen to "need" toys to fully experience their environment and develop in an optimal way. Consequently, children learn at an early age that defining self-worth by what you own, and seeking happiness through the acquisition of material goods, are traits toward which to aspire. Such attitudes are antithetical to creativity, which is characterized by originality and the capacity for critical thinking. A child's sense of self is shaped in numerous ways through creative process or play and, if suppressed, identity formation likely suffers.[140]

Children everywhere are now largely playing with the same mass-produced goods and as a result are pressured to abide by the parameters set by mass-mediated discourse or narratives. Kline interviewed children between the ages of six and eight to assess whether or not television hinders creative expression. He found that the majority of participants in his study either structured their play to match television characters and scripts or incorporated elements from television programs into their fantasies. Kline encapsulated the play dilemma for the modern child: "Although it is difficult to prove that kids are more isolated, consumer-conscious or less creative than they were, say, ten years ago, it is hard to deny evidence of an emergent pattern or 'orthodoxy' of play being promoted through television."[141] Advertisements reinforce for children that engaging in play is so much more exciting if you have the "right" toy and accessories and use them in the "right" way.

Children's books are a good example of how the commercialization of childhood has changed the nature of play. Today, only a handful of megacorporations control the publishing industry. In contrast, between 1980 and 1990 virtually hundreds of independently owned publishing houses and bookstores controlled which books would be printed or sold. Consequently, there has been an overall increase in the number of books available each year but a *decrease* in the number of unique books that were written without attachment to merchandise.[142] Children's books have succumbed to the branding phenomenon and are often in the same retail space as the other branded products. These products range from a line of goods that include graphic novels, television shows, clothing, dolls, blogs, stage adaptations, translations into

multiple languages, family-themed travel, and websites.[143] The underlying message is that children's play should be highly ritualized and
prefabricated as seen fit by marketers, especially if parents want their
children to reach their highest potential.

CORPORATE ENCROACHMENT

In North America, few places remain for children that are devoid of
corporate influence, even schools. Commercial activities are thriving
in schools, where marketers are able to attach their brand to programs
and activities designed to enhance learning. Corporations have also
infiltrated schools using stealth marketing and engagement. For example, they have been known to "assist" in fundraising for school programs and activities by donating their products (typically food). They
also provide incentive programs whereby students are rewarded for
good behavior by receiving a "reward" through a corporate sponsor.
On occasion, a percentage of corporate profits may be donated to
schools with the understanding that such companies can then promote
their products. Corporations also sponsor programs and activities
such as one-off school events. Finally, they engage in electronic marketing in which they provide electronic programming and equipment
in exchange for advertising rights and a captive audience.[144]

CASHING IN ON COOL

The selling of cool has become one of the major child marketing campaigns over the past number of decades.[145] Cool is now revered as a
quality every product tries to be and every child needs to have. Up until
the 1960s, it represented rugged individualism, that person who was
uniquely oneself and embodied diversity. Cool was a person who resisted subjugation and embraced rebelliousness, a trailblazer for the
greater good. Once corporations realized the gold mine that is the saleability of cool, it was co-opted to represent a conformity to style characterized by brands, the opposite of true autonomy.[146] Cool is now said to
be attainable for the right price and a willingness to be swayed by marketers' dictates on chic. The selling of cool can lead to the exploitation of
psychological vulnerabilities, most visible in the marketing of violence,
sex, and drugs (particularly cigarettes and alcohol). Engaging in behaviors that responsible caregivers disapprove of, such as smoking and
drinking, is a large part of what cool now represents. Additionally, how
one looks, in terms of clothing, weight, and overall style of dress, is tied
in with cool. Brands now denote social status, like a caste system, convincing children that cool is the only way to succeed. If, for example,

a teen is not wearing *the* most cool brand of the day, he or she faces the possibility of peer rejection, a sentence seemingly worse than death for many. Behind the indifferent exterior that many exude as they try to embrace cool is inner turmoil and anxiety. There is a tremendous amount of pressure to achieve cool and retain it, all the while hiding whatever insecurities manifest in the process of taking cues from a distant source about what you should look and act like.

Violence in the Media

Children's culture is rife with violence in entertainment, often portrayed as socially acceptable and in some media, such as video games, is treated as "fun"[147] despite the fact that it has long been established that children endure harm watching media violence.[148] This position is backed by the American Medical Association, the American Academy of Child and Adolescent Psychiatry, the American Academy of Pediatrics, and the American Psychological Association, all of whom issued a joint statement in 2000.[149] Yet media tend to showcase hatred, disgust, brutality, rage, and revenge, highlighting our lowest human tendencies with little to no representation of compassion, love, and ethics.[150] Equally problematic, violence in children's programs/movies is often justified, rewarded, accompanied by humor, and portrayed by attractive characters. All of these characteristics have been shown to induce imitation by viewers.[151] Researchers have mapped children's brain activation patterns while they watched violent video clips and found both violent and nonviolent viewing activated regions implicated in aspects of visual and auditory processing.[152] However, areas of the brain activated only during violent programming included those involved in arousal and attention, detection of a threat, episodic memory, coding and retrieval, and motor programming. Put simply, media violence promotes strong emotional responses and "often extremely deranged attitudes in children."[153] Moreover, brain imaging studies suggest that a child's brain does not distinguish between real acts of violence and viewing media violence, even if children are able to report the difference.[154] Additionally, passive viewing of violence induces significant amounts of fear visible in the brain, not all that different from witnessing a live violent incident.[155] In general, exposure to media violence could affect the viewer in the following ways: increased aggression and violent behavior, including bullying; desensitization and increased acceptance of violence as an appropriate means of solving problems in achieving one's goals; increased fear, depression, nightmares, and sleep disturbances; and normalized use of weaponry.[156] Specifically, in a 2010 study, researchers found that more than 75 percent of the children (elementary school aged) interviewed described being frightened by something viewed through media. These children reported both anxiety and sleep disturbance, and approximately 40 percent said they continued to be bothered by the images from the "scary show."[157] Within the context of media, violence is not treated seriously as a human behavior that causes suffering, loss, and sadness for the victim and perpetrator. Rather, it is normalized and promoted as a medium that merely elicits visceral "thrills."[158]

After deregulation in the 1980s, violent content became one of the most lucrative strategies used for marketing to children.[159] This was implemented despite the fact that the National Institute of Mental Health published a report in 1982 stating a clear connection exists between television violence and aggression.[160] Then, in 2004, the CDC published their position that media violence enhanced violent behavior.[161] Yet the majority of toys and other products advertised to children continue to be linked to violent television programs. Indeed, it seems that each successive program launched is significantly more violent. For example, the *Teenage Mutant Ninja Turtles* in the 1980s had an average of 50 violent acts per episode and by the 1990s, *Mighty Morphin Power Rangers* averaged 100 acts of violence per episode.[162] The *Power Rangers* movie, one that was highly violent, grossed over $1 billion. The AAP issued a policy statement in 2009 in which they acknowledged the effects of media violence, imploring paediatricians and parents to take action: "The evidence is now clear and convincing: media violence is one of the causal factors of real-life violence and aggression."[163] According to the National Television Violence study, the highest proportion of violence in television is reported to be in children's shows.[164] Indeed, 70 percent of children's television shows contain displays of physical aggression, a number significantly higher than those for adult programs.[165] Typically, children's television programs average 30 violent acts per hour.[166] By the time a child is 18 years of age, he or she will have viewed an estimated 200,000 acts of violence on television alone.[167]

Approximately 91 percent of movies on television contain violence according to the National Television Violence study.[168] Children now have unprecedented access to adult media with the advent of DVDs, movie channels, pay-per-view channels, and even Web-based movie downloads. Furthermore, advertisements for adult films, including those that are extremely violent, are marketed on television during programming that is seen by children.[169] Regardless, 90 percent of the top-rated PG-13 films have some content that is violent. In 2003, approximately 12 percent of 22 million 10- to 14-year-olds saw 40 of the most violent movies.[170] Many of children's favorite movies are produced by Disney, and while these films almost always contain a "moral message," this does not protect them from the harmful effects of the violence they view.[171] Furthermore, indirect aggression—gossiping, ignoring, dirty looks, social exclusion of others, generally hurting or manipulating other people's feelings—is quite common in animated Disney films with a frequency of 9.23 acts per hour.[172] Importantly, whether or not children can discriminate between fantasy and reality does not inoculate them against the effects of media violence.

Music accounts for more than one-third of adolescents' exposure to electronic media. On average, they listen to 2.4 hours of music per day or more than 16 hours per week.[173] Adolescents, aged 14 to 16 years, listen to approximately 40 hours of popular music per week and children 8 to 10 years old listen to one hour per day. Lyrics have increasingly become more explicit in reference to drugs, sex, and violence. Of the top 10 CDs, there is at least one song with sexual content and 42 percent of all songs have very explicit sexual content. The lyrics of some genres such as rock, heavy metal, and rap are associated with sexual promiscuity, death, homicide, suicide, and substance abuse. Rap, in particular, includes messages of violence, racism, homophobia, and hatred, and violence toward women. Drugs, cigarettes, and alcohol use also tend to be glorified in rap music. Not surprisingly, watching rap music videos is associated with increased promiscuity, misogyny, and use of drugs and alcohol. Frequent watching of music videos has also been related to an increased risk of believing in false stereotypes, perceived importance of appearance (and weight in particular), and increased acceptance of date rape. About 75 percent of 10- to 12-year-olds watch music videos that include a violent content, ranging from 11.5 percent to 22.4 percent.[174]

More than half of the videogames surveyed contain elements of violence, yet 90 percent of games are rated as appropriate for children 10 years or older.[175] Research reveals that 78 percent of boys report owning M-rated games (those deemed for a mature audience).[176] Additionally, a survey of 1,500 ten to fifteen-year-olds revealed that 38 percent had been exposed to scenes of violence while using the Internet.[177]

The Worldwide Wrestling Entertainment Corporation (WWE) is one of the top watched sports programs and is particularly popular among children. Over one million children under the age of 12 watch professional wrestling on television. In fact, in 2007, the number-one show watched by two- to eleven-year-olds was the WWE show *SmackDown*.[178] Fans buy over $44 million of licensed wrestling-themed paraphernalia, ranging from clothing to toys to videos. The WWE claims that it is the number-one entertainment site for males in the 12- to 17-year-old age range.[179] Within each episode of televised wrestling, one can observe 12 uses of weapons, 5 groin kicks, 33 incidents of crotch grabbing, and

21 incidents of simulated sexual activity. Professional wrestling is associated with negative outcomes such as aggression, perpetuating racial stereotyping, desensitizing viewers to violence, and a narrow portrayal of masculinity (e.g., white males are the voice of authority).[180] Research reveals an association between heightened wrestling involvement and increased clinical maladjustment, internalizing of problems, and school difficulties.[181]

Sex in the Media

More often than not, children are learning about sex through the media. Arguably, the group most impacted in this regard is tweens and teens. Music videos, television shows, and movies are rife with implicit and explicit sexual references. Girls get the message at an early age that their value as a person, and that of other women, primarily depends on how they look. Many scholars now hold media directly responsible for the early sexualization of children and its ramifications.[182]

To begin with, approximately 47 percent of high school students reported having had sexual intercourse.[183] Studies have found that more frequent exposure to sexual content in the media during adolescence predicts earlier initiation of sexual intercourse.[184] The United States has the highest rate of teen pregnancy and births among developed nations, according to the Center for Disease Control and Prevention.[185] To put it in historical perspective, compared to the 1940s, young people in the 1990s reported more sexual activity, including a younger age at first intercourse, a leniency toward premarital sex, and less guilt associated with sexual activity.[186] Specifically, more than 20 percent of today's teens are having sex before they reach the age of 14.[187] Persuasion and enticement for sexual activity among adolescents are problematic on two counts: the risk of sexually transmitted infections and unwanted teenage pregnancies. About 435,000 teenagers aged 15–19 years old become pregnant each year in the United States; nearly two-thirds of those births are unwanted for mothers younger than 18 and nearly half for mothers between 18 and 19 years old.[188] Furthermore, the United States has the highest rate of sexually transmitted diseases of any industrialized nation, with almost half of the nation's total sexually transmitted diseases occurring in young adults.[189] For example, cases of chlamydia in young women increased sixfold from 1987 to 2003.[190]

When children learn about sex through the media, they tend to adopt the viewpoints that are persistently promoted. Surprising to many parents, too many children are deriving their sex education and socialization by watching pornography on the Internet. Researchers found that 93 percent of boys and 62 percent of girls were exposed to online pornography as adolescents.[191] It follows that one of the negative effects of commercial culture is the reinforcement of what sociologist Matthew Ezzell (2009) refers to as a "rape culture," that which is embedded within patriarchal privilege.[192] Rape culture refers to the way media normalizes the objectification and degrading sexual targeting of girls and women. Exposure to such images damages both genders; girls learn from early on that their value as a person is primarily dependent upon how they compare to an unattainable beauty, and boys learn a form of masculinity that is detrimental to their psychological health and, as grown men, to their relationships with women.

Exposure to Sexuality and Television

In 2004, a study of approximately 2,000 teens found that television watching with a high sexual content was correlated with a likelihood of engaging in sexual intercourse, specifically twice as likely as their nonviewing counterparts.[193] A Kaiser Family Foundation study revealed that 75 percent of television shows during the "family hour" contain sexual content; this is up 43 percent from 1976. In fact, today's television programming is saturated with sexual content from kissing to full intercourse. And of those shows that had sexual content, only 15 percent covered safe-sex practices.[194] In a study of almost 2,000 teens, it was found that those in the ninetieth percentile of viewing television with sexual content were twice as likely to engage in intercourse as those in the tenth percentile. Even when exposure to television only included talk about sex, the probability of intercourse was the *same* as those exposed to television that depicted sexual behavior.[195]

Sexual Content in Popular Music

While often perceived as less harmful than other forms of entertainment mediums, popular music contains the most references of all to sexual activity.[196] Adolescents are intensely connected to music—it influences their identity development in profound ways. For instance, adolescents often model themselves in terms of dress, behavior, and identity after music celebrities.[197] Longitudinal data show that individuals exposed to degrading sexual references in popular music are, in fact, more likely to engage in sexual intercourse at a young age. Degrading sex refers to the following construct: (1) one person (usually male) is sex crazed; (2) the person's partner (usually female) is objectified; and (3) sexual value is directly tied to physical appearance. About one-third of popular songs include sexual intercourse references in their content; degrading sex was associated with substance use, violence, and weapon carrying. Degrading sex is particularly prevalent in rap and R&B/hip-hop, the most popular genres among young people regardless of demographic characteristics.[198] Research also revealed that watching and listening to televised music videos was associated with an increased acceptance of date rape.[199]

Sexualization of Girls

In 2007, the APA set up a task force for the purposes of compiling data on the sexualization of girls in the media and its concomitant effects.[200] Their findings, based on an extensive review of the literature, are briefly summarized. In mainstream media, more often than not, women and girls are depicted in a sexualized manner and are, thus, objectified. These representations are present in virtually every medium, including television, film, advertisements, music videos, and magazines. To begin with, on television, there are a disproportionate number of males. When female characters appear, they are more than likely attractive and provocatively dressed. In music videos, women are often portrayed exclusively as a decorative sexual object and are far more likely to wear revealing clothing compared to men featured in such videos. Even in cartoons and other animated programs, girls are portrayed as domestic, interested in boys, and highly concerned with appearance. Disney's female characters exude a sexuality that was not present in former times. The content of teen magazines encourages young women to think of themselves as sexual objects and depicts rigid norms of physical attractiveness defined by the consumption of clothes and cosmetics. The media highlights physical "deficits" so that girls who fail to pursue advertised beauty products are portrayed as unpopular "losers." While video games tend to have sparse references to sexuality, only the female characters were found to be highly sexualized.

Approximately 12 percent of all websites are pornographic on the Internet, the majority of which target females. In advertising, the sexualization of women is particularly pronounced. Girls often appear in conjunction with sexualized adult women posing in matching seductive clothing. In fact, the term "Hot Tots" is used to characterize prepubescent girls who dress provocatively and wear makeup to enhance their real age.[201] Products for children also promote the sexualization of girls. For example, the *Bratz* dolls come in sexualized clothing and are marketed to girls as young as four years old. Toy manufacturers also produce dolls for 8- to 12-year-old girls that wear black leather miniskirts, feather boas, and thigh-high boots. The thong, an article of clothing based on what a stripper might wear, is marketed to tweens along with cosmetics associated with the desire for sexual attractiveness.[202] Marketers have convinced parents that babies wearing bibs embroidered with "Supermodel" or "Chick Magnet" is simply cute, and nothing more.[203] Push-up bras for preteens are now a marketable product, as are tanning salons that cater to children.[204] A 2007 survey revealed that 55 percent of six to nine-year-old children wear lip gloss or lipstick and 65 percent use nail polish.[205] Indeed, tween beauty care is big business, and as such, marketers are aggressively targeting these children to sell them whatever they can.[206] For example, Walmart now carries a line of makeup for tweens called "geoGirl" and nail polishes called "Piggy Paint."[207] It would appear that the results of these campaigns have paid off—from 2007 to 2009 the percentage of tweens who regularly use mascara and eye liner nearly doubled.[208] The glorification of teenage culture that corporations have relentlessly imposed on tweens, the encouragement to explore their sexuality prematurely and mimic adult behavior, has all been for the sake of increased profit, not for the benefit of the child.

There are many negative outcomes for girls as a result of being sexualized in the media, which should alert us to how serious a problem it is: 60 percent of all rape victims are girls under the age of 18,[209] and 15 percent are under the age of twelve;[210] 25 percent of girls have experienced child sexual abuse.[211]

Alcohol, Tobacco, Drugs, and Media Exposure

Advertisements for beer, alcohol, tobacco, and drugs proliferate in venues that attract large numbers of children.[212] Advertisements are designed to grab the interest of children by exploiting the same vulnerabilities as those for clothing—"You need this to be and feel cool." Although tobacco can no longer be advertised on television, it is less strictly regulated in the online world. Marketers use sites to create one-on-one relationships with children as a means of attracting them to their products.[213] Interactive media have an edge over television by being able to "read" each learner's knowledge base and adapt messages accordingly. Additionally, the surreptitious presentation of messages about products in online forums can access implicit memory.[214] For example, one tactic is to entice children to interact with online characters who promote specific brands. Research shows that children and adolescents are more likely to smoke, drink, and use drugs when they are exposed to advertisements and programming depicting these types of products.[215] As with the food industry, or with the producers of media violence, representatives in the alcohol and tobacco industry continue to deny a causal relationship between advertising and underage drinking and smoking.

STEREOTYPES

The mediated world that children are exposed to is a type of hyper-reality in which issues of class, ethnicity, race, sexual orientation, and gender struggles are largely ignored. For example, in media simulations there is a dominance of images of white boys and blonde girls. In a 2014 report from the University of Southern California, movies were found to grossly underrepresent visible minorities. The report noted that while almost 50 percent of children under the age of five are non-white, films continue to present a homogenized picture of U.S. culture.[216] Specifically, although comprising 16 percent of the population, Hispanic actors played only 4.9 percent of speaking parts in 2013 blockbusters. Seventeen percent of films had no black characters and black actors were cast in only 14.1 percent of roles. Additionally, television shows for children have become increasingly stereotypic with respect to gender; additionally, more and more programs are divided on the basis of gendered audiences.[217] Furthermore, only about 30 percent of characters on television are female, with the remaining 70 percent being male.[218] The world of television and its cast of characters are thus likely to be driven by the narrow restriction of formulaic writing, rather than be free of stereotypic scripts lacking in vision. The effect of television on conceptions of gender roles remains deleterious to social equality of the genders and gendered identity. The media is, largely, a purveyor of a *uni*dimensional ideology that exudes a militaristic, patriarchal, class-biased, and racist-type imagery that reinforces the existing power structures, detrimental as they are.[219] It should be noted that even advertisements on television portray an inaccurate and unrealistic representation of people of color.[220]

The Disney Corporation is a good example of how "innocent" tales about childhood are full of stereotyping that is not in the best interest of children.[221] In the so-called apolitical atmosphere of Disneyland, children are exposed to gross simplifications of issues surrounding identity and culture. For example, *The Little Mermaid* is all about a white girl whose only goal is to capture the affections of a white male prince. Children are thus socialized to accept female subordination and racial stereotyping in this particular example. In general, children's television can be faulted for its blatant stereotyping based on class, gender, race, and ethnicity.[222] Even television for adults reveals programs that are largely centered on a "man's world,"[223] television that many children will view long before they reach adulthood. The

phenomenon of stereotyping is also prevalent in the culture surrounding wrestling. Wrestling is one of the more blatant genres that promote
stereotypes for men and boys with respect to the expression of physical violence and domination of femininity.[224] In addition, video games
aimed at boys also create gender discrimination in that many of these
masculine-oriented games are misogynistic and homophobic.[225]

UNDERMINING ADULTS

Corporations have made a concerted effort to solicit the business of
children at the exclusion of their caregivers. Why? Children are far
easier to persuade and entice, as they lack the discrimination to choose
based on age appropriateness or otherwise. The drive for cool is so
powerful that the right marketing campaign can easily convince children of their need for certain products deemed to be cool, regardless of
how frivolous they may be. Marketers even take a step further by creating hostility between the child and his or her caregiver as a way of
ensuring the saleability of goods aimed at children. Furthermore, children's consumer culture often involves a subversion of adult values by
incorporating the "carnivalesque," which is characterized by an element of perversion.[226] One of the appeals of consumer culture is that
it coincides with the taboo-breaking of many youth cultural forms.
For example, advertising and television construct school as a dystopia
by depicting how children are governed and restrained, rather than
guided and nurtured. Children's culture is touted to be separate
from, and even superior to, that of education. Children are often encouraged to regard adults as the negative "Other," as "uncool." Many
of Hollywood films, such as the *Home Alone* series, depict adults as immoral, irresponsible, and above all, easily outwitted by kids. By the
same token, these films depict the child as pleasure seeking and self-
indulgent, yet also an autonomous rational decision maker.[227]

EMPIRICAL RESEARCH ON CONSUMERISM, MATERIALISM, AND THE WELL-BEING OF CHILDREN

In her seminal study on consumerism, Schor addressed the question: "How does children's involvement in consumer culture affect
their well-being?"[228] Her research revealed that consumer culture is
harmful to the overall welfare of children. She surveyed 300 children
between the ages of 10 and 13 years in the areas of media use, consumer values, involvement in consumer culture, relationships with
parents, and physical well-being. Her intent was to connect media use,

advertising, and children's involvement in the marketplace and then test to see whether this involvement had any effect on their well-being. Four measures were used as indicators, namely, that of anxiety, depression, self-esteem, and psychosomatic symptoms (i.e., headache, stomach ache, and boredom). Additionally, children were asked to describe their feelings toward their parents to ascertain the quality of the relationship. The results from Schor's study were significant: children who are more involved in consumer culture tended to be more depressed, more anxious, have lower self-esteem, and suffer from more psychosomatic complaints. She also found that the children who spent more time watching television and using other media were more likely to involve themselves in consumer-type behaviors. This finding may be a result of the fact that, with its emphasis on materialism, television induces discontent and causes children to place greater emphasis on brands and products and to adopt consumer values. Also, in this study, higher levels of consumer involvement resulted in worse relationships with parents. Finally, of significance, Schor found no differences based on gender despite widely held beliefs that media comparisons are more difficult for girls than boys. Schor's findings strongly suggest a *causal* relationship between consumerism and negative physical and psychological health. Specifically, high consumer involvement appears to be a significant cause of depression, anxiety, low self-esteem, and psychosomatic complaints.

There has been significant research, both in the past and more recently, which suggests a relationship between media viewing and the acquisition of materialism in children.[229] With enough exposure to media messages which support the view that the acquisition of goods is a desirable undertaking, children seem to cultivate materialism. One study found that even when children expressed some awareness that advertising cannot be trusted, their desire for products was unflinching.[230]

It is also helpful to look at research on adults' materialism and wellbeing to gain further understanding as to the impact of consumer culture on children, considering how closely linked consumerism is with materialism. Materialism can be defined according to marketing professor Russell Belk as: "The importance a consumer attaches to worldly possessions. At the highest levels of materialism, such possessions assume a central place in a person's life and are believed to provide the greatest source of satisfaction."[231] Over the past two decades, a number of psychologists have demonstrated that individuals who strongly upheld values such as wealth, possessions, image, and status reported lower subjective well-being. Specifically, psychologists Tim Kasser and Richard Ryan found repeatedly that when extrinsic, materialistic-type values were rated as high in comparison to other pursuits such as self-acceptance, affiliation, and community feeling (intrinsic values), lower quality of life was reported. When financial success is central to young adults' goals, low well-being, high distress, and difficulties adjusting to life are evident.[232]

A group of social psychologists decided to determine whether the Kasser-Ryan findings in adults could be extended to children. In other words, would extrinsic motives correlate negatively to well-being for children like they do with adults? The researchers found that striving for consumer culture ideals for extrinsic reasons (e.g., appearance, social status), but *not* intrinsic reasons (social cohesion and cooperation), is associated with a lower level of well-being. (The children in this study were between the ages of eight and fifteen years.)[233]

Researchers found that adolescents who hold others in high esteem based on their possessions were at increased risk for personality disorders. Indeed, highly valuing being rich was associated with virtually every Axis I and Axis II psychological diagnosis analyzed in their research.[234] Psychologists Kennon Sheldon and Tim Kasser (1995) reported that young adults with a strong materialistic orientation described fewer experiences of positive emotions. In fact, a materialistic orientation in this study was associated with pursuing one's goals because of feelings of internal guilt and external pressure, rather than for reasons of enjoyment or wholehearted identification.[235]

It is significant and important to note that the negative association between materialism and well-being has been replicated in samples of different ages and cultures from around the world, including Britain, Denmark, Germany, India, Romania, Russia, South Korea, and Australia; German adults and business students in Singapore; and adults in China, Turkey, Australia, Canada, and Singapore.[236] The studies on materialism and well-being reveal that people vastly overestimate increases in happiness based on income: beyond incomes of approximately $60,000, more wealth does little to enhance people's level of happiness in today's market.[237]

Interestingly, Kasser found that for children between 10 and 18, females are more generous than males, and that males are more materialistic than females.[238] Additionally, older children are less frugal and less generous than younger children. Kasser also reported that those low in frugality reported lower self-esteem, more use of cigarettes, and increased incidences of fighting with others. Moreover, those low in generosity reported being less content, having lower self-esteem, drinking more alcohol, and getting into more fights and trouble at school. In this same study, consistent with previous findings, those high in materialistic values reported less happiness, more anxiety, and lower self-esteem.[239]

Successfully attaining materialistic goals beyond average income levels fails to increase one's happiness. At most, a temporary improvement of mood and excitement overwhelms, but it is likely to be brief and superficial. Paradoxically, the more we are surrounded by plenitude, the more we seem to crave. One of the reasons that materialistic values of wealth, status, and image fail to deliver is that they often work against interpersonal relationships and meaningful connections to others—two of the hallmarks of psychological health and quality of life.[240] Pursuit of materialistic values is generally associated with deep-rooted feelings of insecurity and attempts to prove one's competence.[241] It comes as no surprise that despite a quadrupling of the GDP since World War II, Americans' levels of happiness have remained constant.[242]

Twenge et al. looked at whether MMPI (the Minnesota Multiphasic Personality Inventory used to identify mental health symptoms) scores had changed between the 1930s and the present among high school and college students to determine what, if any, generational changes in mental health had occurred.[243] Specifically, they hypothesized that cultural change over the last few decades may be a contributing factor for the dramatic rise in symptoms on the MMPI, indicating increased psychopathology in young people. Large changes over relatively short periods of time cannot be attributed to genetics and are, therefore, likely linked to environment. The data suggest that the rise in mental health disorders among young people coincides with greater emphasis on extrinsic goals, such as material wealth, and less emphasis on intrinsic goals, such as valuing community.[244]

Moniek Buijzen and PattiValkenburg, with the Amsterdam School of Communications Research, conducted a study in 2003 to reinvestigate whether and how television advertising is related to materialism, parent–child conflict, and unhappiness.[245] They found that children who watched television commercials on a regular basis held stronger materialistic values than their counterparts (those who watched commercials infrequently). Because television is replete with advertisements designed to promote and encourage consumption, it is no surprise that it shows up as positively correlated with materialism. The authors also found that advertising exposure leads to an increased number of purchase requests, which contributed to parent–child conflict. This relation was stronger for younger children and for boys. While Buijzen and Valkenburg did not find a *direct* relation between advertising and disappointment, or between advertising and less life dissatisfaction, they did find an *indirect* one. The results showed that advertising exposure led to an increased number of purchase requests, which were associated with increased levels of disappointment.[246]

This chapter has shown overwhelming evidence that consumer culture does harm to children both directly (e.g., poor eating habits) and indirectly (e.g., gravitating toward materialism as a way of life). It is confounding that we, as a culture, are ignoring the obvious and are failing to protect children from corporate predators who view them as "targets" to be had. Why are we sacrificing children for the sake of corporate profit—profit that we will never even experience? Why do we accept so easily that our culture, because it is one that we partake in, is right, democratic, and good for us? It is clear that corporations favor conformity, that kids are primarily all after the same look, technological gadgets, and the desire to embody cool. It is conformity to the norms of consumerism that allows corporations to cash in big—believing in the efficacy of materialism makes one an avid consumer. The argument that corporations are taking advantage of the vulnerabilities of children and adults alike will be pursued in a different direction in Chapter Three. It is there that we will explore what it means to construct one's identity— the core of one's being—as a citizen of a consumer-oriented world. How does consumer culture challenge identity formation, and why should we be worried about it?

3

I Buy, Therefore I Am

At the heart of the struggle between childhood and consumerism, child identity formation is at stake. Children's sense of vulnerability with respect to identity is particularly acute as they strive for a sense of self throughout their growing-up years. Corporations, through advertising, aim to capture a child's attention so as to shape attitudes, motivation, behavior, and ultimately, identity. Of grave significance is the fact that children are invited to believe that what they consume defines who they are and this provides a sense of security. Even those children whose financial means restrict them from the market suffer in terms of identity. They are cast as an "underclass," as individuals with no market value, as "failed consumers" who do not fit the norm.[1]

Advertisers strive to create a convincing depiction of the ideal consumer, the successful, sexy, wealthy individual who owes his or her achievement to the product, whatever it may be. They prey on children's weakly formed identity to convince them of the need to buy, knowing they will wish to emulate the embodiment of cool. Indeed, identity plays an important role in that it affects our perceptions of and responses to brands. At the same time, "branding" is critical to understanding how children incorporate products as aspects of their identity—they do not just wear the brand; they personify the brand. Thus, children are recruited into the adoption of attitudes, roles, and behaviors that they did not consciously decide.[2]

THEORIES AND DEFINITIONS

In the world of modernity and globalization, social scientists believe that identity formation, which has always been vital to understanding of the self, has become problematic.[3] The fast-paced global network in which many of us live is such that we have had to become extremely adaptive to social change.[4] Hence, today many of us experience a continuous developmental crisis, engaged in an identity process that seemingly lasts a lifetime. Identity is considered to be fundamental to personal well-being and merits discussion, particularly in relation to how children fare in consumer-driven societies. Identity can be defined simply as the subjective concept of oneself as a human being.[5] Sociologists Peter Burke and Jan Stets offer a more comprehensive definition, one that includes both the role of the psyche and that of the collective:

> An identity is the set of meanings that define who one is when one is an occupant of a particular role in society, a member of a particular group, or claims particular characteristics that identify him or her as a unique person.[6]

Burke and Stets also stipulate that people possess multiple identities because they occupy multiple roles, are members of multiple groups, and are comprised of multiple personal characteristics. The self is said to originate in the mind and is that which characterizes an individual's consciousness of his or her own being or identity; each of the smaller "selves" operates under the umbrella of the larger identity structure.[7] Identity can be said to be "all inclusive," by virtue of the fact that it encompasses individual, relational, and social levels of self-representation. A person's identity is not to be found in behaviors or in feedback from others, but in the capacity to "keep a particular narrative going" that best characterizes who we think and believe that we are. The traits from which such "biographies" are constructed vary both socially and culturally. Feelings about one's identity can range in extremes from robust to fragile depending upon the "story" that is dominant.[8] Again, identity is located at the level of subjective psychological experience, rather than an objective "essence." Identity, therefore, sustains a sense of self that is alive and within the scope of reflexive control, rather than as that of an object.[9]

Identity can be understood as developing through a complex interplay of cognitive, affective, and social interactive processes, all of which occur within a particular cultural context. There are ongoing pressures toward certain identity states, and away from others, all of which guide the fluid process of identity construction. In addition to having both cognitive and emotional processes, identities encompass functioning at both conscious and subconscious levels.[10] Thus, the concept of identity has several facets, including individual, inner, and psychic dimensions, as well as external, collective, social, and cultural influences that are dependent upon context for understanding.[11]

Consumer capitalism, with its efforts to standardize consumption and to shape desires through advertising, plays a basic role in forming superficial identities, even narcissism. Sociologist Anthony Giddens notes, "the idea of generating an educated and discerning public has long since come to the pervasiveness of consumerism, which is a society *dominated by appearances*" (italics added).[12] Furthermore, consumerism addresses the alienated qualities of modern social life and claims to be the most viable solution, promising the very things narcissistic types desire, namely, attractiveness, beauty, and personal popularity through the acquisition of the "right" kinds of goods. Citizens of consumer cultures live as though their reflection is ubiquitous, searching for the appearance of an unblemished, socially valued self everywhere, in each new fashion style. Hence, the task of building identity in consumer capitalism is fraught with obstacles. Identity has to be created and more or less continually reordered against the backdrop of shifting experiences in the fragmenting tendencies of modern institutions and patterns of consumption. Moreover, identity in its chameleon-like formations directly affects and, to some degree, constructs the perception of the body as well as the self.

Sociologist Zygmunt Bauman proposes that the modern identity is fraught with the same difficulties that come with any addiction, namely, the insatiable desire to shop.[13] In a consumer society, the universal dependency on shopping is the sine qua non of freedom—the freedom to be different, to "have identity." Bauman imagines the modern seeker as one who is guided by seduction, rather than normative regulation, running after pleasurable sensations, but at the same time trying to find an escape from "the agony called insecurity."[14] The consumer-oriented identity strives to be sure of itself, confident and trusting by chasing after objects deemed to be desirable and claiming a promise of certainty. Each attempt is followed by another in an endless cycle—clinging to things solid and tangible, yet chronically unfulfilling. Thus, identities seem fixed and solid only when observed from the outside. Beneath the surface lies a fragile, vulnerable self, torn asunder by an ever-raging desire to appear whole and solid.

In our media-dominated world, we often find ourselves longing after an image, an identity that matches what we see on the screen. In fact, our lived life comes to be seen as unreal compared to that of the screen, regardless of its elusiveness.[15] Hence, the intense engagement of celebrity worship that is so commonly observed in consumer culture. Ironically, the capacity to "shop" for and shed one's identity on a whim, to treat it as a commodity, has come to signify freedom and privilege. We are so often told in the media that the reinvention of the self is possible, is within our grasp. The popularity and normalization of plastic surgeries reflect the commodified nature of the body and indicate the extreme lengths to which individuals will go as they strive to achieve the cultural mandates of beauty. Cleaning, adorning, and exercising the body are now intimately tied to corporate profit. Bodies, in other words, have become commodities to be "bought" and "sold" in keeping with the latest fads and fashions.[16] In essence, consumer culture demands a continual reinvention of the self, one that requires "updating." Erich Fromm, social psychologist of the Frankfurt School, describes modern humans' commodification of the self as a desperate attempt to generate self-esteem—meeting the market standard brings "success," and failure to do so invokes a sense of worthlessness.[17] No longer is valuing the self constituted by the qualities one possesses but by the standards of a market in constant flux. Put simply, fads come and go and so must our sense of self once we align with those fads. This explains the frenetic drive to strive for success as well as a deep-seated fear of failure in keeping up with the dictates of the market. We, of consumer culture, have become reliant on the judgments and opinions of others to the degree that genuine feelings of identity are lost.

Ironically, despite all of the rhetoric about "becoming your own person," individuality is scarce in consumer cultures. The development of one's true nature is often impeded by a continuous stream of media messages that pressure us to pursue paths that we might not otherwise follow. Ultimately, when the genuine self is neglected, relationships take on a superficial quality. Thus, affluent cultures, those which embrace materialism as a way of life, tend to overemphasize competition and devalue integrity, cooperation, and altruism.[18]

One of the greatest challenges to identity formation within modernity is the pace with which the self has to be shaped, altered, and sustained in relation to rapidly changing circumstances of social life, both on a local and global scale. Indeed, the period of consumer capitalism is characterized by swift social, economic, and cultural change, a key feature of daily life, particularly in the West.[19] Modernity also presents special challenges for children, including a quick exit from childhood and expectation of adult behavior, attitudes, and role alignment—all of this long before they are ready.

CHILDREN'S IDENTITY IN MODERNITY:
THE DOUBLE-EDGED SWORD OF TECHNOLOGY

It is widely believed that the pressure on children to establish an identity is now greater than any previous time in history.[20] The "new" media, including video games, MP3 players, iPods, smart phones, and computers, provide endless opportunities to reinvent the self. On average, children are spending five to six hours per day on weekdays in front of a screen and up to seven and a half hours per day on weekends.[21] Schools' use of technology has continued to increase to the degree that recess was eliminated in over 40 percent of primary schools by 2000.[22] It should be noted that the recommended leisure-related screen time guidelines of the Canadian Paediatric Association is limited to less than one hour per day for children between the ages of two to four, and less than two hours per day for children between the ages of five and seventeen.[23] Similarly, the American Academy of Pediatrics suggests children and teens spend no more than one or two hours per day in front of a screen.[24] For many children, technology becomes *the* means with which to express one's "true" identity, a place free from adult intervention.[25] The websites children create and share function as a form of identity expression, self-disclosure, and communication. In 2000, a study reported that girls between the ages of 12 and 17 were considered to be the fastest growing group of Internet users. Girls are more likely to use email and instant messaging, while boys are more likely to download games and music.[26] The use of Facebook, for example, seamlessly allows for the reinvention of the self. The screen seemingly offers a benign place to write about ourselves, to formulate who we are, as we wish to be seen. It is not uncommon for kids to practice on the Internet, expressing emotions and ideas that would be difficult to do face to face. It is, therefore, easy for them to be lulled into a false sense of security and share intimate details with virtual strangers.

Sherry Turkle, a technology specialist who undertook a 15-year study on the use of technology, discovered that anxiety is a key part of social networking.[27] She noted that while technology is clearly a useful tool, it also puts children in a position of constant surveillance. Being accepted into a virtual clique is risky—whatever gets posted online can haunt for a lifetime. Hence, the title of Turkle's 2010 book, *Alone Together*, suggesting that today's young people often feel deprived of attention and security despite having hundreds of cyber-friends. Communication, mediated by technology, has become so inextricably linked to identity that the fear of disconnection is a common anxiety— to feel safe is to be connected. At the same time, online friendships can be demanding and stressful. We like it that the Web "knows" us but have given up our privacy in return. And in a life of texting and messaging, we can accept or just as easily dismiss each other on demand. Professor of education Lowell Monke, who has spent many years teaching children about computers, cautioned: "students must bring at least a budding sense of humaneness to the classroom so they can tell the difference between using the computer for society's benefit and its exploitation."[28] Technology is so familiar today that many children underestimate its enormous power and ability to impact others in positive and negative directions, taking for granted its usefulness.

Narcissism and Personality Disorders

Jean Twenge and colleague Keith Campbell asserted in 2009 that U.S. culture is suffering from a narcissism epidemic affecting both narcissistic and less self-centered people, including children. They note that the rise in narcissism appears to be accelerating—the increase between 2000 and 2006 was especially sharp. Nearly one out of ten Americans in their twenties has experienced some of the characteristics of narcissistic personality disorder compared with only 3.2 percent of those over 65 years old.[29] Narcissism is the "darker side of the focus on the self" and should not be confused with positive self-esteem, which encourages an acceptance of the self and reward of genuine effort.[30] Narcissism is rooted in the belief that you are special and more important than other people, entitling you to privileges that are not necessarily deserved. According to Twenge and Campbell, the central feature of narcissism is a very positive and inflated view of the self. The outcome of such cognition is a fundamentally imbalanced individual with a grandiose, inflated self-image, a sense of entitlement, and a lack of deep connection to others. While narcissists work to keep up their positive self-views and emotions, those around them suffer. Indeed, narcissism is a significant risk factor for aggressive behaviors, as well as for exploiting and manipulating others.[31]

The increase in narcissism is reflective of a massive shift in culture toward a greater focus on self-indulgence and a shallow admiration of self. Despite feelings of worthlessness and emptiness, the narcissist pursues his or her material dreams with gusto, feeding the ravishment of the "false self" all the while dismissing the despair of an empty life.[32] Indeed, consumer culture, with its intense focus on children and adolescents, fuels narcissism by encouraging engagement with materialism and its concomitant, superficiality. As we have seen, children are spending at astonishing rates—in the 2000s they spent *500* percent more than their parents did at the same age, and many of these kids were using money they did not have to earn.[33] The other explanation for a narcissism epidemic could be directly related to the ways in which media reinforce extreme individualism. Environmentalist Bill McKibben points out that for most of human history we have put "the tribe, the gods, the natural world" at the center of our lives, a practice not tolerated in the world of consumption where buying is the new ritual. Keeping people fragmented and hungry for attention has been made even easier with the new technologies that zero in on the psyche with remarkable accuracy.[34] Each of us becomes "known"—our profile with wants and needs miraculously pinpointed—the world of marketing seemingly speaks to us.

American advertising appeals to our desire to be unique or different—yet another feature of narcissism. The emphasis on uniqueness is one of the hallmarks of advertising and children are quick to scramble after any product that defines them as different. Hence, the profitable sale of customized clothing, gadgets, and just about anything that is amenable to a personalized insignia.

Perhaps the most popular cultural message is to repeatedly tell children how special they are. The results are reflected in current statistics: In 2006, 51 percent of 18- to 25-year-olds said that "becoming famous" was an important goal of their generation—nearly five times that of "becoming spiritual."[35] Additionally, a 2006 poll in Britain revealed that children's most popular answer to naming the "very best thing in the world" was "being a celebrity," "good looks," and "being rich."[36] The media plays into the narcissism epidemic with a variety of television shows including TLC's *Toddlers & Tiaras*, which featured young children in beauty pageants.[37] Despite controversy around the show that the children were dressing and acting provocatively, it successfully led to the creation of two spin offs: *Here Comes Honey Boo Boo* and *Cheer Perfection*—both of which showcase a select group of children and their families, turning them into mini-celebrities. The Internet is a place where presenting yourself as better, cooler, and more attractive thrives. Narcissists also thrive on social networking sites like MySpace and Facebook, where self-promotion is the norm. With YouTube, individuals can have their own "show." Unlike traditional media that focus on others' lives and experiences, social networks foster an obsession with "me" by making children the stars of their own stories.[38]

Ultimately, the lack of fulfillment of authentic human needs and desires leaves the narcissistic child bereft. The naturally occurring feeling of emptiness that goes hand in hand with a narcissistic outlook is so buried that there is only the vaguest sense that life is amiss, especially for a child who is still forming his or her personality and character. The nascent narcissist is forever bombarded with the assurance that "this time" true fulfillment can be found with product "X," and so goes the cycle of chronic disappointment followed by high hope.[39] By adulthood, the "false self" has been dominant for so long that it becomes not only difficult to confront but near impossible to override. Even 20 years ago, the problem of the narcissistic consumer was so rampant that a branch of psychology, "ecopsychology," was developed to address this specific issue.[40]

Branding

The 1990s generation of young consumers has been singled out as the most brand-conscious ever by virtue of the depth and breadth of their brand knowledge and preferences.[41] Over the last decade, there has been an exponential increase in the use of brands directed at children. Branding is the process by which corporations use products to create and communicate specific concepts for the purpose of marketing. The overall aim of branding is to associate cultural content with a brand. It would appear that all available space, every desire and thought, will reflect the meaning and values of some brand.[42] Corporations are relying on the value of the image of their product rather than on its quality. There is some evidence to suggest that children are incorporating the associations belonging to brands into their self-concepts, a process referred to as "self-brand connections."[43] Indeed, the intimate entangling of brand and identity is nowhere more evident than in the experience of childhood over the last 20 years. Brand promotion is comprehensive, so much so that the division between entertainment and advertising, and day-to-day functioning, is seamless. As social scientist Beryl Langer describes it: "The colonization of children's lives by the entertainment product cycle has woven Disney, Hasbro, Mattel and McDonald's into the fabric of everyday life for urban children across the globe."[44] Children have been bombarded by brands defined by name products with intrusive and clever advertising strategies such that branding has become a way of life. Through licensing and merchandising, everything from television shows to toys and other products generating sales, keeps corporate brands and logos alive in the minds of children. Corporations invest in grand design strategies to acquire the right logos, constantly reinventing their image in the most eye-catching way. Journalist and consumer critic Naomi Klein exposed how corporations are more about brands than products—a strategy of imprinting on the very identity of those who desperately seek brand "status."[45] Klein writes that "the product always takes a back seat to the real product, the brand, and the selling of the brand [can] only be described as spiritual."[46] Children are an especially desirable brand audience because once hooked, their loyalty could potentially, with the right logo, span a lifetime. While adults are relatively fixed in their brand preferences, children and teens are viewed as exquisitely pliable.

Children as young as three can be avid consumers and devoted media watchers. By age five many begin to show interest in brands and can recognize them in stores.[47] More specifically, conceptual brand meanings, the nonobservable abstract features of a product, begin to be considered by children around the age of eight.[48] Business school professors Jill Ross and Rod Harradine found that early brand awareness and recognition is practically a guarantee of brand loyalty later in life.[49] It has been established that by age 12, children are able to think about brands on a conceptual level and begin to incorporate these meanings into many types of brand-related judgments.[50] However, it is unrealistic to assume that they also have the sophistication required to critically reflect on the true meaning and impact of brands.

Product placement now pervades throughout many types of media from television to video games and aims to harness children's desires with branded images they cannot resist. Journalist Alissa Quart (2003) coined the term "body branding," or "branding of the flesh," because of the explosion in cosmetic surgery on teens 18 and under.[51] Alterations of teens and children, while not all that common, are frequent enough to warrant concern. According to the American Society of Plastic Surgeons, teen surgeries doubled between 2002 and 2010.[52] And between 2002 and 2003 alone, breast implants for 18-year-olds and younger nearly tripled.[53] Boys, typically considered at less risk when it comes to appearance obsession, also engage in harmful behaviors for the sake of looks. For example, data taken from almost 2,800 adolescents revealed that approximately 6 percent reported steroid use and about 35 percent used protein powders for muscle enhancement—in both cases, the majority of users were boys.[54] The quest to transform the self physically, emotionally, and psychologically is one of the outcomes of branding. Hence, identity formation is closely aligned with branded images, especially those that infiltrate deep into the psyche.

Children also experience branding through contemporary consumer culture's obsession with celebrity.[55] Remarkably, a reality television show, *I Want a Famous Face*, showcases young people who subject themselves to plastic surgery so they can look like their celebrity idols. MTV's website exclaims: "Whether it's a Pamela Anderson wannabe or a Janet Jackson hopeful, their goals are not just to look differently, but to look exactly like their favorite stars."[56] Children are "encouraged" by marketers to adopt any aspect of the celebrity's persona that can be sold for profit. The Britney Spears craze several years ago is a good example of how powerful these images can become. The mechanism of identifying with a celebrity directly impacts a child's social identity or that aspect of the self that maneuvers socially. Children's idolatry of sports stars and pop stars appears to have a significant impact on their identity.[57] Since the celebrity is almost always an adult, the "style of life" (cultivation of a particular look) that children come to crave leads them closer to a world for which they are not yet ready.

Research on the Effects of Branding

In 2004, Richard Elliot and Clare Leonard examined the effect of brand-name shoes among poor children aged eight to twelve.[58] This study was important because it is one of the few that explored children's attitudes toward fashion brands and their symbolic meaning. The results indicated that children appear to identify with and desire the perceived positive characteristics associated with brand names such as "being cool." The majority of children in the study said that they would refrain from talking to someone who was not wearing the "right" shoes out of embarrassment. Elliot and Leonard used the term "brand community" to characterize the fact that all of the chilren who participated in their study were united by a desire to own Nike shoes, in particular. It could be said that the children appeared to gauge their status and that of others on the basis of the visibility of certain brands, in this case, Nike. Anthropologist Grant McCracken states that fashion brands are part of a system of meanings that are transferred from within the culture to members of that culture.[59] Within the Elliot and Leonard study, this type of transfer was evident; the child-participants attributed traits such as "cool" and "popular" to the shoes themselves. Sports branding seems to offer children a fairly easy and obvious way of fitting in with their peers, as well as providing a good barometer of status. One of the conclusions underscored by the researchers was that brands invoke "strong attachments" and that the children desperately wanted to be affiliated with the "right" brand.[60] Also, Elliot and Leonard concluded that children desire branded trainers (shoes) to be seen on par with friends who own the same, to appear that they have achieved a certain status.

In a somewhat related study to that of Elliot and Leonard's, boys were found to admit that the opinions they had of their peers was based on their brand clothing.[61] An earlier study by Elizabeth Frost revealed that girls identified cool on the basis of attractive individuals in the "right" clothes and "sad" for those who were not so privileged.[62] Another study of children aged five to twelve found that the consumption of clothing, including branded clothing, appears to be an important way in which they construct their identities and perceive their relationships with peers.[63] What all of these studies have in common is that young children have a fairly advanced recognition and application of the symbolic value of clothing, including branded clothing.

Hence, children seem to have a relatively sophisticated knowledge of clothing consumption both in terms of fashion retailers and the symbolic value of brands. Brand-loyal children represent a lucrative commodity, one that is now in global demand. Perhaps the most disturbing piece of the branding phenomenon is the extent to which it appears to be voluntary and embraced with enthusiasm. As Gitlin observed: "Children today gladly turn themselves into walking billboards."

MATERIALISM IN RELATION TO IDENTITY: RELEVANT EMPIRICAL RESEARCH

In consumer cultures, materialism dominates as one of the central ideologies. Defining the self by one's possessions can contribute to feelings of well-being, as well as those of emptiness and vulnerability.[64] Specifically, three key beliefs are present in a materialistic identity construct: material possessions are a central life goal; material possessions are the main route to identity success and happiness; material possessions are a yardstick for evaluating oneself and others.[65] Dittmar found throughout her studies that personal characteristics were attributed to individuals based on what they owned and how they dressed. In one of her studies, adults were shown a video of a person and asked for their first impressions. Their judgments of qualities such as friendliness and assertiveness differed depending on whether the person was wearing expensive articles of clothing.[66] Highly materialistic adolescents show a stronger tendency to judge the personal qualities of others in terms of the number and quality of material goods possessed.[67] In general, materialism appears to play an important role in social perception. A person's socioeconomic position also influences his or her external views about the world, particularly with respect to economic status and measures.[68]

Dittmar proposed that people often buy consumer goods because of their psychological benefits, rather than their economic and utilitarian value.[69] Additionally, material goods can signify group affiliations and social standing, including sex-role identification, socioeconomic status, or belonging to a subculture. And to some extent, the acquisition of material goods is likely motivated by subconscious desires. Within consumer culture, it appears that for both children and adults, material possessions are regarded as part of the extended self. The loss of possessions is experienced as a personal violation and a lessening of self. Possessions, whether gained or lost, have complex implications for self-esteem and self-evaluation. Interestingly, degree of materialism is a relatively unstable trait, varying with and dependent upon numerous developmental changes.[70] For example, materialism appears to increase from middle childhood to early adolescence. It was found that decreases in self-esteem, which tend to naturally occur between middle childhood and early adolescence, are correlated with increases of materialism. Likewise, as self-esteem increases from early to late adolescence, decreases in the valuing of materialism generally take place.

Kasser et al. used the phrase "materialistic value orientation" (MVO) to capture the aims, beliefs, goals, and behaviors associated with cultures of consumption.[71] They contended that a strong MVO is indicative of the ways in which individuals compensate for worries and doubts about their self-worth. A growing body of research suggests that individuals become more materialistic when they experience environments that do not support their psychological needs. It may also be true that the diminution of interpersonal resources such as love and affection, rather than financial resources, leads to materialistic attitudes and behavior.[72] Moreover, people who strongly orient toward values such as money, possessions, and image or status report lower subjective well-being than their counterparts. It appears that people employ material possessions to compensate for perceived inadequacies in their concept of self. It is important to note that whether people scored high or low in materialism, both groups indicated the presence of positive emotions (happy, excited). However, individuals who were strongly materialistic experienced more negative emotions such as anger, anxiety, guilt, or fear after completing purchases. It may be that consumption is of such importance to those with a strong materialist value that greater expectations of the purchasing process are developed, leaving one vulnerable to feelings of disappointment.[73]

The media is full of images of ideal body types, coveted material possessions, and "idealized" relationships that the majority will never attain.[74] Many young people grow up thinking they have the potential to eventually become a movie star, sports figure, or, at the very least, rich, like those seen on television. It appears that Boomers, when they were young adults, were more grounded than their 1990s counterparts: when given a choice of fame or contentment, only 17 percent of Boomers selected fame compared to 29 percent of the 1990s cohort.[75] It is telling that in 1970, 39 percent of college freshmen considered "becoming very well-off financially" as their number-one objective and in 1998 that number jumped to 74 percent.[76] High school students in the 1990s, a time when consumerism intensified, were twice as likely as high school students in the 1970s to believe that the acquisition of money was very important.[77] Not surprisingly, youth also expect to make a lot of money. In a 2011 survey, teenage Americans believed that once established in their careers, they would be earning $150,000. Yet the average U.S. household income is $50,000.[78] The lure of money is particularly salient in cultures that foster narcissism. Twenge and Campbell exclaim that "Being rich is a narcissist's paradise. When our most cherished hopes are for ourselves, it is extremely easy to be drawn to the appeal of being rich . . . [You] can afford the best of everything (after all, you deserve it)."[79] Yet happiness research conducted across numerous countries confirms that life satisfaction seems to stem predominantly from interpersonal relationships, particularly with a partner and children, as well as bonds with friends.[80] Further, having a high number of material goods does not seem to protect one from mental health disorders. Among affluent youth, substance abuse was linked with depression and anxiety, suggesting efforts to "self-medicate."[81] Indeed, teens in relatively well-off suburban neighborhoods reported significantly higher use of cigarettes, alcohol, marijuana, and hard drugs than their poorer inner-city counterparts. Suburban teens also revealed significantly higher anxiety and depression than did inner-city youth. The problem is so serious that affluent youth have among the highest rates of long-term substance abuse, somatic complaints, and unhappiness of any group of children in the United States.[82]

In a research study of British teenagers aged 16 to 19 years old, it was found that these young people were constructing their individuality according to subcultural parameters that were already well established, rather than forging into unknown or risky territory as a means of defining the self.[83] Specifically, they were using commodities (shoes) to represent "who one is" in relation to the everyday street culture, but in a relatively safe way—conforming while appearing to imbibe novelty. Although the teenagers recognized they were following the crowd, a trend that was popular among their peers, they held onto the belief of achieving individuality. Based on this data, it appears that consumption performs an important role in the solidification of identity. Second, peer relations are closely mediated through the process of consuming, in part to establish "stable" identity formation. Put differently, there is a need to believe we are distinctive individuals, despite conforming to standards established by others. In the West, in particular, we vehemently defend our individuality all the while merging our identity with the most popular trend of the day.

CONSUMER CULTURE AND GENDER ISSUES

Children and adults seem to substantiate their gendered identity through visual imagery, that which is ubiquitously present on every imaginable space in consumer cultures. The appearance industry is something that we pay close attention to, feeling compelled almost as a form of reinforcing identity.[84] Frost sees the obsession with the self as central to issues of control in a complex world:

Concerns with the self, the well-being of the self, the "actualization" of the self, including the body and appearance, have developed in relation to the needs of consumer capitalism to produce individualized consumers with a whole range of personal wants and needs.[85]

Both genders arrive at an understanding of the self and what is expected through dynamic exchange with culture. Specifically, consumer cultures place significant emphasis on appearance in the form of stereotypical models that define what it means to be male or female.

Girls and the Beauty Myth: Relevant Research

For many, perhaps even the majority of women and girls in consumer cultures, appearances are paramount to their self-definition. Mass media is the most powerful and vociferous purveyor of defining the ideal beauty. Girls, in particular, are inundated by such ideals in the form of dolls, figures that appear in comics, cartoons, television, movies, and all forms of advertising. The synergistic effect of such exposure can have a profound impact on a child's developing identity. Girls learn to see themselves as objects to be scrutinized and evaluated on the basis of appearance. They are told by advertisers that their most important trait is their physical facade.[86] This naturally results in a preoccupation with how to improve the body and enhance attractiveness so as to induce social desirability. At the same time, while the cultural ideal is becoming progressively thinner, body weight of girls is increasing.[87] Thus, it stands to reason that they are likely to experience body dissatisfaction, low self-esteem, and identities that reflect both of these characteristics.

Psychologists Helga Dittmar, Emma Halliwell, and Suzanne Ive conducted a study to determine whether children, aged five to eight years, were impacted by the figure of a Barbie doll, historically the most popular doll of all time.[88] Barbie is so extraordinarily thin that her weight and body proportions are not only unattainable but are unhealthy. The image of the ultra-thin female beauty has been linked to the high prevalence of negative body image and unhealthy eating patterns now commonly seen among girls and women. To put the matter in perspective, fewer than one in 100,000 women have Barbie's body proportions. Dittmar et al. found young girls experienced heightened body dissatisfaction after exposure to Barbie doll images. When exposed to a neutral control image, there was no effect.[89] A meta-analysis conducted in 2008 made clear that body image disturbance in women is correlated with media exposure to thin beauty ideals.[90] The same is true of young girls and, considering the most prevalent beauty ideal in Disney and Nickelodeon programming is thin (and white), the effects can be profound.[91]

Girls aged 14 to 18 years old, in particular, have difficulties associated with poor self-esteem emanating from appearance concerns that reflect negative self-perceptions. It is no surprise then that girls in this age group have the highest rate of body dysmorphic disorders, as well as self-harming behaviors.[92] Media-saturated cultures do not easily accept those who fall outside the rigid scripts of gendered expectations.[93] Negative comparing can also be internalized in the form of an "inner judge"—messages that were originally fed from an external source are integrated as an internal mechanism.[94] The inner judge can send us reeling or beaming depending on the messages that are disseminated. Scholar Howard Bloom identifies it as follows: "Our inner judges sentence us sternly or magnanimously depending on the snugness with which we fit our social network's needs."[95] Shame, the fallout of negative inner judgment, seems to have a particular resonance with teenage girls' somatic experiences. Thus, for girls, exposure to media may erode positive identity components whereby inner judges do heavy battle.

From Disordered Eating to Ultra-Masculine: Understanding the "Boy Code"

Like girls, boys also suffer from media effects and, in many respects, on the same types of issues. The media counts on boys wishing to assume the role of characters they see on television or in the movies, many of which uphold traditional masculine constructs. Psychologist William Pollack coined the term "boy code" to capture the kind of constraints that boys face such as having to suppress almost all emotions with the exception of anger and rage.[96] Another aspect of the boy code is to remain cool at all costs, even at academic cost. From elementary grades through high school, boys acquire lower grades than girls; consequently, boys in the eighth grade are held back 50 percent more often than girls. Pollack hypothesizes that one of the significant factors in academic instability for boys is the fear of not being perceived as cool, especially looking *too* smart. Moreover, young men in advertisements are often cast as loners or members of cool all-male groups and are rarely depicted as sons or brothers in a happy home environment.[97] For example, risk-taking behaviors are often attributed as part of a male psychology; bungee-jumping, sky surfing, and fast driving, to name a few, are everywhere in advertisements featuring men.

Chronic and frequent viewing of violent media may influence the display of not only physical and verbal aggression but also *relational* aggression among young children.[98] Relational aggression refers to the transmittance of gossip or malicious secrets or lies, as well as shunning.[99] Television watching has been found to correlate with both physical and relational aggression.[100] Gender seems to be a significant risk factor for violence, as most youth violence is perpetrated by males.[101] Statistically men are 10 times more likely to commit murder than young women; 95 percent of all juvenile homicides are caused by boys.[102] There is considerable concern that the "new media" (video games, music videos, the Internet) are far more salient with respect to aggression than are the passive media (television, movies).[103] And despite data showing reductions in violent crime, youth violence remains a serious problem. Out of all U.S. homicides committed in a year, 10 percent are by individuals under the age of 18 years.[104]

Eating disorders have among the highest mortality rates of all mental health disorders and thus deserve serious attention.[105] While they are commonly believed to be a female problem, 33 percent of high school girls as well as 16 percent of high school boys evidence some symptoms of an eating disorder.[106] Additionally, some estimate that between 30 and 75 percent of preadolescent and adolescent boys are dissatisfied with their bodies.[107] It has been established that media exposure is significantly correlated with disordered eating among adolescents and adults[108] and that media use during childhood is a significant predictor of adult body-image concerns. For example, body dissatisfaction in males has been found to increase significantly when viewing advertisements with male models, especially images of muscular men.[109]

Boys learn early on that a masculine identity is equated with being sexually active and that sexual responsibility is more a female burden than a male one.[110] On the other hand, women and girls are often portrayed by the media in a negative light when they initiate sexual activity. Sexual health topics covered in the media are ambiguous and inaccurate; furthermore, they reinforce traditional gender stereotypes that remain entrenched in our patriarchal society. Furthermore, teen pregnancy is often regarded as a "girl's problem" in which the mother-to-be is considered solely responsible for the child. Even in nonfiction accounts of teenage pregnancy, male responsibility is largely absent. The identity structure of female teens is subject to rapid transformation during pregnancy, some of which is problematic, and as young mothers they often receive little to no male support.

BRAND POWER AND THE MAKING OF IDENTITY

Corporations have always paid close attention to the concept of identity, recognizing its importance in the marketing of products. They have done so by studying the target consumer group's relevant traits and characteristics with regard to culture, ethnicity, age, and gender.[111] Marketers have hoped that, ultimately, their insight into the personalities of potential customers is accurate enough to ensure a hankering for their merchandise. They have spent substantial amounts of money trying to understand how a consumer's identity affects his or her perception and response to brands.

In the past two decades, identity-based marketing has gone a step further. Marketers have assumed control by focusing on the logo, the power of the brand, as a means of influencing identity. In other words, they are now dictating the type of person (identity) that goes hand in hand with their brand. Children, being more malleable than adults with respect to identity formation, are easy fodder. Adults tend to have multiple identities, while children's identities are in constant flux as they develop and mature. Though it feels stable to a child or adult, identity is, in fact, highly sensitive to all sorts of situational cues, and often without conscious awareness. Consumers likely connect more strongly with a brand if it "speaks" to multiple facets of the self.[112] If, for example, we consider an identity of cool, one that marketers know many will yearn for, the product or brand must embody cool in some way. The brand becomes a reminder of the kind of identity we long for or an identity cue. Hence, brands become the very symbols of identity in which we try to match ourselves to fit with the brand. At the same time, children (and adults) are made to believe that striving for cool is uniquely part of their experience, that the brand speaks to them on a personal level. Herein lies the paradox of consumption in cultures where individuality is highly valued. We delude ourselves into believing that our version of cool is unique, unlike any other, yet we all start marching to the same drummer. Our identities meld in such a way that it becomes hard to distinguish one from another, the true self having been cast aside. As Klein described it, "the branded multinationals may talk diversity, but the visible result of their actions is an army of teen clones marching—in 'uniform.'"[113]

4

For and Against the Child as a Consumer

Within the disciplines of sociology, psychology, education, and media studies a debate rages as to whether or not children are being manipulated or empowered within consumer-oriented cultures. This dichotomous banter is characterized by a continuum of positions ranging from those lamenting the loss of innocence and safety of childhood to those celebrating the emancipation and empowerment of children. Furthermore, the debate often distils into a polemic between those who believe consumerism is a negative influence leading to dissatisfaction, disillusionment, and a reduction of overall well-being[1] and those who believe heightened commercialism and consumption is a positive thing that contributes to human betterment and even happiness.[2]

The debate also includes dissension about media and technology. More specifically, media and mass communication technologies have been accused of interfering with and retarding children's physical and emotional development.[3] Media is said, in large part, to be responsible for a burgeoning crisis of childhood.[4] Many of the technologies associated with mass culture, including television, video discs, video games, computers, and other digital display units, it has been argued, are bad for the brain and the body.[5] Media culture and technology are also said to induce anomie and antisocial behaviors,[6] as well as be responsible for reinforcing divisive patterns like racism and sexism.[7] In general, many feel that children's lives should be protected from unregulated advertising.[8] On the other hand, media technology has been praised for its advancement of children's education. Computers and other electronics are heralded for enhancing learning at an unprecedented pace and teaching children to multitask, a "skill" assumed to enhance intelligence. There are those who feel that children have the right and ability to make consumer choices, to exercise free agency.[9]

The anti-consumer position is based on the conception that childhood is, universally, a critical time of development and is independent of cultural variances.[10] This notion is in sharp contrast with the pro-consumer side, which hypothesizes that the human core is superficial and malleable, such that there is no determined state of childhood, that historical context is critical to its understanding and perception.[11] Those who herald consumer culture's benefits believe that the consumer-child is representative of a "new" breed of childhood and that childhood must be viewed as pliable, fluid, and endlessly evolving.[12]

Both theoretical positions are presented with a review of the associated literature to determine their merit and validity as a means of fleshing out the argument. It is through an understanding of this debate that we can further contextualize the impact of consumer culture on children.

CHILDHOOD IS "CULTURALLY CONSTRUCTED" VERSUS A DISTINCT, FIXED PHASE OF LIFE

If we suppose that childhood is not an absolute or fixed stage of development based on a biological category but is, in fact, culturally or socially constructed, meaning subject to the culture of the times, including the education, psychology, socioeconomic ideology, and so forth, then concern about the commercialization or transformation of childhood seems misplaced. On the contrary, some argue that childhood must always be understood within a given historical, social, and cultural context in order to accurately understand its meaning at any given stage of history. Consumer culture may be stimulating children to grow up at a faster pace, for example, but is still viewed as "normal" relative to the times. It can even be said that children are now active participants in forming their own culture in more substantial ways than in the past.[13]

McNeal took the argument that consumer culture is good for children a step further. He claimed that Piaget's theory of child development, which is largely based on a child's interactions with objects in his or her environment, provided a guide about how consumer behaviors contribute to a child's intellectual growth:

Beyond genetics, the growth of the mind and that of the body are largely a result of consumer behavior, of perceiving and consuming commercial objects. Impoverish a child's environment by taking away all commercial objects, and the child is unlikely to become a normal functioning human being.[14]

In essence, McNeal adopted Piaget's theory of child development, then infused it with consumer "language" to produce a new theory, one that claims children are innately possessed with consumer behaviors from the time of birth. He maps out a five-stage learning process of the child consumer that is purported to be nongendered and universal. McNeal does not provide his own or others' research to substantiate his theoretical position; rather, it is all conjecture.

* * *

Those who theorize that childhood is a distinct biological, emotional, and psychological experience unique to children are more apt to view the commercialization of childhood as a negative force. One such theorist is Allison Gopnik, a cognitive psychologist, who suggests in her latest book, *The Philosophical Baby*, that "childhood is a universal fact."[15] She cites recent breakthroughs in neuroscience that reveal how children have different, though equally complex and powerful, minds, brains, and forms of consciousness designed to serve their evolutionary needs. Childhood, she claims, is a distinctive developmental period in which specific brain changes occur that play a prominent role in the metamorphosis to adulthood. Gopnik's findings challenge social construction theory, which states that childhood, especially modern-day childhood, is pliable and dependent upon cultural parameters.[16] Such theory cannot account for the *universality* of children's rights, interests, and needs—those that all children deserve.

In their book *Einstein Never Used Flashcards*, Hirsh-Pasek, Golinkoff, and Eyer, like Gopnik, contend that childhood is a distinctive phase of development that has suffered damage by the deluge of marketing aimed at children.[17] In particular, Hirsch-Pasek et al. maintain that parents have been hoodwinked into believing that they must make their babies smarter and faster through the purchase of so-called educational material. For instance, "Baby Einstein," "Baby Shakespeare," and "Baby Van Gogh" are media products promoted on the basis of enhancing a child's development and are marketed with strong claims, despite a lack of evidence. Hirsch-Pasek et al. assert their theory that authentic play, innately human, is the best means of maturation in children. This view has wide acceptance among scholars in early child development.[18] Parents are urged to protect their children's imaginations by reducing the exposure of ritualized "creativity" that characterizes mass culture.

AGENCY VERSUS DUPES

Marketers of children's toys argue that they do not dictate what children should do with commercial merchandise or the meanings they ascribe, that children are not "cultural dupes." There are some scholars, most notably David Buckingham, who support this view and assert that all consumers (adults as well) have agency, regardless of the intensity of consumer culture and its wares.[19] Agency means that the consumer takes an active role in determining the type of experience he or she will have with media and consumer goods. Furthermore, agency accounts for what individuals actually do with the media and consumer goods, how they veer outside the structuring influence of commercial producers. John Fiske, a strong proponent of the free agency position, suggests that media consumers are not unwitting victims of corporate marketing: "They are not a passive, helpless mass incapable of discrimination and thus at the economic, cultural, and political mercy of the barons of industry."[20] Fiske also credits children with the ability to liberate themselves from the influence of commercial media by developing their own "stories."

The child consumer is now increasingly portrayed as an "active agent," co-creating with marketers on what products are desirable or in establishing the meaning of brands.[21] Co-creation refers to a mindset that embraces the "customers are in charge" ideology. The consumer is deemed competent and should, therefore, be put to work side by side with marketers.[22] The concept of co-creation is also relevant to the notion of empowerment and will be discussed again in the next section.

* * *

It has been suggested that the solution for the child-consumer dilemma lies in consumer education. This begs the question as to how a four-year-old or even a ten-year-old can be "educated," to outsmart marketers and the psychologists who work for them. For instance, Buckingham talks about the intricacies of "media education" and how complex it is to implement within schools, let alone teach.[23] If adults have difficulty understanding how they are being manipulated and losing their capacity for "rational" thinking, then what chance does a child have to embrace a level of critical thinking that has not yet manifested? Martin Lindström, branding expert, states that with the development of neuroscience it will take great effort to withstand the onslaught of consumerism:

Neuromarketing is still in its infancy, and in the years ahead, I believe it is only going to expand its reach. . . . Can we, as individuals, escape the reach of marketers and brands and the new face of advertising that appeals to our subconscious minds? It's not easy to do in today's world. . . . we, the consumers, can [learn to] escape all the tricks and traps that companies use to seduce us to their products and get us to buy and take back our rational minds.[24]

With regard to teenagers, it is not enough to develop agency as a means of warding off consumerism—teens, traditionally viewed as having too much agency, also succumb to consumer demands that are not necessarily in their best interests. Statistics on teens' physical health, including drinking, smoking, and prevalence of psychiatric disorders, speak to this issue. Furthermore, it takes considerable maturation for teenagers to perceive the differences between "realism" and fantasy and develop the wherewithal to grasp the way television messages are delivered.[25] As a result, they are susceptible to all sorts of media influence with a somewhat limited discriminatory capacity.

EMPOWERMENT AND "CO-CREATION" VERSUS DISENFRANCHISEMENT

The "pro" side sees play as serious business to children and one of the important ways they learn to express their power. They believe that children are, ultimately, immune to "scripted" play from toy manufacturers. Ellen Seiter, professor of cinematic arts, maintains that children's involvement in consumer culture vastly expands their capacity to connect with other children all over the world. Specifically, she states that children's "shared repository of images, characters, plots, and themes [provides] the basis for small talk and play, and it does this on a national, even global scale."[26] The fact that children from varying cultural backgrounds share a "language" means that they can operate, to some degree, as a unified whole. As a result of their common identification with consumer culture, children's culture becomes a force of empowerment. For example, children are able to express themselves unfettered by adult rules, authority, and constraints, and to operate with a type of freedom that would otherwise be difficult to impossible to attain.

According to Buckingham, children are achieving "economic empowerment" as they engage in consumer society.[27] The fact that children nationwide (ages four to twelve) influence both directly and indirectly $700 billion of parental spending and also spend $42 billion of their own money means that they must be taken more seriously, not just as consumers but as citizens.[28] Previously excluded from the exercise of social power, children are now being given legitimate access. For example, children now sit on product development boards of corporations and serve as peer consultants for such enterprises as films and new products.[29] Even the issue of children's rights has taken a more prominent position, as evidenced by new legislation in numerous countries with an aim to protect children's civil rights.[30] Empowerment means that children's voices are finally being heard within a cultural and legal venue.

* * *

Children who attempt to achieve "empowerment" through acts of consumption are likely to develop fragile identities and interpersonal difficulties. This is because consumer culture fosters a set of values based on self-interest, a strong desire for financial success, and a self-centered "me" mentality tied to narcissism and competition. Indeed, the idea that individuals should compete against each other in the pursuit of their own self-interest is one of the key tenets of consumer culture. Furthermore, identities built on the valuing of materialism and competition are likely to be shallow and unsustainable. Psychological research has established that individuals oriented toward materialistic values are less empathic, less cooperative, and will likely struggle interpersonally as a result.[31] Children who are influenced to engage heavily in consumer culture have no real opportunity for empowerment, which in its truest form is associated with positive values such as altruism, generosity, respect, and self-esteem.

Today's marketers are touting "co-creation" as a way to engage with the so-called empowered and entrepreneurial consumer whom they attribute as ruling the digitally networked marketplaces. They believe that by "consulting" the customer in market production, by seeking the customer's technical, social, and cultural knowledge, they will gain a market edge that would otherwise be lost to a competitor. The consumer/customer, they hypothesize, should now be regarded as a type of marketing partner, rather than just a potential buyer. As corporations have to increasingly rely on skilled and flexible employees who are able to innovate rapidly in order to keep up with the fast-changing times, who better to partner with than the prospective buyer? Yet Zwick et al. maintain that the co-creating model is more about exploitation than consultation, since the "crux of value co-creation . . . is to provide the surest way of *delivering the customer over to the corporation*" (italics added).[32] By enlisting customers and charging them for their work, the co-creation model must engage a discourse that reframes the traditional methods of consumer control into one of "relationship."[33] It should also be noted that the discourse of empowerment renders marketing to children a morally defensible and an ethically sound undertaking. Yet the mandate of corporations is to provide maximum funds for their shareholders with little other motivation or intention.[34] Ultimately, corporate charters have no interest in empowering their customers, especially if it interferes with profit making.

OPPORTUNITIES FOR CREATIVITY, COMMUNITY, AND SELF-FULFILLMENT VERSUS LOSS OF CREATIVITY

The pro-consumer side sees engagement with media technology as a central part of participation as a consumer, as a means of facilitating purchases, gathering information, and partaking in numerous forms of entertainment. Children are also regarded as the pioneers of twenty-first-century technology. Whether it is through television or the Internet, children are communicating with one another and adults at levels previously unseen or imagined. The result is a complex web of interactions that afford children the opportunity of self-expression and creativity. The media, in general, has become an important tool with which children can express their ideas, views, and needs in order to gain higher levels of fulfillment without continual dependency on adults. Children are creative in their appropriation of consumer goods and media, developing their own meanings from the stories and symbols of consumer culture.[35] Social scientist Paul Willis states that young people's lives are full of expressions, signs, and symbols of a "common culture," partly based upon their use of and investment in media and consumer goods through which they seek "creatively to establish their presence, identity and meaning."[36] For example, soap operas, despite their puerility, nonetheless foster engagement with the viewer. Hence, the viewer is said to be contributing to the symbolic and creative work of culture. As Willis declares: "The audience is not an empty room waiting to be furnished in someone else's taste . . . Young people have an active, creative, and symbolically productive relation to what they see on television."[37] While the artifacts of children's culture originate with corporate conglomerates, children are still able to uniquely develop their own meanings and uses from media.

* * *

It can be argued that true creativity reflects the apex of human intelligence. It is the process whereby we apply ourselves to look at the world in a new way, to solve problems and exercise wisdom, to evaluate ourselves and others. Creativity is the capacity to look at the ordinary as though never before seen, to envision and imagine a new horizon that may lead to uniqueness whether through mental or physical exertion.[38] The sheer volume of toys and other paraphernalia that corporations impose on children is not a direct outcome of a child's creativity. In fact, creativity has no place in consumption because consumable objects are already well-defined in their purpose and utility.[39] Furthermore, it is absurd to argue that technology will lead to increased creativity when the majority of software is solely determined by a programmer. True innovation is not necessary for working on a computer,[40] picking up text messages, or operating an iPod.

CITIZENS OF THE FREE MARKET VERSUS CORPORATE PAWNS

Free-market advocates, those who align themselves with unfettered corporate interests, believe that children are powerful, sovereign beings and are, therefore, in the best position to identify and articulate their own needs. In essence, it is said, they have the capacity to drive the free market. As one of the founders, Geraldine Laybourne, of the children's channel Nickelodeon declared: "What's good for business is good for kids."[41] Marketers advocate that the free market is representative of free choice and the ability to exercise decisions unencumbered by social, cultural, and familial constraints—to be a consumer is to embody such access.

* * *

Children are not unreservedly participating in the mythical "free" market. Rather, they are a *product* of the free market to be bought and sold. If a corporation is able to capture a child audience through such mediums as television programming, movies, DVDs, and so on, the goal is to then sell the audience (just like a product) to sponsoring advertisers. Consumer cultures value the economic worth of children more than their welfare. Children are considered to be up for "sale." They are all too often exploited by self-interested corporations whose mission is to acquire whatever profit they can to please their shareholders, a far cry from drivers of the free market.[42]

ADVERTISEMENTS ARE TRULY EDUCATIONAL VERSUS MANIPULATIVELY PERSUASIVE

Marketers argue that advertisements provide children with the needed information to experience the full embodiment of a consumer modality. They also maintain that advertising teaches children the consumption skills necessary to function in the marketplace, such as evaluating the attributes of different products, as well as teaching children how to shop with discrimination. "Yes," they argue, advertisements can influence choice of brands, but it is ultimately peers and family who are far more influential in dictating consumer spending patterns. While younger children are least able to remember and understand advertisements, considering them more a source of entertainment, there is a dearth of empirical evidence claiming that program-length commercials are designed to deceive.[43] Advertisements make a fairly limited contribution to children's beliefs about the integrity of a product. Again, parents and socioeconomic status are far more significant in this area. There is little to no research that supports the fact that advertising contributes to broader ideologies and values by making an individual buyer more consumerist or materialistic.[44] To be swayed by advertising is to be viewed as incompetent or irrational and thus, uniquely vulnerable to persuasion—an argument used by adults to keep children in their place.

* * *

The argument that advertisements are used only to inform consumers is a gross misrepresentation, considering the extent to which marketers use psychologists and neuroscientists, as well as advanced influence techniques, as a means of getting us to buy. Advertising is not meant to inform or educate; it is designed to manipulate, to exercise control over the audience. Advertising works because it is a refined tactic of persuasion that is generally beyond the capability of most adults, let alone children, to discern.

It has been repeatedly determined that young children do not distinguish advertising from television programming, for example, and are incapable of understanding the persuasive intent of advertising even by the age of 10 years.[45] In 2004, the American Psychological Association (APA) published a bold paper on the negative psychological effects of advertising and strongly recommended an advertising ban for children under eight.[46] For children between the ages of 8 and 12, it has been shown that they are only starting to become aware of the impact of media and its significance[47] and are, therefore, also vulnerable. This explains why cultures, such as Sweden and Quebec, wishing to protect children from marketers, have banned advertising to children under the age of 12 years. It should be noted that Buckingham maintains that media literacy, if applied properly, can mitigate the negative effects of advertising.[48] Yet even he admits that teaching media literacy in schools has been a failure overall because few educational systems seem to understand its importance. It should be noted that in Buckingham's 2003 book entitled *Media Education*, there is no mention of the role of the corporation or that just a few corporations own the media. It seems apparent that media education that ignores this vital piece is somewhat pointless. Furthermore, even when deemed "successful," Buckingham cautions that knowledge alone does not provide immunity from advertising influences.[49] Put differently, knowing that advertisements manipulate does not mean they hold no sway. Indeed, there is evidence that media literacy interventions do not effectively counteract the impact of advertising on children, particularly the younger ones who are most vulnerable to its influence.[50]

COMMUNICATION REVOLUTION BENEFITS THE CHILD CONSUMER VERSUS HARMS FROM TECHNOLOGY

The communication revolution, primarily through the use of digital technologies, engages increasing numbers of children as both consumers and *producers*.[51] Indeed, the pro-consumer side says children now behave as skillful collaborators, navigating around the clock in virtual space, contributing to the creation and production of social networks and other sites.[52] For the first time in history, children are declared as taking control of the critical elements of a communication revolution spurred by advanced media technology, one that is intricately tied to the persona of a consumer. In 1998, Don Tapscott, a business executive and consultant, outlined several themes of what he called the "N-Gen" (net generation) children's culture.[53] To begin with, he claimed that this cohort of children are fiercely independent, characterized by emotional and intellectual openness and the desire to adopt a global orientation in the search of information, activity, and communication. They operate under free expression, strong views, and innovation. This type of attitude involves a level of maturity and investigation more characteristic of adults. In fact, relative to the N-Gen, adults live in a slow-motion world. Finally, this cohort of children is said to have developed sensitivity to corporate interests and a level of authentication and trust to navigate through the world of a consumer. Children's competency when it comes to corporate innovation has no limits.

* * *

Also in 1998, Jane Healy, an educational psychologist and professional educator for more than 35 years, published *Failure to Connect*, in which she described the harm that children were sustaining from increased use of computers. Prescient in her thinking, Healy warned of the dangers in glorifying computer use by children. Nothing much has since changed except that computer use and other digitally mediated technology (i.e., smart phones) have dramatically escalated. The urgency that surrounds the drive by adults to connect children (including preschoolers) to technology is largely motivated by a fear that their intellectual development will be otherwise stunted. Yet the operation of technology is no guarantee of intelligence. As Healy points out: "Precocious technological expertise guarantees nothing. The rungs to the top will be built from a range of uniquely human abilities, not the least of which is creativity, notably lacking in the computer mentality."[54]

There have been many studies by psychologists, neurobiologists and educators, all of which concluded that use of the Internet does not make us smarter. In fact, it can promote distracted thinking, cursory reading skills, and, in general, a superficial style of learning.[55] We now characterize the brain (and mind) as having a quality known as "neuroplasticity," meaning that it is exceedingly malleable. According to journalist Nicholas Carr, Internet use has the capacity to mold children's minds in ways that are problematic. Contrary to marketers' claims, children who grow up with technology are not smarter than previous generations— they just have "different brains," not better ones.[56] Furthermore, the advance of technology could, ultimately, compromise the capacity for contemplation and reflection that comes from the concentration required to read a book cover to cover, a behavior that is fading in popularity. In sum, Carr's position is that technology is implicated in creating new generations of "shallow" human beings.

CHILDREN NEED THEIR PARENTS LESS VERSUS PARENTAL INVOLVEMENT IS CRITICAL

Many of the arguments that contend children benefit from consumerism rely on the belief that they have the capacity to bypass their parents' guidance and that this is a reflection of the advancement of the times. The gap between the narratives, games, skills, and technologies that we knew as children and what our children know now is immense, and the distance continues to grow, rapidly creating a vast chasm. This, it is said, is "a sign of the new millennium," of "progress," of a "new era of childhood." Furthermore, peers are significant to a child's development, which is one of the reasons that children pay such close attention to the latest fads. Peer influence is a normal and healthy phenomenon all children experience.

*   *   *

"Blaming the parents" and depicting them as incompetent has been the mantra of corporations for years, all the while undermining parental roles. Indeed, marketers have successfully displaced parents or extended family from their role in mediating a child's experience of the world. It is said that children have finally been empowered in a way that meets their needs. And the emotions/behaviors that comprises good parenting—"caring, nurturing, cherishing"—are devalued despite reams of literature that upholds the value of front-and-center parenting.[57] The degradation of parents is a deliberate tactic to bypass their approval and to market directly to children who lack the maturity to resist. As Sylvia Hewlett and Cornel West note: "On television, parents tend to be blustering bores, miserly boobs, overprotective fools, or just plain dopey and twerpy. Strong, effective parents are hard to find on television today."[58] Ironically, marketers are quick to blame parents on issues for which *they* hold significant responsibility: child obesity, early engagement of sexual behavior, and generalized anxiety.

Child psychologist Gordon Neufeld and medical doctor Gabor Mate maintain that loss of parental influence is precisely what is wrong with today's youth and why so many of them are anxious, lost, confused, and unduly influenced by their peers.[59] Their book, *Hold On to Your Kids*, goes into great detail about why it is important for children to experience childhood under the umbrella of adult protection and guidance. When parental involvement is jeopardized or absent to any great degree, a child's development can be seriously impaired, leading to any number of psychological problems.

IS THE RESEARCH ON THE PRO-CONSUMER SIDE VALID?

In *Brand Child*, Lindström bases his entire book on a study that he conducted to determine tween attitudes and brand relationships.[60] He offers a cookbook on brand know-how as it pertains to children. Notably, the methodology of the study did not include the design, sample size, data collection, and analyses. As well, the "study" was funded by a private corporation, Millward Brown, a "research agency" specializing in "brands and communication," one that had much to gain monetarily from supporting data. Lindström advocates the use of "nonconscious" methods to instil brand imagery, for which he makes no apology.

The integrity of the research reviewed, including the overall design and analyses, tends to be more robust from those who cite harm as opposed to those who cite benefit. Interestingly, the majority of those who vociferously align themselves on the pro-consumer side have some affiliation with marketers. Those on the anti-consumer side tend to be academics from varying fields, including sociology, psychology, and neuroscience, as well as child advocates and social activists. Both McNeal and Lindström, staunch marketers that they are, now concede that corporations are preying on children in ways that they cannot resist. For example, McNeal states on the last page of his extensive treatise:

Parents have put their children pretty much in charge of their own consumption levels. If children ask for more, they get more. The net results are too many children taking risks, getting fat, becoming unhealthy, not studying enough, not sleeping enough, and, in general, *endangering* themselves through overconsumption[61] (italics added).

ARE BOTH SIDES FLAWED?

In his book *The Material Child*, Buckingham attempts to reframe the problem of the child consumer by suggesting that both sides of the debate are rife with misplaced conceptions. The commercialization of childhood battle cry is one full of rhetoric about moral panics and the dangerous, corrupted childhoods that children now experience. By the same token, he stated that marketers' insistence that children are savvy, autonomous consumers is overstated. Buckingham believes that the situation is more complex than either of the two polarities represents and that understanding the child consumer in the modern world is a complex and diverse field. He is also highly critical, like Daniel Cook,[62] that children are largely absent in consumption theory and writings. Buckingham goes on to say that much of the research, including Schor's (2004), Linn's (2004), Quart's (2003), and the APA's, to name a few, is weak and generally inconclusive. Buckingham states that children should not be "singled out as a special case" from that of adults, that they do not have "different needs and vulnerabilities" and thus do not require "different forms of provision and intervention."[63] He goes on to write that children are not "merely passive or incompetent consumers" and that "claims about the power of advertising and marketing are often absurdly exaggerated."[64]

It may be true that children, like adults, use commodities as a means of self-expression, identity formation, and even have the skills of being a type of consumer from an early age. However, recent evidence from the field of developmental psychology and the burgeoning research in brain science makes clear that children's needs are vastly different from adults. For example, it is critical to children's mental health that from birth onward, they receive emotional and psychological safety from appropriate caregivers.[65]

Some scoff at the view that children are innocents or dupes and maintain that the histrionics about children's consumption ultimately harms them because it distracts from the real issues concerning income inequality and other social problems that impact diverse groups of children.[66] Yet exploitation of children by corporations does not cancel out the effects of income inequality or make it appear less significant. In fact, vast differences in socioeconomic status are, in large part, driven by corporate culture.[67] As noted in a recent Oxfam article: "In developed and developing countries alike, we are increasingly living in a world where the lowest tax rates, the best health and education, and the opportunity to influence are being given not just to the rich but also to their children."[68] The article is clear that this is a result of corporate power dominating and coercing governments.

While it is true that North American children experience the world differently depending upon socioeconomic status, ethnicity, familial history, and so on, *all* are impacted by the harms associated with consumerism. It is also important to note that the "pro" side of the child consumer debate has infinitely greater resources than the "con" and is the side that, up to now, is clearly winning the debate, regardless of the lack of evidence. Children continue to lose.

CONCLUSION

Without question, consumerism leads the twenty-first century as the dominant ideology. Indeed, it is the only ideology to have survived the twentieth century with any great success. Affixed to a "capitalism" label, its power as indicative of a democratically operated free market is almost undisputed. It is so naturally a part of our lives that we see no need to critique consumerism. Corporations have simply come to regard children as a means to their own ends: increased profit, a better bottom line, and most important, a lifetime of brand loyalty. Somehow we fail to accept these facts and to be outraged. Yet we are quick to protect our children in so many other ways. Marketers have become extremely adept at manipulating children's emotional needs, unabashedly using whatever available information they have to ensure their financial success.[69] Children have been losing their grip on childhood as a result of the gradual but steady encroachment of media into every aspect of their lives. Though corporate interests in children had commenced by the early twentieth century, the trend for more permissive regulations (especially under Reagan in the United States) has resulted in a daily onslaught of advertisements that many adults, let alone children, cannot consciously process. The revolution in technology added to the venues in which marketers could attract the child consumer, including the Internet, DVD players, computers, iPods, smart phones, video gaming, and so forth. Children are seen as a viable market all on their own without the supervision of parents. This dramatic cultural shift has led to a fiercely competitive market to capture children's attention. Marketers have upped the ante, imposing their logos on the minds of preschoolers too young to even recite the alphabet.[70]

Under the dubious justification of "empowerment," corporations were able to deftly forge ahead with new goods, brands, and media with virtually unchallenged speed and ingenuity.[71] The depiction of the child consumer has been fashioned in such a way that marketing and advertising toward children appear as a benign, even liberating undertaking. Ironically, since the 1990s, marketers have touted that children are better equipped to resist the power of advertising than their counterparts of several decades ago. They have argued that the "free" market inherently teaches children to become savvy, discerning consumers. The discourse of empowerment, not unlike that of social-ization, renders marketing to children a morally defensible and ethi-cally sound undertaking. Indeed, the language of "choice" resonates with everyday notions of freedom and citizenship in the capitalist world. The child consumer has been reconfigured to stand for indi-vidual autonomy rather than corporate exploitation. Corporations have thus successfully co-opted children's empowerment by equating choice with the consumption of heavily sponsored products.

Currently, resistance to the commercialization of childhood and criti-cism of the corporate grip on children are slowly developing. For ex-ample, the following groups have formed in the past few decades: Commercial Alert, Center for a New American Dream, Campaign for a Commercial-Free Childhood, American Academy of Pediatrics Committee on Public Education, Alliance for Childhood, and Who Minds the Child? Since consumer culture is so dominant in the West, resisting and rejecting those aspects that are less than desirable is chal-lenging, particularly after being socialized and steeped in such culture from childhood. Thus, the process of "branding identities" may partly explain why children, and even adults, suffer under the illusion of free agency and are unable to discriminate the degree of effect that consum-erism imparts. Undoubtedly, it will take concerted effort to muster a dissenting voice, one counter to the slow drip of implicit assumptions that keep the corporate market alive at a psychological level. Children are particularly vulnerable and generally unable to engage in self-reflec-tion. By the time they are adults, consumer ideology is likely established as an integral part of the self. Hence, resistance efforts are up against a tall order of corporate power, money, and sway. In the United States, corporations were given the legal standing of the rights of a "person" in the mid-1800s (an exploitation of the Fourteenth Amendment) and since then have continued to accrue more rights, freedoms, and authority than the average citizen. We feel at their mercy in efforts to protect the environment and children, and in the lobbying of governments for self-ish interests. We show deference where none is deserved.

It is essential to continue research on the impact of consumerism, particularly the *ways* in which it operates on children given the in-creasing role it plays in their lives and the extent to which it seems to detract from physical and psychological health. While current litera-ture demonstrates some of the outcomes or harms of consumer cul-ture, it also leaves many unanswered questions. We do not really understand what it is like for a child to have grown up in the most in-tense targeted-media campaign in human history, that which began in the 1990s, especially from their perspective. It is not clear how young people perceive the experiences of their childhoods and what it is like to have human relationships mediated by commodities. If relatively high consumer involvement leads to anxiety and depression, what is the mechanism by which this manifests? Is it that consumer culture leads to a perpetual dissatisfaction or feelings of futility about never "having it all"? How is it that children learn to be "good" consumers, to operate within consumer cultures and retain their identity? And what of the resisters, those who see through the charade that consumption is equated with happiness and are able to reject the consumerist lifestyle—how are their experiences different? What understanding do young people have about how consumption connects us to economic and ecological injustices of other global citizens? These are the type of questions that empirical researchers have yet to address and which are paramount to our analysis in understanding what it is like to be surrounded by media, all the while attempting to forge one's own path. I addressed many of these questions through the research that I conducted and these will be reviewed in later chapters. But first it is important to understand how the mechanisms of persuasion operate. Much of the pro side of the debate dismisses the power behind advertising and other media techniques aimed to persuade children to buy and participate in consumer culture. Just how easy is it to resist advertisements and persuasive rhetoric? How do we convince someone to alter his or her identity, to be persuaded to behave in a particular way? Are we exercising free will or choosing when we gravitate to a particular brand? Are we predominantly in charge of our own identities? With the right "weapons of influence," we can be persuaded to change our identity, our behavior, and our beliefs far more easily than most of us imagined.

5

Conformity, Creativity, and the Mechanisms of Persuasion

Consumer culture appears to be inhibiting the creative process in children's mode of expression, including their capacity, or lack thereof, for play characterized as innovative or unique.[1] During their formative years, children should, ideally, be allowed the freedom to develop creative skills that prepare them for a whole host of external (social) and intrapsychic challenges.[2] Those living in consumer cultures may experience their creativity as constrained or confined by technology use and scripted formulas for what play should look like and how it should be experienced.[3] The primary emphasis of consumerism is on media providing information to *passive* learners about how to think, behave, and experience the world. At the opposite end of conformity is the capacity to develop novel ideas or ways of solving problems, both of which reflect the creative process at work. A highly original person is characterized by a willingness to push the boundaries in unusual, even socially undesirable ways, in the face of adult authority or rejection from peers. In order to utilize creative potential, an individual must be relatively free from the obligation to conform to others' expectations. The need for approval and affiliation must be secondary to a striving to be different, to be a nonconformist for the sake of personal integrity.[4]

Contrary to popular belief, much of the research on conformity suggests that it is a relatively easy state to induce, especially under the auspices of an authority figure or group pressure.[5] It remains to be seen the extent to which children growing up in consumer cultures from early childhood are able to resist conforming to many of the norms of popular culture or whether, in large part, they capitulate to the dictates of consumerism. Of course, it is likely that a child's creative expression falls somewhere in the middle and is representative of a rejection of some consumerist norms and adoption of others.

The trajectory or development of a child's morals, values, and sense of self is brought about by a myriad of determining influences, including family, peers, schooling, socioeconomic status, genetic makeup, psychological traits, and culture. All of these factors merge in a synergism of influence, the outcome of which is the formation of an identity. For the purposes of this chapter, I will focus solely on cultural influences, specifically, those of the media, in order to isolate factors that contribute to conformity to popular norms. Understanding the ways in which children adopt conforming behaviors and attitudes requires an investigation of the ways and means of persuasion and compliance gaining, particularly those salient in the media. The extent to which media can influence children, while difficult to measure in totality, appears to be substantial, especially considering the use of neuro-marketing and other persuasion techniques that are now regularly employed.[6] Children tend to adopt cultural norms with ease, readily copying and imitating from those in their environments.[7] As a result, they are vulnerable to the ways and means of marketing experts who hone their skills across a variety of media, including print, television, and the Internet. While corporate "persuaders'" tactics do not mirror an Orwellian style of thought control, many of their tactics aim for a high level of compliance with respect to consuming.

Many of us would vehemently deny that we could be influenced by the likes of powerful autocrats and that it is fair to lump all persuasion techniques together as if they merit the same consideration. Yet, persuasion, even propaganda, in the modern capitalist democracy is not to be underestimated.[8] Randal Marlin, a philosophy professor who specializes in propaganda, cites the actions of some corporations as equivalent to propagandist tactics. As an example, the marketing of the McDonald's fast-food chain fits under Marlin's definition of propaganda which he defines as "the organized attempt through communication to affect belief or action or inculcate attitudes in a large audience in ways that circumvent or suppress an individual's adequately informed, rational, reflective judgment."[9] He also refers to the branding scams (e.g., with this product you will achieve this lifestyle/image) as being a type of propaganda, which implicates many forms of advertising.

Understanding the mechanisms by which norms are transferred, maintained, and accepted and the ways in which they are rejected (nonconformity) is important when considering the effects of consumerism. Of particular importance is the concept that persuasion is being used as a tool to ensure a high degree of compliance through the adoption of consumer values by children. Corporations are able to generate a groundswell of support for thousands of brands using a plethora of effective techniques that will be described and explored. In short, media have the opportunity to influence and persuade children as never before and they appear to be succeeding. It goes without saying that a minority of children, for whatever reasons, choose to deviate from popular norms and blaze their own trail. Their capacity to express creatively is useful in explaining what nonconformity means in a practical sense. The concern is that within consumer cultures this type of individual appears to be few and far between.

WHAT IS PERSUASION?

According to professors of communication John Gass and Robert Seiter, persuasion can be defined as "one or more persons who are engaged in the activity of creating, reinforcing, modifying, or extinguishing beliefs, attitudes, intentions, motivations and/or behaviors within the constraints of a given communication context."[10] Persuasion is not simply about changing one's own or another's mind, but it can also involve reinforcing or strengthening beliefs not yet solidified. On the flip side, persuasion can also refer to attempts to extinguish or eliminate beliefs and attitudes.

CONFORMITY AND NORMS

Conformity refers to the specific movement from a stated position to a contradictory one. For example, one may start at a point that is contrary to that expressed by a comparison other or group, otherwise defined as a norm.[11] Famed psychologist Robert Cialdini and his colleague M. R. Trost define social norms, those specific to social behavior, as follows:

Standards that are understood by members of the group, and that guide and/or strain social behavior without the force of laws. These norms emerge out of interaction with others; they may or may not be stated explicitly, and any sanctions for deviation from them come from social networks, not the legal system.[12]

Cialdini and colleagues[13] categorized existing definitions of norms into two types. Norms that describe that which is actually occurring, or what others are doing, are referred to as *descriptive norms*. Individuals often assess the descriptive norms of a situation when they are uncertain of how to act. Descriptive norms are depicted throughout the media in images (billboards, magazines), enactments (movies, Internet, television), and verbal messages (radio). The second types of norms, *injunctive norms*, have a moral element, meaning rules or beliefs about what to do when confronted with an indeterminate situation. Injunctive norms do not necessarily depend on a specific group and usually originate from social or cultural standards that are widely shared.[14] These are the norms that individuals commonly refer to when referencing behaviors that are deemed acceptable within a given culture. Like descriptive norms, injunctive norms are also displayed throughout the media in a myriad of ways. For example, gift giving on the occasion of a person's marriage is a type of injunctive norm. Generally speaking, norms can reinforce the status quo and sustain behaviors, attitudes, and values deemed to be acceptable. For descriptive norms, the extent to which each of us demonstrates normative behavior will vary: a majority may conform to normative behavior, making the norm salient, or few may conform when the norm is obfuscated. Similarly, for injunctive norms, what others believe we should do may be quite evident, meaning the injunctive norm is relatively easy to surmise. Alternately, what others believe should take place may be unclear to us, making the norm difficult to discern. Regardless, descriptive and injunctive norms can be found in all forms of media influencing, guiding and pressuring children at varying levels of their development. In today's world of fast-paced technology, transmission is relatively easy and efficient for both types of norms.

Regardless of the method of transmission, we both influence and are influenced by norms and their environment in an iterative or repetitive process.[15] The creation of subcultures, for example, can occur when enough of us consistently deviate from an established set of norms, thus creating our own mini-culture.[16] Subcultures can eventually become the norm, especially if they are picked up by media and commodified, perceived to be "cool," and thereby lucrative as well (e.g., hip-hop music and its concomitant lifestyle). Environmental conditions must be somewhat conducive for a subculture to thrive and go against the grain.[17] Indeed, our need to conform cannot be underestimated. Oftentimes, we conform to norms for fear of punishment or social ostracism. At other times, we voluntarily go along with a norm at a subconscious level because we have been socialized to accept its appeal or legitimacy.[18]

NONCONFORMITY

Nonconformity, in its simplest form, is defined as the adherence to norms, values, and behaviors that are different from the dominant culture. The process of nonconformity is best understood when the motivation behind behaviors and beliefs are made transparent. Hence, it is important to differentiate whether nonconformity is adopted as a means of rebellion against external pressures (i.e., not truly chosen) or due to personal choice (i.e., genuine). Behaviors that are experienced as deriving from free will tend to be assimilated within the self and are more likely to be maintained over time. For instance, we could choose *not* to conform, believing in a true expression of the self, hence, disregarding some of society's values. Nonconformity can also take on the face of defiance as a way to rebel against external pressures. In other words, sources located outside the self can determine behavior.[19] For example, children may adopt nonconformist behaviors as a way to rebel against parents, authority figures, or society in general and to defy the adoption of extrinsic norms. Thus, children may do the opposite of what is demanded simply because they feel controlled. In this case, the nonconformist behavior, while intentional, is not truly chosen. Rather, it is a reaction against the loss of freedom or "rights" and an attempt to regain a sense of autonomy. This type of nonconformist behavior is unlikely to persist over time because its regulation is predominantly characterized by tension rather than by solidity. Pressures from the environment can topple our willpower to maintain a nonconformist stance, especially in the face of competing demands. In sum, it appears that nonconformity, although reflecting an intentional action, is not always driven or regulated by the self and may, therefore, be quite transient.[20]

DEVIANCE AND NONCONFORMITY

Deviance, a subset of nonconformity, has traditionally been defined as behavior that violates norms or that is labeled and evaluated negatively. Sociologists Alex Heckert and Druann Heckert offer a typology of deviance that suggests four types of outcomes: negatively evaluated underconformity (negative deviance); negatively evaluated overconformity (rate busting); positively evaluated underconformity (deviance admiration); and positively evaluated overconformity (positive deviance).[21] Negative deviance is any type of behavior or condition that the majority regard as unacceptable and that evokes a negative response. Examples include the mentally ill or criminals—groups that underconform to established norms and are usually judged in a pejorative light, even if unfair. Rate busting refers to overconformity behaviors and conditions that surpass norms and that are negatively evaluated. For example, gifted and overachieving students, those who *over*conform, are often subjected to a construction of "nerd," or "geek." They are regarded as rate busters with respect to intelligence, while simultaneously perceived as devoid of social skills, clumsy, and replete with other undesirable characteristics. Nonconformity or deviance can also be positively evaluated. More precisely, it refers to behaviors that the majority deem as unacceptable, yet invoke a positive response overall. Examples include outlaws who have been elevated to the level of hero such as Jesse James, Butch Cassidy, and Bonnie and Clyde. These historical figures are infused with mythological or symbolic characteristics that match the quintessential archetype: Robin Hood. A final category, positive deviance, suggests overconformity (that which exceeds the normative standards) that is positively evaluated. For example, altruists like Mother Theresa are revered for their "positive deviancy." Positive deviancy does not typically threaten the dominant order, unlike negative deviancy, which does.

Heckert and Heckert's typology of deviance is relevant when analyzing and assessing nonconformity to popular norms, those that support and reinforce consumer lifestyles. Restraint from shopping, for example, may be viewed as either negative deviancy or positive deviancy depending upon the values of the culture. Refraining from shopping can be regarded as "un-American" and bad for the economy. In less materialistic cultures than the United States and Canada, minimal shopping behavior may be highly desirable and positively viewed. Clearly, deviance is complex, and our reactions to it must be assessed within a cultural or societal context before judgment can be made.

CIALDINI'S SIX WEAPONS OF INFLUENCE

Research reveals that there are six basic principles that govern the process by which one person might influence another. Cialdini coined them the "six weapons of influence": reciprocation, scarcity, authority, social validation/proof, liking, and consistency.[22] In the pages that follow, these six principles will be elaborated upon in order to understand how corporations influence children and adults to accept and believe in the products and accompanying lifestyle they wish to sell.

Reciprocity

We feel obliged to give back to others in the form of behaviors that we receive. Human beings have molded their cultures around the principle of reciprocity. Scientific research reveals that the gifts we give are more likely to be effective when they are viewed as meaningful, tailored to an individual, and unexpected. Free product samples received by mail or in person at the mall play on the notion of reciprocity in that they are presented as "gifts." The receiver then feels a level of obligation to respond by giving back or buying other products.

Scarcity

We typically associate greater value with things that are rare, dwindling in availability, or difficult to acquire. Examples include the mad scrambles to purchase the most popular Christmas toy that threatens to be out of stock. Advertisers use the scarcity principle regularly to infuse a given product with greater desirability.

Authority

We operate in a culture of expert endorsement, relying on the "right" information to make sound decisions. We seem to be swayed by impartial experts more than by those who benefit directly by their convictions. Regardless, real, perceived, or faked, an authority figure tends to induce conformity. Advertisements regularly use the presence of an authority figure(s) when talking about a product—everything from toothpaste endorsed by dentists to toys that will supposedly enhance a child's learning, according to "experts."

Social Validation

If we believe a choice is made in our best interest, we often look to the behavior of others for validation. In circumstances that leave us feeling uncertain, social proof has the greatest persuasive power. Advertising heavily relies on social validation by portraying desirable actors using the saleable item. Advertisements for children's toys or cereals almost always depict a child happily enjoying the target product. Advertisers love to inform us when a product is the "fastest growing" or "largest selling" to persuade us that it is worthy of buying.

Liking

Put simply, we prefer to say "yes" to and comply with the requests of those we like. There are three specific elements of liking: similarity, praise, and cooperation. We tend to like others who are similar to ourselves. Advertisements for children include actors who are quintessentially average in behavior (though above average in appearance). We also tend to like, and therefore, be more persuaded by those who express compliments and praise. Advertisers often relay how deserving their audiences are of having their product. Thirdly, we are more drawn to those who cooperate with us toward mutual goals. Advertisements often use a discourse of "we" and "us" to convey a sense of comradery and understanding of our personal needs.

Consistency

We strongly favor consistency between what we publicly say and how we behave. Once established, we often feel obligated to uphold our earlier commitments. The principle of consistency is applied regularly in the phenomenon of brand loyalty. Once we commit to a brand, we feel a sense of obligation to stick with it, to prove our ability to be consistent.

Cialdini emphasizes that his six weapons of influence are often applied in conjunction with one another, synergistically, to produce a more potent and persuasive effect. Influence and influence "peddlers" are a fact of life. Indeed, influence tactics have been integral to human survival and social groups for thousands of years.[23] Unless one becomes aware of persuasion techniques and recognizes the strategies being implemented, we are doomed to be helplessly manipulated. While adults have the intellectual capacity to sometimes discern when they are being persuaded, children are far less able, if at all. Cialdini cautions:

> The blitz of modern daily life demands that we have faithful shortcuts, sound rules of thumb in order to handle it all. These are no longer luxuries; they are out-and-out necessities that figure to become increasingly vital as the pulse quickens. That is why we should want to retaliate whenever we see someone betraying one of our rules of thumb for profit . . . [that] we cannot allow without a fight. The stakes are far too high.[24]

RESEARCH ON CONFORMITY

Social conformity is a natural process on one level that, simply, represents the tendency to be influenced by one another. Conformity is more than mimicry, however, and generally involves social learning; it is the process by which humans discern the rules of society.[25] There are two types of social conformity: the adoption of a widely accepted societal norm and group conformity.[26] One of the most compelling experiments on the effects of conformity was conducted by Solomon Asch in 1956.[27] Asch recruited seven to nine college students and told them that they would be participating in an experiment involving visual judgment. Next, the students were asked to look at two large white cards; a single vertical line appeared on the first card and three vertical lines of different length appeared on the second card. Each student was asked to report out loud in the presence of the group which of the three lines on the second card was the same length as the line on the first card. According to Asch (1965), the experiment began in a mundane fashion but changed rapidly:

One person near the end of the group disagrees with all the others in his selection of the matching line. He looks surprised, indeed incredulous about the disagreement. On the following trial he disagrees again, while the others remain unanimous in their choice. The dissenter becomes more and more worried and hesitant as the disagreement continues in succeeding trials; he may pause before announcing his answer and speak in a low voice, or he may smile in an embarrassed way.[28]

The dissenting student in the experiment did not know that all of the other students in the group were planted by Asch and told beforehand to give the wrong answers. Asch wanted to see what a person would do when he or she was giving correct answers that were different from those of the near-unanimous group. The results of the study revealed that conformity was common. When under group pressure, 75 percent of the subjects gave the wrong answer in at least one of the trials. So, put somewhat differently, in most cases a minority of one will capitulate in the presence of a unanimous majority. The desire to conform in order to receive acceptance and approval is so powerful that it can cause us to deny our own perceptions. Interestingly, those who participated in the experiment agreed, nearly without exception, that independence, speaking one's own mind, was preferable to conformity. Asch was confounded by his results, especially that the tendency to conform and call "white" "black" was so common. In a meta-analysis of Asch-type experiments done over succeeding decades, there was little conformity found when the majority consisted of only one or two subjects and a dramatic increase when the majority numbered three. Above a majority size of three, the results were the same; that is, increasing amounts of conformity did not occur.[29] Asch's experiment was repeated on children between the ages of 3 and 17 years.[30] The results showed that the younger the child, the greater the conformity and likewise, the older the child, the less the tendency to conform. Similar to Asch's experiment, another research study found that a single subject is likely to conform when encountering four other individuals who disagree with their position; if only one of these four sides with the subject, this appears to empower the subject to uphold his or her dissenting position. We can conclude, therefore, that in situations in which we are not the lone dissenting voice, we are more likely to uphold an unpopular or contrary decision.[31]

How do we explain Asch's results? It has been proposed that when we make a decision in a group, we are motivated by two things: wanting to be right and wanting to be liked.[32] Conforming to a group can occur because the group has informational influence that appeals to our desire to be right. We then conform to the group because we think the group may be correct. The other type of influence that plays out of conformity to a group is normative. This means that even when we are sure a group is wrong, we choose to conform in order to gain rewards (liking) and avoid punishments (disapproving) that are associated with agreement and disagreement, respectively. New research shows that when we are rejected socially it affects the same part of our brain as physical pain.[33]

We tend to conform more to a group of individuals who are similar to us than to a group we perceive as different.[34] Moreover, we tend to experience positive emotions when conforming to a group that we identify with socially. Likewise, we experience negative emotions when conforming to a group that is less similar.[35] Overall, as far as conformity under group pressure is concerned, women show somewhat higher levels than men.[36] Differences in gender, with respect to conformity, were also found in a study by Michael Guarino and Pamela Fridrich, who tested to see if subjects in a cafeteria-type line would select a dessert if the person in front of them did so. The study revealed that 77 percent of the women conformed to the dessert-choosing behavior of the person ahead of them, compared to only 43 percent of men.[37]

Humans tend to view behavior as correct to the degree that they see others doing it, though clearly, there are differences in how each of us perceives the prevailing degree of conformity. Cialdini and his colleagues found that priming and salience of the norm increased compliance. They demonstrated this phenomenon experimentally by observing the likelihood of people littering based on the amount of litter visible in their environment; the greater the amount of litter, the more people conformed to the littering norm.[38] On the flip side, when subjects got messages about norms that were similar to anti-littering, littering decreased proportionately. Self-identification with a group also tends to increase conformity to the norms of that group.[39] This is especially true if we regard ourselves as members of an in-group.[40] In general, adults acquire norms that pull in two directions—loyalty to an in-group and upholding egalitarian principles (even toward those in an "out-group"). Undoubtedly, we each have a plethora of different norms stored in the brain, but what we do in a given situation greatly depends on context, as we shall see.

Milgram's "Obedience to Authority" Experiments

Milgram's now famous experiments on the effects of authority demonstrate chillingly how easily situational circumstances can lead human beings to wreak great suffering on innocent others.[41] In short, Milgram set up a scenario in which a subject (Teacher) was instructed to deliver continued, intense and dangerous levels of shock to an actor (introduced as a Learner) if he failed to provide the right answer to a bogus question on memory and learning. Hence, the Teacher participant thought the Learner was also a participant. The Teacher was situated at a desk that contained 30 switches ranging from 15 volts to 450 volts. Each time the Learner made a "mistake," the Teacher was instructed by the experimenter to give him a shock. The intensity of the shock increased with each "error" that the Learner made. Conflict arose when the Learner began to indicate that he was experiencing discomfort. Learners were, in fact, confederates of the experimenter and never received a real shock. By 285 volts, the Learner actor expressed his discomfort with an agonized scream. Despite the fact that many of the Learner actors expressed extreme stress and protests, the majority of subjects continued on to administer the highest level of shock (450 volts). Milgram was flabbergasted.

Psychiatrists, graduate students, and Yale faculty had all predicted, before the experiments began, that virtually every subject would refuse to obey the authority figure-experimenter. They believed that only a pathological 1 to 2 percent would proceed to 450 volts and not the 65 percent that actually did. The significance of the experiment can be seen on many levels, the most important of which, as Milgram noted, is the obedience to authority. "It is the extreme willingness of adults to go to almost any lengths on the command of authority that constitutes the chief finding of the study and the fact most urgently demanding explanation."[42] Milgram was disturbed by what he saw as the "banality of evil," that ordinary people with no pathology could shock a victim out of a sense of obligation to uphold the demands of an authority figure and not from any peculiar aggressive tendencies.[43] Moreover, even when the subjects were made aware of the destructive effects of their actions and were asked to carry out actions of an amoral nature, relatively few had the fortitude needed to resist. Many found themselves continuing in the experiment, even though they were clearly conflicted in their behavior. The subjects divested themselves of responsibility by attributing all initiative to the experimenter, whom they believed was a legitimate authority. They upheld the role of authority even when there was no threat of material loss or punishment.

Milgram's experiment is a stunning example of authority as a weapon of influence, and it may explain the acceptance of authority figures in the media, especially those who address children. Indeed, children receive messages across all channels of media from knowing adults and peers directing them to take specific action by purchasing a product or adopting a particular physical appearance. Milgram warned back in 1975 that the effects of unfettered authority are quite threatening:

In growing up, the normal individual has learned to check the expression of aggressive impulses. But the culture has failed almost entirely in inculcating internal controls on actions that have their origin in authority. For this reason, the latter constitutes a far greater danger to human survival.[44]

It is highly questionable as to whether or not today's children are psychologically equipped to disagree with and reject the authority figures they encounter in the media throughout their day. Even in extreme circumstances, Milgram was able to demonstrate how easily control and compliance can be attained. Nearly 50 years after the controversial Milgram experiment was conducted, social psychologist Jerry Burger, under somewhat milder conditions, obtained the same results.[45] Western culture has not evolved to a level at which blind obedience to authority is no longer a danger or likelihood. The experiment in conformity that is mass consumption requires us to compromise our values all the time, whether it be to ignore harm to developing world labor markets that manufacture our "stuff" or the devastating effects on the environment.

Zimbardo's Prison Experiment: Conformity under Systemic Influence

Psychologist Philip Zimbardo's legendary 1971 Stanford prison experiment also demonstrated that conformity to adopted roles, even to the harm of oneself and others, is extremely potent.[46] Before the experiment began, all 24 participants were established to be physically and mentally healthy with no history of crime or violence. Each of the student volunteers was randomly assigned to play the role of prisoner or guard in a setting designed to convey a type of imprisonment. The experiment was established to ensue over a two-week period without break. Yet it took just a few days for the Guards to become abusive to the point of sadistically tormenting their Prisoners. The Guards invented a variety of psychological tactics to demonstrate their dominance over their powerless charges. Nakedness was a common punishment, as was placing Prisoners' heads in nylon stocking caps, chaining their legs, repeatedly waking them throughout the night for hour-long counts, and forcing them into humiliating "fun and games" activities. Dozens of people had come to the prison-like setting, had seen some of the abuse, or its effects, and made no protest. Everyone involved, either directly or indirectly, with the exception of one lone research assistant, obeyed without question. Zimbardo was eventually forced to terminate the study after only six days because it was running out of control. It had been convincingly demonstrated that, once again, situational variables can, and do, overpower many individuals even when cruelty is being inflicted. Zimbardo attributed the behavior of the subjects of his experiment to the need to belong, associate with others, and accept group norms. He added "the need to belong can also be perverted into excessive conformity, compliance, and in-group versus out-group hostility."[47] Further to this, Zimbardo clearly stated that the *system* in a given culture provides the institutional support, authority, and resources that allow situations to unfold as they do.

The person is an actor on the stage of life whose behavioral freedom is informed by his or her make-up—genetic, biological, physical and psychological. The situation is the behavioral contact that has the power, through its reward and normative functions, to give meaning and identity to the actor's roles and status. The system consists of the agents and agencies whose ideology, values and power creates situations and dictates the roles and expectations for approved behaviors of actors within its spheres of influence.[48]

For children immersed in the system of consumer capitalism, situations at the most intimate level of media direct them to specific roles reinforced by that system. Theirs is not to question but to dutifully comply according to the dictates of the market. As Zimbardo's experiment showed, under the right system or circumstances, we can be made to do and believe just about anything, even if contrary to our own well-being. One of the critical messages from the Stanford prison experiment is to be sensitive about our vulnerability to subtle but powerful situational forces and, by such awareness, develop the ability to overcome those forces through deconstruction of the system in which they exist. This capacity is way beyond the means of many adults, and relatively impossible for the majority of children whose cognitive functioning is still maturing.

RESEARCH ON PERSUASION AND CONFORMITY WITH CHILDREN

Up until about the age of eight, children do not understand the persuasive nature of advertising, believing instead that advertisements are merely providing information.[49] At least a couple of variables, family influence and getting older, seem to decrease children's vulnerability to advertising. First, some scholars maintain that if children are exposed to media education taught by adults, their ability to critically assess what they are viewing in the media increases, thus providing them with a better understanding of the nature and purpose of advertising. Second, as children become older, they are less susceptible to the persuasive appeal of advertisements, but they become more susceptible to peer pressure. However, while they may be less susceptible, they are not immune. There are numerous studies that link drinking intentions to the exposure to and liking of alcohol advertisements.[50] Additionally, longitudinal research suggests that the effects of media exposure may exacerbate body image disturbance and that exposure to an idealized thin or muscular image can sometimes result in symptoms that resemble an eating disorder.[51] This causal connection is more pronounced with individuals who are at high risk for developing an eating disorder.

Educational psychologists Kyongboon Kwon and A. Michele Lease sought to determine whether the relationship between "friendship group norms" and children's "intended conformity" to those norms is greater when they strongly identify with their friendship group.[52] They found that children who have a high consensus with their friendship group membership reported feeling a greater sense of connection and belonging, as well as more positive emotions toward their friendship group. For children, it appears that when they strongly identify with a group, they are more likely to adopt the beliefs and behaviors that are accepted by the group; the converse is also true.

It is widely believed that young people engage in smoking and other risk behaviors (e.g., illegal drugs, alcohol) because of peer pressure.[53] A frequently applied theoretical model of peer influence assumes an *active*, explicit form of peer influence. Yet the findings of survey studies operating within an active peer influence assumption are inconsistent.[54] An alternative explanation for the influence of peers can be found in a social cognitive/learning theory of psychologist Albert Bandura, who suggested that individuals observe and imitate others' behaviors so as to accrue positive rewards like belonging to a group or simply being liked—hence, *passive* (imitation) peer pressure. It is important to note that we often imitate the behavior of others spontaneously and unintentionally and are not necessarily aware of engaging in conformist acts. For example, young adults (aged 16 to 25) seem to engage in smoking because their social environment passively evokes such behavior and less because they are actively pressured.[55] Nonetheless, it appears that social conformity plays a significant role in the types of behaviors that individuals adopt. Adolescents were found to conform to the drinking behavior of both pro-alcohol and anti-alcohol norms established by peers.[56] However, they did not conform equally to all peers; as expected, they conformed more with popular than unpopular peer norms. In general, as children mature, parental influence will usually decrease while conformity to peer groups increases. Pre-adolescents begin to use clothing to conform to peers as early as age eight. One of the most visible ways of "fitting in" is to physically resemble others who are deemed to be socially desirable.[57]

SOCIAL CONSENT IN CONSUMER SOCIETIES

Nonconformity, even in democratic "free" societies, implies a sort of threat to the habits of others. This is true in an obvious way when nonconformist behavior directly challenges the morality or even rationality of conformist behavior.[58] Each of us develops what might be called a "practical identity"—an internalized set of habits, routines, expectations, and so forth. It is this identity that allows us to navigate through daily activities without having to continually contemplate the effects of our actions on others. In essence, our lives are built upon this set of unreflective expectations and practices—sociologist Pierre Bordieu called this the "habitus"—for which some degree of overall conformity is clearly necessary.[59] When faced with nonconformism, we often perceive this as a threat to our identity. Also, social disapproval is often aroused by nonconformity and the nonconformist is generally subjected to a fair degree of scrutiny.[60] Survival needs (e.g., food, housing, and clothing) require that we conform to and accept the mechanisms of production that not only sustain but, at times, also stifle us. Oftentimes, it is our dependence on others, or the perception of dependence, that stops us from pursuing even the most elementary of rights. What we see in consumer capitalism is the tendency toward imitative conformity, the inclination to adopt behaviors as an assurance for social acceptance and survival. Even in situations in which confusion and fear are consequences of conforming, we generally react to these feelings by conforming further still. In general, we disdain the thought of collective scrutiny and fear being the object of collective rejection or hurt. Rather, we often turn to others to examine their wants on the assumption that they would make us happy as well. For example, within consumer cultures there is mass conformism to shop and acquire objects whether one needs them or not. Yet we know from studies on materialism that this type of behavior is not fulfilling, despite being one of the fundamental principles and contradictions sustaining consumer capitalism.[61]

Consumer capitalism fosters a fierce level of competitiveness and ranking on a scale of privilege such that differing groups are often pitted against each other on the basis of status. Individuals often build their self-esteem and identity according to whether or not they hold a dominant position over someone else.[62] Humans strive to increase their subjective well-being, in part, by contrasting themselves with those in a so-called lower hierarchical stratum. With the exception of those at the bottom, downward comparison contributes to an internal satisfaction, another motivating force that results in conformity.[63] We learn to adapt to the conditions in which we find ourselves and then rely on the gratification those conditions present, however meager. This gratification is tied to what is known as secondary gains, those which also become a means of reinforcing conformity. The person who calls society to task on moral grounds of economic inequality, for example, is at risk of facing disapproval; actions based on moral principles are the most threatening form of nonconformity. This can be accounted for by the fact that most humans have a deep emotional need to think of themselves as behaving ethically. It is important, in other words, that individuals not conceive of themselves as bad or evil but as fundamentally good. It is this need that solidifies conformity, even in the face of obvious injustice.[64] Thus, believing in a just world leads directly to consensual conformism and, at times, even to brutal forms of victim blaming. Ironically, it is not only oppressors and third parties who commit themselves to believing that the world is just—the oppressed do so as well. Victims learn to rely on the belief that the world is just, in part, because it helps them to survive victimhood. English professor Patrick Hogan believes it is the limitations of our moral reasoning, meaning an unrefined sense of right and wrong, that may render our ethical decisions consensual, thus squelching dissent.[65] An ideology that fosters consent, like consumerism, operates both by encouraging positive beliefs and ensures contrary (or questioning) beliefs are less popular. Furthermore, those who fail to attain the "American dream" are taught that they are to blame. Indeed, underprivileged groups often internalize their failings, believing themselves to be solely responsible, all the while defending consumer capitalism despite its obvious inherent injustices for women, minorities, and children.

Social Dominance Theory and Conformity

According to Jim Sidanius and Felicia Pratto, we are predisposed to structure and to maintain social organization based on hierarchies. Starting with this hypothesis, they developed "social dominance theory."[66] Essentially, the theory states that societies are made up of hierarchies which consist of dominant hegemonic groups at the top, contrasted with a number of subordinate groups at the bottom. Further, all societies exhibit three hierarchical systems: a gender system, an age system, and an arbitrary set (based on factors such as ethnicity, religion, or social class). More specifically, in the gender hierarchy it has been the case for centuries that women have less social standing and political power compared to men. In the age hierarchy, children and young adults generally concede to the social power of adults and middle-aged persons.[67] The arbitrary-set system is:

filled with socially constructed and highly salient groups based on characteristics such as clan, ethnicity, state, nation, race, caste, social class, religious fact, regional grouping, or any other socially relevant group distinction that the human imagination is capable of constructing.[68]

Social dominance theory is built on the premise that hierarchies are upheld by several predispositions (psychological) that most of us possess: the tendency to exaggerate differences between social categories; the tendency to favor in-groups over out-groups; the tendency to be especially responsive to threats rather than to potential gains. Each of these tendencies contributes to a person's predilections to imagine group boundaries, stereotype out-group members, and hold prejudicial views against the generalized "other."

Much of what sustains group dominance can be explained by human beings' general tolerance of oppression and group discrimination. Hierarchies of domination and subordination are also bolstered through the process of establishing legitimacy by the spread of ideologies and by the inadvertent collaborative role of individuals in subordinate positions to support existing hierarchies. The cultural ideologies of any given society are usually so thoroughly embedded and widely recognized that it is relatively easy for ideology to be evoked at a person-to-person level and so influence a person's behavior to enact such ideology. Sidanius and Pratto also introduced what they call the "behavioral asymmetry hypothesis," which explains that out-group members actually favor in-group members.[69] Put differently, the reflections by members of both dominant and subordinate groups not only result from their power differentials but contribute to them. As Sidanius and Pratto note, "it is subordinates' high level of both passive and active cooperation with their own oppression that provides systems of group-based social hierarchy with their remarkable degrees of resiliency, robustness and stability."[70]

Social dominance theory offers considerable insight into understanding how powerfully the process of conformity plays out in daily life. Children, in particular, are born with a predilection for either dominance or subordination, adopting the characteristics of their in-group or out-group members. Breaking out of the mold of a consumer lifestyle poses a threat to one's hierarchical positioning and could result in a drop in status from the dominant in-group to subordinate out-group. Faced with rejection, children are under enormous pressure to conform, to uphold values, beliefs, and behaviors that reinforce the normative hegemony of their given culture.

INDIVIDUALITY: THE FACE OF CONFORMITY

The omnipresent and potent ideology of individualism permeates consumer culture, and those who argue in its favor declare that children have never been afforded such opportunity for self-expression.[71] Yet, as we are seeking the outward appearance of uniqueness or specialness, at the core, many of us hold conformist convictions. In other words, says cultural critic Hal Niedzviecki, outer individuality obscures inner conformity.[72] Niedzviecki sees Americans clamoring after fabricated and instantaneous stardom, for example. U.S. culture places great value on the celebrity to the degree that many of us will do whatever is necessary to inch toward a celebrity lifestyle. Niedzviecki comments that "many of us are starting to feel the pressure to 'realize' ourselves as a 'mythology.'"[73] It is no longer enough to be well-educated with a responsible vocation. Now, the bar has been set for megawealth and fame. The hallmark of the new conformity, externalized performance and internal normalcy, can be found in the myriad of reality TV shows. Losers are portrayed as those content to stick with the crowd, while winners are willing to take a risk by reinventing themselves and daring to stand out. Indeed, one of the hottest items to be sold on the Internet is the self. Internet dating, for example, is a huge industry, ranking among the top five uses of the Web. Corporations are more than willing to fan the flames of specialness by offering opportunities to personalize everything from beer to portable technologies. The rise of conformist individuality is confirmed by the plethora of such goods and opportunities to convey uniqueness to the world. The pressure to constantly reinvent oneself and come up with a good enough "story" can lead to perpetual anxiety, fear, and depression—the autonomous self is virtually lost. At one time, we were relatively content with our status in the middle. Now, we strive for something better and faster. The quest for opportunities to express our narrative places a tremendous pressure on identity construct as we strive to "make it" in the media and be perceived as special. At the heart of the new conformity is a fantasy about successful self-reliance when in reality we are beholden to the system of buy and sell. Yet the message of pop culture is almost always that of an ordinary person who triumphs by bucking the system, becoming the admired exception. Thus, it is no surprise that television features recurring characters whose lives are more exciting, triumphant, and different than the ordinary citizen. The message or pressure to turn one's life into a success story is found everywhere in consumer culture. Niedzviecki summarizes: "Once film was the only peddler of the fantasy of transcendent reinvention. But now there are also pop songs, TV shows, video games, celebrity magazines. This material all promotes a whole new relationship to the self: a philosophy of 'I'm Specialism.'"[74]

The power and allure of pop culture is deep—the myth that anyone can attain stardom is perpetuated throughout. In the struggle to ensure that our fantasies somehow become a reality, we seem more and more to be disconnected from the self. The World Health Organization cites depression as the leading cause of disability in developed nations with 350 million cases globally.[75] Local cultures are shrinking as pop culture and its products spread and as does the addictive promise of the new conformity. Increasingly, the culture is set up largely to ease the way for individual striving. To quote Niedziecki: "Intense individuality fenced in by intense regulation . . . breeds intense conformism in the form of pseudo-individuality."[76] It has become near impossible for us to break free of pop culture because of the ensuing isolation. Ironically, we are often separated from one another in modernity by failing to connect in a truly meaningful way despite being hooked on technology. There are free cyber-communities that almost anyone can join as long as they conform to the particular restrictions or mindset of the group. However, they seem to serve no real purpose other than to provide us a place where we can be noticed, and where the narrative of our lives can be manufactured, seemingly infused with meaning.

COMPONENTS OF CREATIVITY

Creativity can be defined as "a person's capacity to produce new or original ideas, insights, restructuring inventions or artistic objects, which are accepted by experts as being of scientific, aesthetic, social or technological value."[77] Hence, creative ideas or products are not only novel but also have a certain value or meaning either for the creator or their culture. Essentially, creativity involves three basic features: novelty, unconventionality, and validity.[78] Based on psychologist Sandra Russ's writings, for a product to be judged as creative it must be (1) unique, original, and novel; and (2) useful and aesthetically pleasing according to the standard of the particular discipline from which it derives.[79] In environments that are conducive, children have tremendous capacity to generate and express themselves creatively. Indeed, all individuals possess creative abilities to some degree and can produce creative acts, given the right circumstances. Russ considered the following attributes as key in the creative process: "tolerance of ambiguity; openness to experience; possessing unconventional values; independence of judgment; curiosity; preference for challenge and complexity; self-confidence; propensity for risk-taking; and intrinsic motivation."[80] Being sensitive to problems and problem finding are other important cognitive capacities of the creative individual. Breadth of knowledge, insight, and evaluative ability are also essential to the creative act. Those environments that allow for, even encourage, the expression of such traits are thought to be found in democratic societies. Yet democracies do not guarantee individual freedom when corporations are

given too much power. Ironically, ideas and objects deemed to be original and creative often become commoditized in capitalist cultures, losing their novelty as they are adopted en masse.

There are two broad *affective* processes related to creative cognitive
ability.[81] The first is having access to affect-laden thoughts. This refers
to what Russ called "primary process thinking and affective fantasy in
daydreams" as examples.[82] The second, being open to affect states,
means the ability to experience affect is critical to the creative process.
It would appear that children and adults who have access to affect-
laden thoughts and fantasy are more creative than individuals who are
less able to access this material. Additionally, children who are able to
express and experience affect in play are more creative than children
who are less able. A growing body of research indicates that, in particular, positive affect is associated with enhanced creative problem solving in a variety of settings.[83] For example, young adolescents showed
increased verbal fluency when positioned in a positive-affect condition.[84] It appears that self-confidence is also important in helping a
child to persist in a task, try alternative solutions, and tolerate repeated
failures before a novel or good solution comes to mind. Curiosity and
intrinsic motivation also play an important role in the persistent pursuit of problem solving. It is also important that the creative process,
however difficult, provides a source of pleasure.[85] The release of dopamine, the pleasure-producing neurotransmitter in the brain, may occur
simultaneously as creative analytical investigations unfold.[86]

Children's play is extremely important in the creative process because play is the arena in which children have the opportunity to express affect-laden thoughts and affect states.[87] Play helps a child with a
number of vital processes: expand vocabulary and link objects with
actions, develop object constancy, form event schemas and scripts,
learn strategies for problem solving, develop divergent thinking ability, and a flexibility and shifting between different types of thoughts
(narrative and logical).[88] Over time, the child who engages in genuine
play, relatively unfettered by corporate scripts, may experience greater
affect when actively working on problems. Indeed, the type of play
most important to the development of creativity is pretend play or that
which involves the use of fantasy or make-believe and the use of
symbolism.[89]

In sum, most researchers agree that no single cognitive, affective, or
personality trait is sufficient to ensure creative processes will emerge,
and there is no concrete way to predict how creative someone might
be. It is possible, even likely, that creativity can cause tension because
it often leads to nonconformity. Indeed, in very general terms, creative
behavior is deviant and can easily upset activity that is guided by a

routine—and most children's activity is routine, if not outright stereotyped in consumer cultures.[90] Thus, most characteristics of creative children are perceived as "out-of-order" and as "nonconformist," trying to avoid social norms and discipline. This is true in the school system, for example, where creativity can be met with authority and the striving for social unanimity.[91]

It appears that children's capacity for creativity in the United States is in steady decline, as evidenced by a massive study conducted by Kyung Hee Kim, an educational psychologist.[92] Her research team reviewed 300,000 scores from 1966 to 2008 derived from the Torrance Test of Creative Thinking, a standardized test that has reliably predicted creative capacity in children. Between 1990 and 2008, especially in the kindergarten through sixth-grade age group, test scores were observed to have fallen significantly. The researchers attributed part of this decline to the sharp rise in computer use and television watching, as both activities require little to no creative response or action. Hee Kim also believes because schools are structured for rote learning and standardized tests, the infrastructure necessary to foster creativity is largely absent.

AGENCY-STRUCTURE DICHOTOMY

In order to understand the factors contributing to an individual's expression of creativity or capacity to act independently and freely, we must turn to the debate of agency versus structure. Structure encompasses many aspects of the components of culture (social class, religion, gender, ethnicity, and so on), meaning those tacit rules and resources that guide our behaviors, attitudes, and values. Structure has a strong social component and can be said to encompass those "social arrangements, social relations and social practices which exert enormous power and constraint over our lives."[93] In contrast, agency refers to the ways in which individuals exert themselves within a given culture to shape the very systems within which they are situated. As sociology professor Gil Richard Musolf describes, "agency emerges through the ability of humans to ascribe meaning to objects and events, to define the situation based on those meanings, and then to act."[94] The agency versus structure debate is essentially reduced to a question of cause and effect. Do cultures or social structures influence and shape an individual's actions (e.g., conforming to the norms), or does the individual act freely in a way that influences the social structure around him or her (e.g., rejecting customs)?

Sociologist Anthony Giddens developed a theory of what he called "structuration" as a means of accounting for human action that accepts both structure and agency.[95] Giddens argued that agency is not solely a type of self-expression but rather is representative of our *interaction* with each other. Hence, we must remember that social structures, those that appear to impose on each of us, are "continually created and recreated in every encounter, as the active accomplishment of human subjects."[96] Giddens tried to resolve the polarities that the agency versus structure debate inevitably renders. Rather than arguing on the side of voluntarism and its opposite, determinism, it makes more sense, according to sociologist Stephen Fuchs (2001), to treat agency on a continuum: "Agency, creativity and genius are not essential properties that some persons 'have' qua person. Rather, they are . . . more likely in some situations, on some occasions, and in some networks than others."[97] In summary, social structures operate in a multitude of ways influencing the expression of agency positively or negatively. Some subsets of culture are highly conciliatory with respect to agency, while others consider it adversarial.

This book focuses on a structural analysis, yet structure cannot exist without agency. Agency surfaces in structural social systems with either the intent to conform or rebel, not necessarily in an opposing manner, but simply to exert one's intent in a direction different from that of the status quo. It would be too simplistic an argument to suggest that we are completely controlled, "mere robots, programmed to conform to a structured pattern."[98] It is clear that structures not only limit the latitude one may digress; they also provide the right environment from which creativity and freedom can flourish. At the same time, to diminish structural influence is to overrate our capacity for self-efficacy and individualism. Hence, the reason why some scholars argue that it is best to conceptualize both structure and agency as flexible parts of a scale.[99] After all, structures are the outcome and production of individual action, and agency is always shaped by social structure, often reflective of *collective* choices. The tendency is to conceive choices as individually driven and representative of individual freedom; yet we must also remember that choices are always the outcome of social influence.[100] Perhaps agency is best conceptualized as the process in which an individual exercises social choices that are limited by structurally bound alternatives.

Social psychologist Erich Fromm suggested that Western cultures cultivate the *feeling* that each of us is the "center and active subject of his powers," that the full experience of attaining individuality is to reject *obvious* authoritarian constraints.[101] He defined well-being as the capacity to be creative, independent, and live in the world with a satisfaction of *being* rather than *having*. Fromm explains that obedience to the self, to one's own convictions, is life affirming, whereas obedience to a person or institution is a submission, an abdication of autonomy. To follow one's own convictions and judgment is to be true to oneself, to be an "I." This description is the essence of agency, the ability to be disobedient not for the sake of rebellion but for the purpose of affirming the self. As Fromm puts it, "Freedom and the capacity for disobedience are inseparable; hence, any social, political, and religious system which proclaims freedom, yet stamps out disobedience, cannot speak the truth."[102] Why then are we so fearful of and adverse to disobedience if it is in our best interest? Fromm believes this is largely understood by the desire for safety, strength, and perhaps most important, a sense of identity, even if illusory. Thus, to have agency is to be disobedient with respect to the infrastructures that restrict creative, self-fulfilling development. Ultimately, agency refers to the rejection of beliefs, norms, and customs that restrict the capacity to evaluate critically.

When talking about children, the question of agency versus structure becomes even more complex than when considering that of adults. As children mature, we expect that their agency is emboldened, more prominent and representative of their burgeoning mind and concomitant behaviors. Typically, we attribute the child's agency as peaking in adolescence. Yet the agency of children more likely develops and gets expressed throughout the entirety of childhood. While a child's social life is fundamentally structured by family, school, church, community, and so on, such systems also support a wide range of possible choices that have the capacity for creative expression and determinism. Thus, for children living in consumer cultures (and elsewhere), striving for free expression is critical to their development as autonomous human beings. And as Fromm stressed, to disobey and forge one's own niche, to reject aspects of consumer culture, may be all that stands between a creative life of integrity and becoming "one of the herd."[103]

NEURO-MARKETING AND THE MALLEABLE MIND

Neuroscience has now established that the mind is malleable throughout one's lifetime, especially during the sensitive period of early childhood.[104] Our beliefs, experiences, memories, even the very self are malleable, changeable, and moldable to the degree that warrants serious reflection on the reliability of both memory and belief.[105] Neuromarketing is one of the tools that has advanced considerably and is being used to influence us below the level of conscious awareness, thereby reducing our reactance to losses of freedom of mind.[106] The mind is no longer separable from the activity of the brain—according to neuroscience, it is the "product of the brain."[107] So advanced is the "science" of neuro-marketing that corporations can now sway us to buy before realizing we have been subjected to a form of advertising.[108] For example, there is now experimentation in using brain scans to see which parts of the brain are activated when exposed to specific advertisements. Advertisers have moved way beyond surveys, focus groups, and depth interviews and are now experimenting with uncovering subconscious motivations.[109] Case in point, the Zaltman Metaphor Elicitation Technique (ZMET) is a patented market research tool that taps into the subconscious mind through nonliteral or metaphoric expressions.[110] The whole purpose is to help marketers gain information on what motivates consumers and which advertisements might then be most effective. Researchers hope to uncover the deepest workings of the mind that per-suade us to consume, those pathways that cannot be attained through mere rational thought. As for children, their burgeoning brains are fod-der for the corporate advances that manipulate and control how a child thinks, reacts, and responds to various stimuli in the form of advertise-ments. A far cry from creative process.

Conscious versus Subconscious Processing: Twenty-First-Century Marketing

Generally speaking, the subconscious is conceptualized as an auto-matic mental process that is spontaneous, uncontrollable, and immedi-ate—something that just *happens*.[111] Furthermore, the subconscious is understood to be that mode of thinking, desiring, and becoming that is not immediately accessible to conscious deliberation, yet drives much of behavior.[112] We now understand that differentiating between subcon-scious and conscious thoughts and decision making has become in-creasingly blurred. In other words, conscious decisions are laced with subconscious influences.[113] Neurologist Robert Burton (2008) believes that the distinction between conscious and subconscious thought has been grossly misunderstood.[114] When failing to experience intentional-ity, we are under the illusion that thoughts are simply *un*intentional, that they somehow "occur to us" or are part of the subconscious. Ultimately, we like to believe that most of our thinking is conscious (cognitive, analytic, reflective, systematic) and distinctly different from subconscious processes. All of us, to lesser or greater extents, can think and act consciously and rationally (the scientific method is built on this ability). However, conscious deliberation is not always what it seems. Despite conventional beliefs, subconscious cognition determines much of goal setting, attitude formation, and even decision making.[115]

Vision takes up approximately one-third of the brain's resources. It is no surprise that quite a lot of brain activity takes place in the observa-tion of others.[116] Mirror neurons refer to those that fire when an action is being performed and even when that same action is only being observed. For example, watching another person experience physical pain triggers pain-related regions of the brain. These mirror neurons can even be activated when we are reading about the behavior of others. Mirror neurons not only help us to imitate others but are also responsible for human empathy; they send signals to the limbic system or emotional region of our brains that then help us tune in to one another's feelings.[117] As consumers, our mirror neurons may fire when we observe shopping experiences other than our own and, ultimately, influence our purchasing decisions. We have all experienced how seeing a certain product over and over makes it more desirable. Mirror neurons do not work alone; often, they work in tandem with the release of dopamine, which creates a feeling of well-being that we crave.[118] Therefore, shopping can *chemically* contribute to our level of happiness, at least in the short term, due in part to a flush of dopamine. Scientists have even isolated an area in the frontal cortex of the brain called "Brodmann area 10" that is activated when we see products that we think are cool. This area of the brain is associated with self-perception and emotions activated by social behaviors. Lindström offers this warning: "[Buyers] beware. Because the future of advertising isn't smoke and mirrors—it's mirror neurons. And they will prove even more powerful in driving our loyalty, our minds, our wallets and our buyology than even marketers themselves could have anticipated."[119]

Lindström found, when conducting a rather massive series of experiments on neuro-marketing, that more activity in the reward and craving centers of the brain occurred when subjects viewed subliminal images associated with the product, rather than more overt images. For example, images paired with cigarettes such as a Ferrari vehicle or a beautiful sunset triggered more cravings among smokers than the logos of the cigarette packs themselves. Subliminal advertising is powerful because it is so easy to let our guard down, not believing we are under the influence of an advertiser. Lindström proposed that once we stop protecting ourselves from the seductive power of an advertisement, the brain is no longer on high alert and, therefore, responds only at the subconscious level to the stimulus presented. Big tobacco's effort to pair desirable images with smoking, with an aim for the subconscious, was highly successful, particularly in films where smoking is still portrayed. The tobacco companies were able to bypass government regulations using these methods and subvert traditional advertising in which the product is front and center. In response, the Surgeon General declared in 2012 that watching movies with onscreen smoking is a causal factor in children's initiation of smoking. Indeed, the CDC estimates that because of this exposure to smoking in movies "6.4

million children alive today will become smokers, and 2 million of these children will die prematurely from diseases caused by smoking."[120] Hence, banning cigarette advertising did not deter smoking nearly to the degree that was hoped for because the images associated with smoking became far more potent than the tobacco logos. The implications of Lindström's finding are that we can be persuaded to buy almost anything without having a clear understanding as to why. Marketers have tremendous latitude in finding the most potent associations with which to sell their products.

Brands

One aspect of Lindström's neuro-marketing research was to examine the effect of various brands on the brain with those participants who identified as being religious. He found that these particular brain scans were the *same* whether shown powerful brand images or religious icons. This shows how salient brand images have become.

Somatic Marker Hypothesis

The somatic marker hypothesis indicates that whether we know it or not, we are swayed by emotional factors in decision making.[121] The brain develops shortcuts or "somatic markers" triggered by past experiences of reward and punishment. These markers (anchored in the nervous system of the body) serve to connect an emotion with a specific response generated by the brain. For example, we may associate a particular brand of shampoo with a good feeling based on the images in the advertisement for that specific product. Thus, when shopping for shampoo, the marker is activated—we feel good and decide on a purchase, believing to have done so on a hunch. Somatic markers allow us to make quick decisions with little deliberation. Advertisers work to create somatic markers in the neurology of consumers to increase the likelihood that their products will be chosen. It is estimated that over 50 percent of all purchasing decisions by shoppers are made at a subconscious level, and not spontaneously, at the point of sale. Fear, too, can create some of the most powerful somatic markers, as Lindström describes:

Practically every brand category I can think of plays on fear. I predict that in the near future advertising will be based more and more on fear-driven somatic markers as advertisers attempt to scare us into believing that not buying their product will make us feel less safe, less happy, less free, and less in control of our lives.[122]

We are living in an age of propaganda in which the dexterous and subtle use of images, slogans, and symbols plays on our prejudices and emotions. Most of us are convinced that we make our decisions voluntarily and on our own initiative. Increasingly, the goal of modern propaganda is not to inform and enlighten but rather to move us toward a particular point of view that benefits the corporation. For example, neuroscientists have already studied how our brains make decisions about how much money we are willing to pay for a product.[123] It seems likely that neuroscience research will continue to provide information to corporations about how to work our subconscious impulses in their favor. The successful persuasion tactic of today is one that convinces a "target" to adopt the point of view of the communicator and lessen the possibility of negative ruminations.[124] The use of neuroscience tactics, combined with the weapons of influence already well established in corporate culture, will make it very challenging for children to generate their creative potential and resist conforming.

The constraints and parameters of consumer culture are such that many children appear to be living a prescribed life, one short on true creative expression. The media continuously preach at and reinforce children to accept popular norms and conform to the system on all levels. It then becomes extremely challenging to break free of a conformist lifestyle, to forge an identity that is genuine or autonomous. Younger children are especially vulnerable where identity is less a choice and more an intuitive process until they reach an age where active decision making can occur. Milgram, Zimbardo, Asch, and others have demonstrated that conformity is a powerful drive that many succumb to, particularly under the influence of authority or group pressure. Creativity, on the other hand, should be fostered, encouraged, and allowed to flourish unfettered by the constraints of some of our social norms. Creativity is the means through which the self finds integral expression beyond the mimicry of superficiality that so characterizes popular culture. Creative expression has become a relatively scarce phenomenon in children whose lives are scheduled and orchestrated according to the whims of media technology. The pull to conform to the habits of a consumer is powerful and thus requires complex navigation to offset the negative outcomes that go hand in hand with this lifestyle. Understanding the intricacies involved in resisting the pull of conformity could potentially reveal how the creative process is developed and nurtured in consumer societies, and help to unveil variables that may mitigate degrees of conformity. It may be that children have little awareness of succumbing to the tenets of consumer culture and are unable to recognize the face of nonconformity. As Niedzviecki skillfully points out, the "new" individuality resembles the old conformity—it is thus easy to be duped into believing one's creative expression is genuine rather than hackneyed. The acquisition of commodities sets up the paradox of locating uniqueness in and through objects that are mass-produced so that some degree of self-expression is always under threat. By the same token, the quest for authenticity may slide dangerously toward artificiality.

6

Democracy versus Consumer Capitalism

Having reviewed the evidence up to this point, we should ask ourselves whether or not it is substantiated by respected theoretical scholars. A chapter on theory should provide critical answers along with deeper layers of understanding as to how and why North American consumer culture has left children vulnerable. In general, a good theory attempts to establish a causal connection between sweeping events or movements, such as the advance of capitalism and the rise of a consumer culture. Specifically, a social theoretical discussion helps explain the effects of a system on the players presumed to be impacted. So, who were the theorists who pondered the inception of mass culture and its effects? Those chosen for this particular discussion are from varying backgrounds and were writing at different times, yet remarkably, each of them came to similar conclusions, namely, mass culture was undermining democracy and denying its citizens their full potential for well-being.

This chapter focuses largely on the writings of a group of left-wing intellectuals who would later become known as the Frankfurt School. Together, their work has been said to be the beginnings of what would be called "critical theory"— the analysis of the ideological and economic role of commodity processes in capitalist society. These scholars were interested in theories of consumption, particularly how a commodity takes on value beyond its function. The theories of Theodor Adorno, Max Horkheimer, and Herbert Marcuse, just a few of the Frankfurt School scholars, were chosen because of their understanding of mass culture and their ability to hypothesize about and provide analysis on the effects of consumerism. These scholars were especially concerned that the "massification" or homogenization of culture in Western democratic society was eliminating diversity altogether. The second half of the chapter reviews more current political theorists, Stuart Ewen, Benjamin Barber, and Sheldon Wolin, who critique the effects of mass culture where the Frankfurt School left off. They each examined the integrative role of mass consumer society and the new values and political and societal structures that developed as a result of, or concomitantly with, the specific transformations that converged into what would be labeled consumer culture.

The crux of each of the theoretical perspectives examined in this chapter is that citizens of capitalism are participants as well as victims in the formation of modern consumer culture. They are victims in the sense that consumerism is about commodified culture in which goods are no longer produced for their intrinsic cultural value but are sold merely to accrue profit for corporations whose interest in culture is largely absent. Whether we review the theories of Adorno and Horkheimer, Marcuse, Ewen, Barber, or Wolin, we see a commonality. Each of them links mass culture with a form of mind control, meaning individuals are psychologically and socially influenced. Culture, propagated by media, becomes a form of rationalized and systematic control of labor and leisure that leaves the consumer a pawn, subservient to a system that keeps him well in check. Consumers become less able to resist the economic and social systems spun by mass culture, all the while being told they operate in a "free" society with limitless choice. What appears to be a system capable of fulfilling wants and needs endlessly is, in reality, servicing a small sector of society, namely, the plutocrats and oligarchs who control the economic infrastructure, including policy and implementation, driven by media propaganda. Thus, the urging to consume, propagated by mass media, fulfills a corporatist agenda and, as such, the capitalist elite are directly tied to the creation of mass consciousness. Contemporary society is incapable of progressing (and is arguably regressing) beyond its present state as consumerism is reinforced relentlessly and re-established wherever it appears threatened. Modern-day capitalism perpetuates itself through the creation of desires for which it offers only spurious gratification. Children represent tomorrow's consumer and must be brought "on board" at an early age for the system to perpetuate its functioning.

Adorno, Horkheimer, and Marcuse were all writing about the dangers of consumerism long before anyone took issue with the seemingly free cultures of democratic societies, those that appeared in sharp contrast with the obvious totalitarianism of Europe and the former Soviet

Union. Even if some of the details of their analyses were specific to their time, their diagnoses of the predicament of mass culture hold true to the present. Indeed, the economic organization of modern capitalist societies reveals itself to be an instrument of control and self-destruction. They recognized that under capitalism all production was driven by the seeking of profit for the sake of acquiring further capital, and that this system was inherently flawed and dangerous to its citizens. While many would argue consumer culture by no means represents a totalitarian state, there are similarities: both represent an oppressive loyalty to a system that depends on the conformity of its citizens to perpetuate values that are not in their best interests.

By 2007, when Barber wrote *Consumed*, it was clear that capitalism had gone asunder, spiralling out of control and reducing society to a puerile form of self-indulgent citizens who were losing their civic or democratic liberties. Finally, Wolin (2008), with his recent publication *Democracy Incorporated*, characterizes how democratic participation in capitalist cultures is marginalized and managed by a corporate ideology that justifies the overtaking of all forms of governance. The chapter's theoretical analyses offer an in-depth look at each of these perspectives and show how the arguments build on a time-driven trajectory of increasing control from the "totalitarianism" that Adorno, and Horkheimer and Marcuse describe, to Barber's depiction of "totalism," and finally to Wolin's warning about the specter of "inverted totalitarianism." Additionally, Ewen's theory will be discussed for the purposes of gaining a historical perspective on how consumer culture came under the control of corporate America and the subsequent manipulation that ensued.

Throughout this chapter there is an underlying and more obvious critique of capitalism. Whether we refer to it as "consumer culture," "consumerism," "mass culture," or the "culture industry," modern capitalism is reflective of a corrupt system in hyperdrive that is running roughshod over people and the planet. This is not to say that a more humane, ethical form of capitalism is not possible and desirable—*regulated* capitalism when aligned with democratic principles has merit. Indeed, capitalism has a history of serving Western civilization relatively well with what were once unlimited resources. As Bloom described, "Nearly every faith, from Christianity and Buddhism to Islam and Marxism, promises to raise the poor and the oppressed. But only capitalism delivers . . . [and] lifts the poor and helps them live their dreams."[1] There are countless examples of the ways in which capitalism has benefited society from the printing press to the railway. However, even Bloom acknowledged that when the ruling principle is solely one of profit, when humane and ethical considerations are absent, capitalism is "not at its best."[2] Indeed, those at the helm of modern capitalism today, including the energy sector, the financial sector, and multinationals have virtually disregarded any moral imperative. The economic guru of the twentieth century, Milton Friedman, famously stated that expecting corporations to demonstrate "social responsibility" is a "fundamentally subversive doctrine," that their only purpose is profit making.[3] In keeping with this point of view, capitalism has devoured everything in its path regardless of the fallout, particularly in the last 50 years when the stakes were raised by ecological/human devastation. Corporations have worked hard to mask their transgressions against humanity with slick public relations campaigns set to distract scrutiny. Case in point: though one of the most notorious abusers of third-world sweatshop labor, Nike successfully used sport "superstars" to elevate their brand image through television advertising.[4] At this juncture in history, it is in spite of capitalism that democracies are fighting to stay in the game, to protect the rights of all and resist "rule by corporation." If corporate culture dominates or dictates governmental policy, as each of the theorists point out, then democracy is in peril. What does this mean for children? The likelihood of accepting corporate values or lack thereof, of conforming, dramatically increases and makes them easy fodder for the adoption of a consumerist way of life.

"THE CULTURE INDUSTRY": ADORNO AND HORKHEIMER

Adorno argued that popular culture or mass culture is not only lacking in aesthetic taste, but, more important, it demands a rigid *conformity* of style. The central theme of Horkheimer's and Adorno's essay, *Dialectic of Enlightenment*,[5] includes the image of consumers easily manipulated by mass culture. The characterization of society is one in which authoritarianism encroaches and eventually dominates with little resistance from its citizens. Adorno repeatedly underscores a theme that would resonate deeply throughout his writings on mass culture, the role of the "culture industry" as an agent of social and intellectual control.[6] By culture industry, Adorno was referring to mass-produced cultural artifacts (movies, popular music, and most of the content of radio and television broadcasts) that are manufactured or contrived by those in power, the political and economic "aristocrats," for the purposes of accruing profit. The problem of the culture industry, he asserted, is twofold: it perpetuates itself at an inferior intellectual quality, and secondly, fails to provide a critical analysis of the systems that support it. There is no denying that the culture industry is a fabrication largely imposed upon the public by corporations; it is one of tight regimentation and control, sidestepping any breakdown or anarchy. Whether it is film, radio, popular novels, or magazines, the same stock of character types, plot structures, and narrowly conceived outcomes repeat themselves in a monotonous, agonizingly formulaic, barrage that continuously reinforces the status quo. Even the most carefully constructed critique or argument is inevitably corrupted by virtue of its stereotypic form. This type of formation is potentially dangerous, especially when dissenting views are shunned and considered deviant relative to a normatively acceptable view. This depiction is a far cry from those who advocate the existence of a "free" market.

MEDIUMS OF MASS CULTURE: THE DELIVERY OF CONTROL

Adorno argued that television has a "totalitarian" impact even when specific programs have an overtly democratic or critical message because of how these messages are communicated.[7] Like Marshall McLuhan's famed phrase "the medium is the message,"[8] Adorno saw debates about content as missing the point entirely and only diverting attention about the form of the medium to an irrelevant concern about programs themselves. He stated: "The majority of television shows today aim at producing, or at least reproducing, the very smugness, intellectual passivity, and gullibility that seem to fit in with totalitarian creeds even if the explicit surface message of the shows may be anti-totalitarian."[9] It is the mechanism of delivery in the culture industry that fails to produce a mediated and consciously reflexive relationship between the viewer and that which is observed. The individual is eventually overpowered and unable to withstand the all-encompassing force of mass culture (of which television is one of its most powerful instruments). Adorno continued: "The repetitiveness, the selfsameness, and the ubiquity of modern mass culture tend to make for automatized reactions and to weaken the forces of individual resistance."[10] As the sway of conformity chips away at rebuttal, media viewers find themselves in consolidation with, and even defending, the status quo. Life is no longer fully lived but is deceptively programmed for the citizens of the culture industry, who are all the while receiving the message that individuality is valued.

Television has proven to be an effective means of enforcing conformity through the tireless assault of overt and hidden messages justified as "information" by those in control. The pseudo-realism projected from television infuses life with a false meaning, one which viewers can scarcely see through. Hence, the television show presents a distorted image of life itself, such that a "widespread hostility toward effective self-reflection" intensifies under the pretence that what is being viewed is an honest portrayal of modern life.[11] It is not that the television consumer is entirely duped; rather, we are powerfully drawn to believing what appears on the screen. Peter Weir demonstrated this phenomenon well in his movie *The Truman Show*, a dramatic illustration of what happens when television becomes "living the life" and not just a delivery system of sound bites open to interpretation. Reality television shows including *American Idol, Amazing Race, Face Off, The Voice,* and *America's Next Top Model* are all designed to convince us how ordinary lives can embrace stardom and celebrity. Indeed, reality television has successfully dominated the airwaves because audiences identify with the featured "stars" and tend to believe what they see on the screen as an accurate portrayal, seemingly oblivious of the editing and rehearsing that takes place.[12]

Adorno took a particular dislike to modern music, lamenting the loss of diversity and arguing that one of the roles of such music is the prohibition of free speech.[13] It was not only that he was an inveterate snob; rather, he believed that popular music was comprised of an agglomeration of musical phrases that are no longer consciously mediated in the form of a coherent whole. Put simply, popular music lacks integrity, serving only to meet immediate sensual gratification. And because mass culture is designed to produce an immediate impact, the details lose their specificity. For example, popular music exhibits a limited range of musical techniques that are forever rearranged. Consequently, a narrow repertoire is established in which the most successful forms are imitated in a circle of seemingly never-ending repetition. Popular music successfully hides its repetitive form beneath the pseudo-free-style and lyrics that promote rebelliousness. Adorno alleged that we become so conditioned to popular music as to lose our capacity to think critically about what we are hearing. Moreover, the intended meaning of classical music becomes apparent only after a considerable degree of listening skill has been acquired; listening to serious music should, therefore, be a type of educational experience. Popular music fails to convey meaning and, thus, no listening skill is necessary due to its standardized format. The purpose of popular music is partly to ensure a specific, uniformed response among listeners. Like all digitized mediums, popular music strongly invokes a level of conformity from its audience.

The culture industry seeks to undermine critical thinking, a process eased by the ways in which ordinary persons capitulate to its force. It, superficially at least, performs the role of cultural reproduction yet bears no critical stance. Ultimately, we relinquish the capacity to think critically about our positioning in relation to culture. In fact, the wishes and desires of individuals become so tightly controlled that their entire life-world becomes rationalized by the very system that controls them. For Adorno, critical feelings are expressed or created by genuine art—engagement in art fosters reflexive capacities.[14] He maintains as well that the net result of musical fetishism and regressive listening is one of an alienation that is as radical as it is submissive. Popular music has become a means of social control, a means of fragmentation, and a means of stultification of the mass audience. Perhaps the most profound irony of this "condition" is that consumers are lured into believing there is some form of meaning where there is none and seek comradery where there is little.

What of the music video, a specimen foreign to Adorno? Even at its worst, music incites some individual imagination, but the music video is greatly lacking in this respect. Instead, the listener/viewer of music videos experiences an onslaught of visual cues accompanying each sound bite, both of which dictate in a precise matter what to think about or imagine. Adorno was prescient when stating that "[music] serves in America today as an advertisement for commodities which one must acquire in order to be able to hear music."[15] Big-name stars such as Madonna, Michael Jackson, Taylor Swift, and Justin Bieber have all sold their "brand" through music videos by commoditizing themselves.

Adorno and Horkheimer believed that the monopolization of the culture industry in the hands of a few corporations created standardization with little tolerance for anything else.[16] The underlying goal of media—mental cloning—aims to ensure allegiance/obedience to the larger corporate culture that dictates the way life should be lived. Indeed, the culture industry ultimately manifests as a mono-culture. Film production, primarily motivated by money, churns out formulaic plots under the guise of new content. The examples abound: *The Fast and the Furious* films one through eight; *X-Men*, which spawned a plethora of superhero films; the spy thriller *The Bourne Identity* followed in series by *The Bourne Supremacy, The Bourne Ultimatum*, and *The Bourne Legacy*. Furthermore, the culture industry incites rapacious viewing of television series and films that feature beautiful characters basking in material pleasures with emotionally satisfying lives that mock reality.

PSEUDO-INDIVIDUALITY AND PSEUDO-REALITY

Horkheimer and Adorno maintained that the masses of the culture industry are deluded into believing that the world mediated through technology (movies, television, radio) is the same as the "real" world:

[The] more intensely and flawlessly [the movie producer's] techniques duplicate empirical objects, the easier it is today for the illusion to prevail that the outside world is the straightforward continuation of that presented on the screen . . . Real life is becoming indistinguishable from the movies.[17]

The illusion of total freedom is, in truth, a mirror image of mental incarceration. Those who defend the products of the culture industry are quick to highlight its emancipation from the tyranny of style of a dated modality. Yet these claims, from Adorno's and Horkheimer's perspective, prove to be hollow: "Having ceased to be anything but style, [the culture industry] reveals the latter's secret: obedience to the social hierarchy."[18] Further to this, the culture industry is central to the elimination of individuality because of its stereotyping of behavior and expressions that renders genuine emotional display into mere empty gestures. The result is a kind of pseudo-individuality—thus, what "is individual is no more than the generality's power to stamp the accidental detail so firmly that it is accepted as such."[19] Individualism becomes a *commodity* in the culture industry, something that is determined by society, though professed to be naturally occurring. Pseudo-individualism also rang true for Niedzviecki when he talked about the mass conforming that is taking place under the guise of individual expression.[20] For example, torn faded jeans that are "distressed" with ripped fabric, one-shoulder-bare tops and sweatshirts, "skinny" jeans for women, and low-hanging pants for men were all co-opted by corporations as a desirable look, and paradoxically claimed to represent a unique demeanor for each buyer.

Adorno believed that "people give their approval to mass culture because they know or suspect that this is where they are taught the mores they will surely need as their passport in a monopolized life."[21] Mass culture becomes self-sustaining as a model for ensuring conformity because of powerful (innate) needs that characterize most of us, such as the need to belong, the need to be liked, the need to be seen as successful, and so on. Adorno felt that the totality of mass culture culminates in the demand that no one be different. Thus, the "monopoly shuts its doors on anyone who fails to learn from the cinema how to move and speak according to the schema which it has fabricated."[22] Conformity becomes the scaffold for the survival of the culture industry, constantly fueled by newly invented schema that plague its citizens and their struggle to keep abreast of the latest fashion; failure to do so is akin to a psychological "suicide."

Today anyone who is incapable of talking in the prescribed fashion, that is, of effortlessly reproducing the formulas, conventions, and judgments of mass culture as if they were his own, is threatened in his very existence, suspected of being an idiot or an intellectual.[23]

Hence, a world of monotony scaled down from one of pluralism and diversity becomes the new norm.

COMMODIFICATION OF CULTURE

Horkheimer and Adorno lay much of the blame for the standardized, pseudo-individual (or customized) products of mass culture on the process of "commodification," meaning everything and anything can assume the form of a commodity. With the rise of the culture industry, aesthetic freedom began to erode; cultural production became increasingly organized as a profit-making industry and, thus, was subject to all the restrictions that conformity for production's sake demands. This penetration of the commodity form into aesthetic culture was particularly damaging. When we think of culture, we like to believe that it is born from the expression of free will and thought, and not simply the product of a massive campaign as so many cultural icons in the West have become:

Art for the masses has destroyed the dream . . . not only are hit songs, stars, and soap operas cyclically recurrent and rigidly invariable types, but the specific content of the entertainment itself is derived from them and only appears to change. The details are interchangeable.[24]

Commodification imposes the most precise, extensive, and insidious control over cultural activity that has yet existed in human history. The entirety of the culture industry is premised on the rational organization of mass-produced "cultural" production. Essentially, genuine art has been largely replaced by that which is devoid of integrity and marketed for quick sale. Since today's culture is made specifically for the purpose of being sold, the production of true art is, thereby, all but eradicated. Under such circumstances, art simply cannot flourish and inevitably succumbs to the forces of mass production, devoid of true meaning.

Culture—the way it is perceived, produced, and consumed— is now determined by the activities associated with capital. Culture has become an industry rather than an inspiration and reflection of, among other things, human ingenuity. Goods, services, and people are no longer understood in terms of their intrinsic worth or merit but, rather, are based on their market value: "Purposelessness for the purpose declared by the market."[25] Within the culture industry the commodification and rationalization of labor results in relatively precise control over the minds and bodies of workers; human activity is subordinated to the demands of efficient production. In essence, work and leisure become opposite sides of the same coin as both involve subservience to the dictates of the market.

THE MECHANISM OF CONFORMITY

Horkheimer and Adorno contended that the culture industry does our thinking for us, resulting in restrictive cognitive processes or patterns: "[The culture] industry robs the individual of his function. Its prime service is to do his schematizing for him."[26] Television programs, popular music, films, and even novels have been so extensively organized, sorted, and classified that there is little left to interpret. Perhaps most important, the thrust to conform in mass culture is so powerful that it often overtakes any impetus or will to resist. Horkheimer and Adorno describe the consequences of such a system where "not to conform means to be rendered powerless, economically and therefore spiritually—to be 'self-employed.' When the outsider is excluded from the concern, he can only too easily be accused of incompetence."[27] Ultimately, conformism and cultural reproduction feed each other in a cyclical pattern, repeating the same endlessly. We now receive our cues from an environment so limited in scope as to render any form of creative dissonance almost impossible. The capacity for reflective thought and action erodes under the barrage of disparate sound bites and visual flashes of sensory data so characteristic of modern film and television. In short, both the products of the culture industry and the manner in which they are consumed inhibit the fostering of critical thought. The absence of such paves the way for mass deception common to the consumer's world—that fulfillment is to be found in a buy-and-consume modality. Horkheimer and Adorno describe this phenomenon thus:

The principle dictates that he should be shown all his needs as capable of fulfillment, but that those needs should be so pre-determined that he feels himself to be the eternal consumer, the object of the culture industry. Not only does it make him believe that the deception it practices is satisfaction, but it goes further and implies that whatever the state of affairs, he must put up with what is offered . . . Paradise offered by the culture industry is the same old drudgery.[28]

The commodification of culture also means that culture is experienced as monotony and a series of trivial experiences. Essentially, mass culture is littered with predetermined ideas, plots, and imaginings. Adorno further suggests that, increasingly, we lose our capacity to recognize, understand, and experience contradictions within the culture. The culture industry promotes identification with mass-produced products, negating the possibility of critical perspective. It holds, therefore, that the citizens of capitalism, exhausted by the labor process and tempted by easy promises of the culture industry, bypass reflective cognition and critical analysis in order to submerge themselves in the "pseudo-immediacy" of the moment. Ultimately, individualism falsely stems from the belief that the culture industry is providing new experiences, when in fact it is rehashing the same mold over and over. Mass culture thus cultivates a fictional sense of agency. Most important, Adorno views the buying and selling of culture as the buying and selling of identity (false as it may be): "The masses are not primary, but secondary, they are an object of calculation; an appendage of the machinery. The customer is not king, as the culture industry would have us believe, *not its subject but its object*" (italics added).[29]

The commodification of culture in modernity leads to the exclusion of many critical impulses that had previously been nurtured by aesthetic practice. Art had been one of the few sites of political resistance in which the status quo was challenged; with the private world virtually eliminated, colonized by the forces of mass culture, true art has had little chance of survival. While art may have been the language of truth, a new "pseudo-language" associated with mass culture has become prominent. Horkheimer and Adorno view the effects of commodification as more than just repressive or prohibitive. It takes on a far more sinister profile. The commodification process has the ability to, and does, strip us of our potency. However, we are not mere dupes. Each of us participates in spite of our intuition in the culture industry, partially aware that much of what we are fed through media is a lie:

The phrase, the world wants to be deceived, has become truer than had ever been intended. People are not only . . . falling for a swindle; if it guarantees them even the most fleeting gratification they desire a deception which is nonetheless transparent to them. They force their eyes shut and voice approval, in a kind of self-loathing.[30]

Indeed, self-deception becomes a necessity in a world of lies. Furthermore, individuality transforms into a familiar persona of sameness that everyone scrambles to adopt, desperate to fit in:

The sacrifice of *individuality*, which accommodates itself to the regularity of the successful, the doing of what everybody does, follows from the basic fact that in broad areas the same thing is offered to everybody by the standardized production of consumption goods. But the commercial necessity concealing this identity leads to the manipulation of taste and the official culture's pretense of individualism, which necessarily increases in proportion to the liquidation of the individual.[31]

The culture industry must keep us entertained, even laughing, as a means of smothering and defusing the latent rage from that part of the self that recognizes we are pawns. We find ourselves tolerating and even enjoying the fraudulent pleasures fed to us through a humor that stymies interest in social and political revolt.

Ironically, we treat the artifacts of the culture industry with a kind of half-conscious tolerance, even amused scepticism, *including* values that oppose the system itself. Given that the culture industry has a monopoly over the production and distribution of culture, it is able to integrate and absorb any and all dissidence. Conformity is thus guaranteed with the eradication of critical messages while at the same time using such messages as evidence of pluralistic tolerance. Paradoxically, the presence of dissenting voices even helps to sustain the lies, the myth that unmediated experiences are not only possible but are frequently occurring and that we are truly free agents.

THE CULTURE INDUSTRY AND TOTALITARIANISM

Adorno unabashedly depicts the culture industry in terms that invite comparison to fascism:

[The] voice of the monopoly will tell them as they wait in line precisely what is expected of them if they want to be clothed and fed. . . . Anyone who fails openly to parade their freedom, their courtesy, their sense of security, who fails to observe and propagate the established guidelines, is forced to remain outside the pale.[32]

Just as no one really believes fascist propaganda, no one really believes advertising's claims, and yet in both cases, we are compelled by the force of the message, both implicitly and explicitly. Advertised culture, in essence, constitutes a command for obedience to the social order, not unlike a fascist regime. Power will remain in the hands of a ruling elite even when the intention of cultural production is to operate in a "free" market. Where once individuation was highly valued, now imitation of the dominant modality is rewarded. Adorno leaves little optimism for the future. He predicted a world in which virtually all possibility of rectification would be squelched and was most disturbed by the fact that the culture industry dehumanized people and eroded their sense of freedom.

ONE-DIMENSIONAL MAN AND TOTALITARIANISM

The notion that so-called democratic societies could operate in a totalitarian manner was not unique to Adorno. Herbert Marcuse, in his well-known treatise, *One-Dimensional Man*,[33] contended that, in "advanced" societies, the development of consumer capitalism constitutes a profound threat to freedom and individuality. The main thrust of *One-Dimensional Man* suggests that capitalist societies are "totalitarian" because the capitalist mode of production and the "vested interests," or what Marx referred to as the ruling class, use technology to manipulate needs and to indoctrinate, manage, and administer society in accord with their own interests. It is in this sense that capitalist societies are totalitarian, controlled by the hegemony of capital. Indeed, as capitalism and technology continue to develop, society is expected to increasingly adjust to the economic and social apparatus and, ultimately, submit to its administration. As a result, conformity is rampant throughout consumer-driven cultures. Like Adorno, Marcuse believed that under capitalism citizens lose their capacity for critical analysis; hence, a "one-dimensional society" and "one-dimensional" man.

Marcuse's theory argued that those possessing the most capital control the activities of the state, including its media and social institutions. The motivation behind such control is to maximize economic gain, maintain social domination by eliminating opposition, and fuel the capitalist "machine": "The brute fact that the machine's physical (only physical?) power surpasses that of the individual, and of any particular group of individuals, makes the machine the most effective political instrument in any society."[34] The crux of Marcuse's one-dimensionality, therefore, is that the instruments of culture, including mass persuasion, manipulation, consumerism, and controlled gratification function to lure individuals toward a capitalist lifestyle that is to embrace one-dimensionality. By doing so, we lose our autonomy and freedom. Eventually, we relinquish the power to know what we need and want, to choose or deny and be able to resist obstacles. Indeed, one-dimensional man is incapable of knowing his true needs because they are not his own but are instead administered, superimposed. Individuals under such conditions are not able to resist domination; rather, they embrace popular culture, imitating and submitting to the powers that be. As such, one-dimensional thought and behavior begin to take form, develop, and eventually become habitual. As a result, we lose our ability to imagine alternatives, to transcend one-dimensional thought and society, to control our own destiny—to become a subject rather than an object of domination. One of the more serious consequences of surrendering one's subjectivity is the tendency to conform to the cultural whims of any given time.

Within Marcuse's analysis is also an outline of how mass consumption produces "false needs." He is explicit about how noncoercive social control powerfully "persuades" the individual to conform, submit, and adopt the norms of sameness:

"False" [needs] are those which are superimposed upon the individual by particular social interests in his repression . . . The result then is euphoria in unhappiness. Most of the prevailing needs to relax, to have fun, to behave and consume in accordance with the advertisements, to love and hate what others love and hate, belong to this category of false needs.[35]

It would appear that capitalism's freedom and democracy are based on manipulation and a new form of social control found within mass culture and its source of propaganda—advertising: "The products indoctrinate and manipulate; they promote a false consciousness which is immune against its falsehood. And as these beneficial products become available to more individuals . . . the indoctrination they carry . . . becomes a way of life . . . [that] militates against qualitative changes."[36]

Paradoxically, societies built on slogans of freedom, steeped in the proclamations of the advantages of consumer capitalism (such as the access to goods and services), rely on constraints or restrictions as a condition of success. It is only when we are relieved of the burden of false needs, and the ongoing manipulation to market such needs, that freedom is attainable.

As with Adorno and Horkheimer, Marcuse recognizes that failure to conform to the status quo threatens one's survival. Thus, "the intellectual and emotional refusal 'to go along' appears neurotic and impotent."[37] We are seen as becoming incapable of grasping or identifying the true nature of our interests, attributing false motives to the causes of our suffering. Consumer needs for money, possessions, property, and security are binding to the extent that they perpetuate conformity and alienate labor. For Marcuse, the "benefits" of consumer culture are repressive and the needs created are false because this type of culture binds individuals to a way of life that actually restricts their freedom and possibilities for happiness. It is a way of life that impedes development of a more rational social order. Ironically, the representation of liberty can serve as a powerful instrument of domination. The freedom to choose goods and services does not signify freedom if the system in which they are delivered sustains social control.

Throughout *One-Dimensional Man*, Marcuse argues that freedom and individualism are being eroded in late capitalist societies and, at the same time, dissenting views are "quickly digested by the status quo" to inoculate against any possibility of reform.[38] Marcuse, like Adorno, identifies mass culture as an agent of "manipulation and indoctrination" to the extent that consumable goods have been reified to a point of utter alienation from the self: "People recognize themselves in their commodities; they find their soul in their automobile, hi-fi set, split-level home, kitchen equipment . . . Control is anchored in the new needs which it has produced."[39] It is thus the consumer's endless quest for products that keep him or her vulnerable to the dictums of mass culture. In Marcuse's view, advertising agencies or corporations contribute to the pseudo-individualism that is prefabricated and synthesized within capitalist cultures. The system is such that freedom has become a pseudo-freedom, locking us in a bondage we fail to recognize.

Marcuse maintains that consumer culture has become a mode of domination through the hegemony of corporations whose structures keep it intact. Mass culture bombards us with ideologies, images, advertisements, and values that reproduce and legitimate the way of life that capitalism offers. Mass culture, in this view, promotes conformist behavior and conventional values as an instrument of socialization. Finally, Marcuse makes claim to capitalist society as reconfiguring into a totalitarian state by virtue of the fact that capitalism permeates every aspect of culture and easily operates through the manipulation of needs by vested interests (corporations). In essence, the ruling elite is able to control the interests of ordinary citizens, including their demands and the type of lifestyle needed to maintain consumptive behavior patterns.

THE INCEPTION OF MASS CULTURE

In *Captains of Consciousness*, Ewen traces the origins of mass culture to the 1920s when industry engaged in a process of socialization that aimed at inculcating loyalty among those whose labor was being solicited.[40] It was during this time that many industries had begun to employ mass production as part of their manufacturing. The impetus of industry was to lure the masses into a modality of more buying power. Marketers strove to establish an ideological bridge across traditional social gaps—region, class, culture, religion—which would work in their favor. At the same time, the movement toward mass production severely changed the character of labor in that workers had become a decreasingly significant unit of production. Marketers sought to soften the blow by speaking of "economic freedom" and "industrial democracy" as the rewards promised for industry labor.[41] Shorter hours and higher wages were deliberate strategies used to habituate the American population to the demands of mass production, as was more leisure time. Increasingly, new priorities demanded that the worker spend his wages and leisure time bolstering the consumer market. Ewen maintained that entry into and participation with the consumer market were presented as a "civilizing" experience. And yet the discrepancy between wages earned and that of industrial growth was significant, so much so that marketers realized they needed to habituate people "psychically" to accept consumerism as an equitable way of life.[42]

Advertising's main role was to create a dependable consumer, to feed the needs of mass industrial capitalism. Thus began the long-term relationship between industry and psychology; "experts," particularly psychologists rooted in the school of behaviorism, were hired to research how people responded to varying stimuli. Advertising was seen as a way of controlling the distribution of a product through stimulus-reward patterns: "Advertisers were concerned with effecting a self-conscious change in the psychic economy . . . Advertising literature, following the advent of mass production methods increasingly . . . appeals to instinct."[43] One advertising strategy was to offer products that claimed to ameliorate social and personal barriers. Further, a new cultural ethos was being projected by advertisers—social responsibility and social preservation—tied to the consumption of goods. Indeed, it was felt that capitalism, through an appeal of instincts (of which social insecurity was major), could "habituate men and women to consumptive life."[44] Thus, the functional goal of advertising was the creation of desires and habits previously "dormant," so that fulfillment of personal needs would become dependent on the market.

One of the outcomes of advertising on a mass scale in the early twentieth century was the production of a homogeneous "national persona"; consumption took on a cultural tone in keeping with an ideological creed of nationalism and democracy. Common desires, rather than common ethnicity, language, or class, began to define the "American type."[45] By transforming the notion of "class" into "mass," business hoped to persuade us to seek the fulfillment of needs for class "advancement" through the consumption of goods. Ironically, advertising offered up visions of individualism as a strategy for people to extricate themselves from the masses, all the while fomenting a homogenous "groupthink." Advertisements intimated that through the use of certain products success was guaranteed—"the capitalist notion of individual 'self-fulfillment.'"[46] Additionally, advertisements targeted everything personal—bodily functions, self-esteem—suggesting products as effective remedies for social maladaptation. The lone citizen on his own terms was thus pathologized. Ewen noted that "advertising offered the next best thing—a commodity self—to people who were unhappy or could be convinced that they were unhappy about their lives."[47]

Consumerism developed throughout the 1920s in a way that suggests the mere selling of products was no longer an adequate goal. Rather, broad-scaled strategies aimed at selling a *way of life*. Consumerism emerged not as a gradual progression from earlier patterns of consumption but rather as "an aggressive device of corporate survival."[48] Marketers believed their job had an educative role concerning cognition and behavior. Indeed, widespread within the literature of the 1920s and 1930s is this notion that people need to be educated about the benefits of the products of mass-produced culture, to be acculturated. Industrial development became far more than a production process. It became a propaganda machine advocating a "better" life.

Ewen, like Adorno, noted how art transformed from a means of expression to a sales tool and weapon of manipulation. Thus, creativity was sacrificed to the authority of commerce. In large part, the arts were conscripted as part of the broad cultural movement that characterized consumerism, namely, the eradication of indigenous culture. Furthermore, where art was once regarded as a source of "truth," markets co-opted the new "art" of advertising as the only legitimate form of truth. For those who sought to indoctrinate the masses to the logic of consumerism, the elevation of the goods and values of mass production to the realm of "truth" was a primary task. In particular, advertisements began to dictate "reality," regardless of their veracity. Under the guise of consumer protection, advertisers equated their message with "truth" as a means of dominating ordinary citizens. As Ewen explains:

Within such a vision of the future, the notion of the truth was "of interest" to the "citizens of industry," who were not expected to recognize or to particularly care about what was of social importance for them. Only the "great international broadcasting organization" was to determine what was important and what was not.[49]

Aspects of the "good life" associated with home and community were attacked and demeaned as a way of turning over authority to corporate enterprise. It was the corporation and its systematic attempt to commoditize sensual gratification that claimed to know better. Businessmen became diligent in their task to eradicate attitudes antithetical to the consumption ethos. Under the guidance of psychologists, the implementation of "mass psychology" was unleashed so that public opinion could be controlled.[50] As the industrial machinery produced standardized goods, so did the psychology of consumerism attempt to forge a mindset of consciousness en masse.

The political ideology of consumption depicted democracy as a natural expression of American capitalism, if not a by-product of the commodity system. The association of the consumption of goods with political freedom made such a configuration possible: "Within all of the democratic pronouncements, the essential political impulse was one of entrepreneurial domination, a structure in which *political* choice was limited to the prescriptions formulated by business and *politicized* in its advertising."[51] Consumerism developed into an ideology that not only supported big business economically but also politically. Through buying, individuals were democratically legitimizing the ideology and practices of marketers. Ewen maintained that American industrial barons, in essence, became the "social directors of the nation."[52]

In drafting an affirmative conception of human characteristics, the business community was setting up itself . . . [as] a model of emulation . . . The authority of industry was being drawn as a sustaining *father* figure while the traditional arenas of social intercourse and the possibility of collective action were pictured as decrepit, threatening, and basically incapable of providing any level of security.[53]

The advancement of consumerism penetrated social relations as marketers developed a new definition of family, one which would jive with the goals of industry. Ewen claimed that in the early days, corporations worked to successfully encroach on the authority of the home whose productive capacity was being outmoded. While the family still provided a semblance of social life, its erosion as the center of production was a dramatic shift. People were inundated with the message that industry, rather than the home, would determine how the family thrived; thus, compliance with industry's values and norms was relatively easy to obtain. Furthermore, industrial propaganda repeatedly claimed that the economic well-being of women and children was again sustained by industry rather than family. The cultivation of the successful household imaged in terms that revered family was now characterized by a shift away from family: "Love, like democracy, had become implicated in a broad patriotic program which revolved around the mass distribution of commodities, focusing the human psyche on the issue of accumulating goods as a primary social bond and activity."[54] The conditions of both production and consumption were simultaneously connected in a newly espoused ideology where the "proper" roles of each family member required faith in the authority of big business. And, with respect to children, their consumption of goods and services provided a much desired conduit between the family and marketers.

For businessmen, the fact that childhood was increasingly a period of consuming meant children represented great potential. Advertisements began to convey the message that the needs of children were better understood by industry; such advertisements were a microcosm of the steps taken to shift authority from the family to industry and the psychologists they employed. The symbolic ascendancy of children meant the infiltration of daily life by corporations that sought to ensure a family structure ruled by the ideals and desires of children. Indeed, adults were instructed to look toward children for an understanding of the new age of social behaviors and customs. Children were heralded as having the capacity to cope with modern life above and beyond that of their elders.

Despite the firm roots of patriarchal dominance in families, Ewen believed that the male role was stripped of most of its social authority except insofar as wages were concerned. At the same time, women were elevated to a "managerial" status with respect to the running of the household. Why such a dramatic change in strategy? It was understood early on that women would greatly influence family purchases. In order to appease demands for equality and freedom, businessmen appropriated feminist values into the discourse of consumerism. Even when it came to mothering, marketers aimed to convince women that modern science, as a subsidy of corporations, should guide their role as mothers. This campaign had enormous success; by 1929, more than 80 percent of the family's needs were satisfied through purchases made by women. Advertisers were convinced that it would be through women that the values of mass production would best be conveyed. Women were repeatedly told that through consumption their children would achieve a level of lifelong security and happiness. Additionally, the discourse of "free choice" was linked to the consumption of mass-produced goods affording women a "new and liberated role."[55] Ewen was clear that every aspect of family life was seen as a business opportunity:

For each aspect of the family *collective*—the source of decision-making, the locus of child rearing, the things which elicited affection in response—all of these now pointed outward toward the world of commodities for their direction. Corporate America has begun to define itself as *the father of us all*.[56]

Ewen theorized that industry's "captains of consciousness" successfully sold capitalism as a benign force from which all meaningful relationships would be constituted. The culture of the marketplace actively worked to generate an image of positive regard, to detract from the less appealing aspects of modernity, including the monotony of work, the decay of traditional social arenas, and the political repression that was encountered by those who resisted corporate politics. In fact, corporate ideology contended that a bolstered consumer society was more than capable of neutralizing political opposition. Ewen detailed how the market surreptitiously infiltrated the very social fabric of America in the early stages of consumer culture:

Brand names had inserted themselves into the idiom of daily expression, prepackaged foodstuffs were increasingly the culinary fare of the population. The automobile—perhaps the archetypal commodity—was no longer merely an idiosyncratic mode of transport but an artifact of multidimensional significance within the culture.[57]

Marketers succeeded in posing an idealized, "consumerized," and, increasingly, advertised vision of society made up of people who were basically inadequate and thus dependent on industry for success. Ewen argued that this process was not a random evolution over time;

rather, it was calculated and deliberate. Ultimately, corporations chose to depict human beings in a pejorative light for the purpose of generating and prolonging behaviors, attitudes, and values conducive to consuming. The plan proved to be a raging success.

CORPORATE RULE

> Marketing has become the center or the "soul" of the corporation. We are taught that corporations have a soul, which is the most terrifying news in the world. The operation of markets is now the instrument of social control and forms the impudent breed of our masters.[58]
>
> —Gilles Deleuze

Ewen, Horkheimer, and Adorno all theorized that the production, distribution, and sale of goods for the masses were deliberate means of mind control on the part of the capitalist elite whose power culminates within the corporation. Furthermore, culture, propagated by media, is a form of rationalized and systemic control of labor and leisure. The consumer is, in essence, a pawn, beholden to the system and relatively well controlled by a continuous bombardment of "entertainment."

Since Adorno's writings, mass culture has grown in terms of its potential to influence society to the degree that the corporation is now the most powerful institution of our time.[59] Horkheimer and Adorno observed at the time of their writing that those who control the culture industry wield enormous influence over civil society, as well as political society. The culture industry is a means of keeping social order, reinforced by political, social, and economic initiatives and, more specifically, the cultural and social institutions under corporate domain. Regardless of the existence of democracy, and often because of democracy, dominance can be maintained with the appearance of consent. Capitalism can, therefore, be defined as part of the core structure of the social order that has gained ideological dominance. Social dominance and cultural control are essentially achieved through the corporations of mass media. Horkheimer and Adorno state that:

All are free to dance and enjoy themselves, just as they have been free, since the historical neutralization of religion, to join any of the innumerable sects. But freedom to choose an ideology—since ideology always reflects economic coercion—everywhere proves to be freedom to choose what is always the same.[60]

Consent in the form of compliance is willingly given by consumers who are themselves "captivated by the myth of success" and believe in capitalist ideology such as the "free" market and the opportunity for upward mobility like the capitalist elite whose dominance eludes them.[61] Enlightenment has all but disappeared and is not possible within the confines of the culture industry where society is suppressed by and subservient to the ubiquitous financial machinery. Horkheimer and Adorno showed that as the culture industry developed into a tool for mass domination, the commercialization of all aspects of society were at its core. They also argued that this process is leading to the intellectual impoverishment of society, favoring commercialization over individuality and authenticity. In their view, the culture industry projects a disguised form of ideological propaganda, employing "pop culture" to mask oppression, all the while reducing cultural standards. Hence, creativity takes a backseat to the mechanisms that gave rise to mass-scale conformity.

THE INFANTILIST ETHOS AND TOTALISM

Benjamin Barber, a political theorist, proposed that present-day consumer capitalism, driven by methods of manipulation, generates faux needs. In particular, *Consumed* discusses how capitalism has shifted from serving nations and their citizens to an indulgent capitalism, driven by an "infantilist ethos."[62] By "infantilism," Barber meant that markets are consciously indulging a youthful culture via advertising, marketing, and branding for the purposes of increased profit and not for any revitalization of culture. This "ethos" spurned a new style of identity politics in which ownership of branded goods defines us even more than race, religion, nationality, and so on. Not only is adult consumer culture embracing an infantilist modality, children themselves are becoming the new market target. The misuse of populace terms like "autonomy," "empowerment," and "choice," typical of an infantilist ethos, are co-opted as part of the rationalization of selling to children. Barber is harsh in his criticism of "corporate predators" that defend their motives as deriving from an "altruistic ethic," all the while applying self-serving and immoral means.[63] As Barber sees it, we have moved from an era (1800s and preceding) when corporations were under the authority of government and in which capitalism served society and abided by its democratic principles, to one of capitalist narcissism in which corporations feel entitled to assert their demands. The infantilist ethos tolerates and promotes the dumbing down of adults, even as it appears to sanctify the maturation of children into "empowered" consumers. In other words, the infantilist ethos generates a set of habits, cravings, and attitudes that encourage and give credence to immaturity.

Barber characterized infantilization through three archetypal dualisms: easy over hard; simple over complex; and fast over slow. To begin with, while the tensions between easy and hard have challenged every culture, modernity is perhaps the first in which adult institutions lean heavily on the side of easy, even rewarding easy and penalizing challenge. As Barber described, "weight loss without exercise, marriage without commitment, painting or piano by numbers without practice or discipline . . . athletic success through steroids."[64] Lying, cheating, and deception have become rampant in today's culture in keeping with the "easy way." Barber maintained that the great civilizations have generally been characterized by their capacity to utilize nuance and complexity in their thinking, behavior, and ideology. Not so in consumer culture, which leans toward the easy route because it is so enticingly profitable: "Fast foods and moronic movies, revved-up spectator sports and dumbed-down video games, for example, [are] linked in a nexus of consumer merchandising that the infantilist ethos nourishes and promotes."[65]

Teenagers, in particular, are an ideal market segment for a society steeped in an easy-over-hard modality. With the means to spend money (lots of it) and sufficiently conditioned to consume a whole host of commodities, but possessing juvenile taste, they are naturals at sustaining "easy over hard." Remaining ignorant and youthful, often disregarding the worth of others, requires nothing more than a motivated narcissism.

Speed has become the modern quintessential expression of a youthful persona whether child or adult: "time whipped, time mastered, time accelerated, time overcome."[66] For example, video games are all about trying to induce a rapid neurological response to stimuli. Such goods are intrinsically tied to the perpetuation of youth, representing one of the most successful sectors of merchandising to children, as well as enticing adults to consume children's commodities. In a culture of fast over slow, speed is associated with the intelligence to reach conclusions in the blink of an eye and analyze within fixed time limits. Speed is seen as the promise of a thrilling experience. Not only do we like the sensations that speed provides, we love to view this endlessly on the screen. Indeed, the most consequential speedup of our time is the onrush of images that technology so adeptly provides. As an example of a lifestyle devoted to speed, Barber cites the "emblem" of American-style consumerism for the rest of the world—namely, fast food. The fast-food franchise has cropped up in astounding numbers both in North America and globally to the extent that a countermovement ("slow food") became necessary to preserve indigenous culture's relationship to eating.

Consumer culture reduces the complexities of life to a few simple axioms, the most prominent being "we are what we buy."[67] The infantalist ethos also rewards or reinforces a simplistic form of entertainment, as evidenced by the number of puerile movies, reality TV shows, video games, and so on. Even the most basic but important source of survival—eating—has been reduced to a fast, simplistic meal accompanied by a whopping number of calories that lacks in nutrition and flavor. The fact that adults are embracing many of the styles designed for children in a desperate quest to hold onto cool is another example of a reductionist culture. Ironically, the infantalist ethos is pressuring children to grow up as fast as they can, to dress like adults, smoke, drink, and engage in sex, yet also embrace the childishness in adults who long to hold onto their youth. Barber cites numerous examples of simple over complex, particularly when it comes to media. For example, the news has successively lost its depth of reporting, falling from "hard" to "soft" news to mere "info-tainment." Fox News, now wildly popular, distorts issues, reducing them to a polemic about liberalism versus conservatism, bypassing all the nuances associated with the complexity of issues facing today's world.

Infantalization plays out across the board in consumer society, privileging digitized images and pictures over words for their speed, efficiency, and simplicity. Barber believed that infantilism culture's preference for easy, simple, and fast, gave rise to a celebration of individuality over that of community. Hence, the infantalist ethos is reinforced by a creed of entitlement in which "human beings are seen first of all as individuals—what political scientists might call rights-bearing legal persons—rather than as family members, lovers, kin-people, or citizens of the civic community."[68] Barber felt that for the first time in history, people have come to view economic survival as a "controlled regression"; again, a culture that promotes puerility rather than maturity. The motivation to infantilize society is solely based on an "instrumental need to sell unnecessary goods to people whose adult judgment and tastes are obstacles to such consumption."[69]

The infantilist ethos has helped to create a culture conducive to slackness in conjunction with an obsession for shopping and spending—a potent combination. At odds with the democracy or free market it once helped launch, Barber saw how laissez-faire liberalism continues to mistake popular values with the repression of freedoms. Commodification philosophy is more than just a threat to democracy. It is *the* source of capitalism's most troubling problems today, says Barber, namely, its incapacity to meet the needs of the poor. Indeed, capitalism is now about promoting faux needs all the while ignoring the real needs of those in developed and underdeveloped societies. Barber argued that market dictates tell us what we "need" and simultaneously, proclaim to have all the answers. Within this catch-22, we somehow accept our dilemma, participating in the charade as though oblivious.

Within the main core of consumer culture is a process of privatization in which all aspects of human exchange and relationship are commoditized. Barber believed this represented more than just an economic ideology. Privatization acts in league with the ethos of infantilization to embrace and reinforce narcissism and a type of foolhardiness. Additionally, privatization confuses liberty with the fulfillment of wants and thereby distorts how we understand civic freedom and citizenship, often ignoring, even undermining, the meaning of the state of well-being:

Privatization turns the private, impulsive me lurking inside myself into an inadvertent enemy of the public, deliberative we that is also part of who I am. The private me screams "I want!" The privatization perspective legitimizes this scream, allowing it to trump the quiet "we need" that is the voice of the public me in which I participate and which is also an aspect of my interests as a human being.[70]

Consumer capitalism reinforces a cult of "me" on the model of the narcissistic child and discourages "we" thinking of the kind seen in acts of cooperation and altruism. It is the combination of capitalism reconfigured by an infantilist ethos and a privatization ideology which is corrosive to civil society. Infantilization acts to continuously induce the preference for the private and the trivial by upholding the image of an impetuous child as the ideal shopper, and the shopper as the ideal democratic citizen. We are in essence, ruled by a divided sense of liberty that renders itself to chronic dissatisfaction in both the private and public realm.

Barber was clear that the forces of capitalism play a vital role in forging identities conducive to buying and selling. Ultimately, the commercialization of identity responds to and reflects the infantilist ethos in significant ways. For example, commercial identities tend to be shallow or lacking in depth, all the while undermining agency, community, and democracy. Identity formation is now conceived almost entirely based on our commercial persona:

Branded lifestyles are not merely superficial veneers on deeper identities but have to some degree become substitute identities—forms of acquired character that have the potential to go all the way down to the core. They displace traditional ethnic and cultural traits and overwhelm the voluntary aspects of identity we choose for ourselves.[71]

Brands are no longer associated with the specific content of the products and services they label; they are instead affiliated with a lifestyle and desired persona only remotely linked to the products and services they represent. And it is in this process that they become com-pelling new purveyors of infantilism. The challenge of building brand loyalty is one of the key reasons why companies are so very eager to engage young consumers. For consumer identity, appearances are of maximum importance, especially to youth who are obsessed with ac-quiring the right look. Barber maintained that "in a commercial society where identities are linked to cars that people 'wear' and churches they 'shop' for, it is little wonder that identity can be bought, borrowed or stolen."[72] Thus, branding and privatization turn out to work in tan-dem. As identity drifts from public influences rooted in religion and nationality (even familial influence) toward arbitrary commercial stan-dards, those associated with brands, identity itself is privatized. For Barber, this means that identity politics are part and parcel of the infantilist ethos which mistakes the brand for true identity and con-sumption for an aspect of personality.

Barber exclaimed that not only is consumer society privatized, com-mercialized, infantilized, and branded, it is also "totalizing," in that all aspects of being are devoted to consumption. Barber opined that Adorno and Horkheimer overstated the ills of mass culture by label-ling it a totalitarian society. He does, however, agree that consumer culture is both "totalizing and homogenizing."[73] By this, he meant that consumer society robs liberty of its civic meaning (or democratic meaning) and threatens pluralism—a point of view also held by H. and A. Pluralism in this case refers to the inclusion of behaviors that enhance human well-being and flourishing. Furthermore, one of the consequences of "totalism" is that consumers buy products and en-gage in services they do not necessarily need or want—a capitulation to the forces of the market. The market consciously aims at producing a firm and encompassing grip on all aspects of life, demanding a total immersion. Thus, the market controls

each and every of our waking moments and [infiltrates] the psyche's most remote and private geography. This is a necessary condition for capitalism success: an all-consuming people who shop or think about shopping, who conceive or exercise consumer wants, all the time.[74]

Barber described five forms of market domination, the first being *ubiquity*. The market is everywhere we turn—every open space (e.g., on the bus, the clothes we wear, on buildings, on park benches) invites a brand logo or advertisement. Second, the market is *omnipresent*, it is always "on" engaging our time at a frenetic 24/7 pace. Another indica-tor of the totalizing and homogenizing character of consumer culture is its *addictiveness*. In a hyperconsumer society, addiction has a cultural and economic dimension. By creating "addictions," marketers have an ideal means of securing their presence with little effort. The fact that we even have a disorder of shopping addiction speaks volumes about the extent to which our consuming behavior controls us. Fourth, the market has the capacity for *self-replication* as it operates and proliferates with such little opposition or regulation. Self-replication means market monopolization is a prime goal. As for the consumers, their conformity within the market services the frenzied process of self-replication. Commodification is the venue by which consumer cultures reproduce, aiming to create monopolies of taste and behavior. As Barber describes it, "to commodify is thus to colonize, to impose singular meanings on multi-dimensional goods."[75] Consumer capitalism has an endless capacity for self-replication at the cost of diversity and thus interferes with, even prevents, pluralism. The last form of market domination can be labeled as *omnilegitimacy*. By this, Barber referred to the ways that commerce successfully places consuming at its core, virtually unchallenged all the while shutting out rival influences. Consumerism is constantly propounding its legitimacy, not just in economic terms but at a gut level as well. Indeed, the goal of marketing is to impose a legitimacy of positive feeling not only on the products and brands it peddles but also on the entire process by which it runs.

One of the outcomes of consumer capitalism gone "hyperdrive" is the disintegration of identity formation, the hollowing of individual sovereignty. Barber goes a step further than Marcuse, claiming that consumers are less one-dimensional than *no*-dimensional as their identities are literally manufactured, bought, worn, and discarded; the self transposes in the car, computer, Nike shoes, or whatever other objects resonate with the desired image. The end effect is the eradication of unique character traits and the multiplication of consumer clones.

Barber leaves us with only a margin of hope that totalism and homogeneity can be staved off. He concludes that in order to lessen the impact of the infantilist ethos, we must reclaim our citizenry, resist the hold of marketing and branding on identity so as to mitigate the destructive impulses of consumers who are disconnected and self-serving. As long as consumers find themselves trapped in a cage of infantilization, reinforced by privatization and an identity based on branding, true democracy remains at peril.

INVERTED TOTALITARINISM

> The corporation's legal mandate is to pursue, relentlessly and without exception, its own self-interest, regardless of the often harmful consequences it might cost to others.[76]
>
> —Joel Bakan

The whole sphere of the culture industry, which Horkheimer and Adorno suggest is controlled by the creators of popular "entertainment," is also interwoven into the economic infrastructure, that which is at the heart of corporate dominance. Today's culture of capitalism includes a small number of elite corporations that wield control over political decisions, financial investments, or money industries, as well as media in all forms. The corporation as an institution is virtually unchallenged, sovereign, holding tremendous power over the lives of ordinary persons. The ability to shape culture largely rests with those who take control of channels of communication under the guise of consenting democracies. Countries like the United States and Canada are beholden to the corporation for this reason. The Frankfurt School scholars, despite all their criticism of modern capitalism, could hardly imagine the degree to which culture has been generated in the hands of just a few corporations.[77]

Wolin (2008), a political theorist, believes that we are currently witnessing in the United States the most advanced form of corrupted democracy, what he labels "inverted totalitarianism."[78] Wolin is quick to say that inverted totalitarianism is something entirely new, distinctly different from the twentieth-century totalitarianism of a Stalin or Hitler; rather, it is a type of political system so entrenched in corporate politics as to be essentially under corporate rule. For Wolin, democracy in the United States has been steadily eroding since the time of the New Deal following the Great Depression. The New Deal was conceived as a means of redressing inequalities within American society, but when World War II broke out, it was superseded by governmental control of the entire economy. The war had a profound effect in halting the momentum of political and social democracy and contributed to the increasingly open cohabitation between the corporation and the state. To a large extent, Wolin attributed the diminishment of democracy to the rising power of global corporate interests and select elitist groups (plutocrats like the Koch brothers), particularly those associated with the presidency of George W. Bush (2000–2008).

Wolin used the term "inverted totalitarianism" as primarily representing the political coup by corporate power and concomitant demobilization of citizenry. While classic totalitarianism uses available technologies to control, intimidate, and manipulate in order to force societies into a preconceived totality, inverted totalitarianism is not found in ideology or overt expression such as public policy. Rather, inverted totalitarianism "projects power inwards" and gains its dynamic by the conflation of the state with other forms of power (e.g., evangelical religions), particularly private governance represented by the corporation.[79]

Wolin cites some of the symptoms of inverted totalitarianism as including preemptive wars (Iraq), widespread use of torture (Guantanamo Bay), domestic spying (National Security Agency), and widespread corruption in both government and corporate infrastructures (2008 economic meltdown). Tendencies in American culture now point in a direction away from self-government, including the rule of law and egalitarianism, toward "managed democracy." Fiercely capitalistic, the United States, and Canada under prime minister Stephen Harper, have both prided themselves on adhering to a *decentralized* power structure in which no single person or governmental agency could or should attempt to direct. The economy is said to be working best when left alone so that the free market can operate unfettered. Yet Wolin claimed that laissez-faire economics has produced and sanctioned trusts, monopolies, holding companies, and cartels. As a result, economic ideology reinforced by business corporations and science and technology has overtaken, even replaced, politics. "The emergence of the corporation marked the presence of private power on the scale and in numbers hitherto unknown, the concentration of private power unconnected to a citizen body."[80]

Wolin argued that our current situation is comprised of unprecedented combinations of power distinguished by their "totalizing tendencies" that challenge political, moral, intellectual, and economic boundaries on a continual basis.[81] One such power base is the media conglomerate, which has restricted the free dissemination of ideas to that of a "managed" system.[82] For example, the media representation of the 9/11 terrorist attacks established salient images of American vulnerability minus a more complex analysis of what had happened. In the aftermath of 9/11, the American people were propelled into a world of pseudo-reality in which mendacities shaped decisions despite obvious distortions of facts.[83] Such conditions lent themselves to abuses of executive and judicial power characteristic of inverted totalitarianism. It relies on "private" media rather than on public agencies to disseminate propaganda that reinforces the so-called official version of news. It is important to note that inverted totalitarianism is not driven by personal rule but by "abstract totalizing powers" seemingly difficult to hold accountable for their lack of direct actions.[84]

Inverted totalitarianism is sustained by encouraging political *disengagement* of citizens rather than mass enlistment typically used in totalitarian states. In classic totalitarianism, the conquest of total power is a conscious aim of those heading a political movement. With inverted totalitarianism, the figurehead is the product of the system rather than its leader. In fact, inverted totalitarianism is largely independent of any particular leader and requires no specific authority to survive. It is best understood by examining how corporate heads hold sway over society and wield power within political and social systems. Wolin characterizes this process as follows: "Inverted totalitarianism has emerged imperceptibly, unpremeditatedly, and in seeming unbroken continuity with the nation's political traditions . . . an inversion occurs when seemingly unrelated, even disparate starting points converge and reinforce each other."[85] Inverted totalitarianism disclaims its real identity so as to normalize deviations from true democracy. For example, George W. Bush sanctioned the use of torture and imprisoned individuals without due process, all the while pontificating about the sanctity of the law. Totalitarianism attempts to realize an ideological conception of (or normalize) a system controlled from the top down. Inverted totalitarianism claims to endorse democracy on a global scale, yet it supports governments legitimated by bogus elections or, even worse, dictatorships. In the case of the United States, its government alleges to be the showcase, the ideal of how democracy can be managed without appearing to be suppressive. Capitalism, democracy's twin, is thus virtually uncontested in the West.

Wolin believes that corporate power has skyrocketed, and while ostensibly nonpolitical in its origins, corporations are now unrestrained by constitutional limits or democratic processes. The recent U.S. Supreme Court (2009) decision allowing corporations unlimited campaign contributions in any and all election processes (including presidential) is a prime example of how government colludes with corporate rule. Wolin's theory developed from the premise that democracy and totalitarianism are not mutually exclusive. He opined that it is possible for inverted totalitarianism to evolve from a presumed "strong democracy" instead of a "failed" one.[86] In other words, inverted totalitarianism does not require the overthrow of an established, legitimated system. On the contrary, it operates by defending the very system in which it thrives. Governments "infected" with inverted totalitarianism exploit political and legal obstacles, especially to facilitate certain favored forms of corporate power, while squelching rival ones. This is possible, in part, because U.S. law upholds the corporation as having the legal rights of a person.[87] Wolin notes: "Our totalizing system . . . has evolved its own methods and strategies. Its genius lies in wielding total power without appearing to . . . or enforcing ideological uniformity, or forcibly suppressing dissident elements."[88]

While the scope of government has receded, corporate power has increasingly assumed governmental responsibilities and services, many of which were deemed to be the special preserve of state power. To the extent that the corporation and state are inextricably linked, "privatization" has become the norm for a significant number of government services. State defiance of corporate control is now a mere aberration, having been pressured to relinquish its power too many times. Wolin contends that privatization encompasses a major component of managed democracy by diminishing the political and its democratic content. Perhaps what characterizes inverted totalitarianism's greatest harm is the abdication of governmental responsibility for the well-being of its citizenry. Wolin continuously repeats that the ethos of the twenty-first-century corporation is one of competition rather than cooperation, of aggrandizement and profitability at the expense of community: "The [corporation] is both the principal supplier of political leadership and the main source of political corruption... 'Shareholder democracy' belongs on the same list of oxymorons as 'Superpower democracy.'"[89] Inverted totalitarianism marks a political moment when corporate power is no longer a purely economic phenomenon within the confines of "private enterprise." As a co-partner with the state, the corporation has become more of a political entity and the state more market oriented. Corporate power infiltrates government in the form of lobbyists and contributes to the degradation of political dialogue through privately organized media. The $700 billion plus corporate bailout in 2008, described by Congresswoman Kaptur as an *economic coup d'état*[90] that Congress sanctioned and implemented, is a stark example of Wolin's theory in practice and how the welfare of ordinary citizens is disregarded when pitted against corporate interests.

THE CLONING OF MASS MIND

The corporate teaching that we can find happiness through conformity to corporate culture is a cruel trick, for it is corporate culture that stokes and feeds the great malaise and disconnect of the culture of illusion.[91]
—Chris Hedges

Perhaps the most striking feature of this chapter has been the overlapping repetitiveness or similarity of each of the theorists considering their diversity in historical time, culture, and orientation. They all came to the same conclusion that capitalism, as an ideology, demands culture and humanity itself become subordinate to economic imperatives, even at the demise of democracy. History appears to be moving in a regressive direction for each of these theorists in which escape from cultural influence and its concomitant, economic dominance, is increasingly remote. As a result, what were once citizens of the free world are now clones of mass culture, those who believe their "individuality" has been preserved when, in fact, their actions and attitudes confirm an entrenched level of compliance. True individuality is about establishing a position of moral autonomy and, when appropriate, finding the courage not to cooperate, a process that holds little merit in mass-produced consumer cultures. The culture industry does the bulk of thinking for us like in a cult in which members are told to follow the leader with blind faith. The promises of happiness/salvation never quite deliver. We even become numb to our disillusionment. As media critic Kono Matsu stated, "Dreams, almost by definition, are supposed to be individualistic and imaginative. But what does it mean when a whole culture dreams the same dream?"[92]

The culture industry seeps into thought, emotion, language, and behavior, and its products provide the normative framework of expression. It is the means with which we experience the social and material conditions of our lives. What of the receiver of such culture? We now have the technology and power to create a virtual world at the beck and call of the consumer. The result is a vehement defense of individuality, paradoxically seen to be upheld by the mechanisms of mass culture and spurring us to guard popular cultural values against all other authorities, even government. Yet it is widely admitted that the basic incentive of culture production is profit making, not human betterment. Were there any doubt that acquisition of capital is a prime motive, a mere surface glimpse will reveal the gross misappropriation of wealth between the ordinary citizen and industry. Somehow the mendacity is never exposed in a way that catapults a cultural revolution of a magnitude necessary to evoke real change. Pockets of dissent are isolated and rendered ineffective (Occupy movement) as generations of new believers, those raised in the swath of the culture industry, know of nothing else.

In the case of adults, there is room to charge that the embrace of mass culture is a conscious choice. Horkheimer and Adorno were under no illusion that the masses are dupes or merely suffering from false consciousness. Their final conclusion in *Dialect of Enlightenment* purported that "the triumph of advertising in the culture industry is that consumers feel compelled to buy and use its products even though *they see through them*" (italics added).[93] Perhaps the most alarming aspect of the culture industry is that we feel compelled to partake without having critically examined the reasons why, as though operating out of some instinctual unconscious drive. Even so, Horkheimer and Adorno held out some hope for resistance and creativity for adults, though this was not a well-developed piece of their theoretical treatises. Their central message remained that the ubiquity of consumerism, the power of media, and the mass production of culture all helped to create a totalizing cultural ethos. Many have elaborated beyond Adorno's central theses decades after their publications, including more current academics who concur that hyperconsumerism continues to erode both culture and the political environment that supports its dominance.[94]

In the case of children, however, the argument of "knowing yet still persuaded" becomes increasingly more difficult to make. From infancy, children are being introduced to consumer culture and media such that a world without it is unimaginable. Children's most elementary mode of expression—play—has become the target of marketing strategies, allowing corporations to "define the limits of children's imaginations."[95] As we have already seen, children are so immersed in mass culture that they spend an astonishing amount of their day with media. When not engaged with technology, the modern child is encouraged to play with mass-produced toys and games, all of which have been carefully scripted. As Stephen Kline chillingly noted, "Imaginative play has shifted one degree closer to mere imitation and assimilation."[96] Even for adults, there is little variety within the culture industry despite an endless array of consumer products seeking to disguise their ever-sameness with trivial differences.

Media of all forms, the prominent distributor of the culture industry, is now the main, though largely unacknowledged, educator. For children, the omnipresence of television, computers, DVDs, and so on, and the amount of time devoted to their viewing, far surpass that of schooling. As marketing criteria begin to dominate all aspects of children's lives, they underwrite the most important modality of socialization, namely, children's imaginations. We are preoccupied with safety from physical harm, yet we have ignored the psychological and emotional harm to children that results from unfettered access by corporations. We must ask how it is that, as a culture, we have abdicated our responsibility to ensure children retain freedom of mind. We allow a battery of professionals from psychology, sociology, and neuroscience, among others, to apply themselves to the child market as a means of ensuring the continued "successes" of the corporation. The rights of children in this regard have been cast aside.

7

Deconstructing Consumerism: From the Voices of Young People

There is a considerable gap in the literature as to how young people experience and understand the meaning of consumer culture *throughout* their lives, and because little is known about these phenomena, or how accurately present theories address them, I felt further research was needed. My qualitative research process followed an inductive, data-driven format in which individual interviews were conducted. Each interview was analyzed to identify codes or recurring concepts. The codes were then organized into larger categories from which themes were identified in accordance with researchers Juliet Corbin's and Anselm Strauss's methods.[1] The study incorporated an open-ended interview guide (Appendix 1) aimed at soliciting responses related to the experiences associated with consumerism. The interview questions were used as a guideline to elicit rich descriptions, and they served as a tool to encourage discussion. Critical theory was applied as an analytical mechanism with which to further understand and interpret the interview data. Critical theory is concerned with analysis of the constraints placed on individuals by race, class, gender, and other constructs that act as barriers to personal and social emancipation. In summary, critical theory supports an examination of the personal while considering the context of larger social, political, gendered, and economic parameters.[2]

The interview data were reduced to clusters of meaning, and then coded so that similar concepts across interviews could be connected and subsequently analyzed. Once the analysis had been completed, a reanalysis of the data occurred; this time, each emergent theme was viewed in a contextual framework (critical theory framework) to shed light on the larger cultural factors that may have influenced or contributed to the type of data collected. Critical theory recognizes that privileged groups within a culture often have an interest in supporting the status quo to protect their advantages and, therefore, seek to identify who dominates in specific situations.[3] Hence, for a qualitative research study, critical theory invites inclusion of subjective experience as a valid process with which to understand social phenomena. Thus, the aim of the research was to extend beyond a micro-level and place the research findings within a macro context—political, sociological, and psychological—that has broad implications at a societal or cultural level.

The intent of this study was *not* to determine whether or not consumer culture can be harmful—the literature reviewed in previous chapters demonstrated clearly some of its ill effects. Rather, my research study was an exploration to uncover the means with which such harms manifest within the context of cultural values and beliefs. The purpose of the study was to determine how individuals who are 18 or 19 years old have experienced consumer culture, both in terms of the past, the present, and what they perceive or hope for in the future. Hence, the interview guide included numerous questions related to the participants' childhood, teenage, and nuclear family years, including what they hoped for in the future. Children who were born in the 1990s (i.e., the research participants) have been heavily targeted by corporations whose aim was to inculcate in them a desire for a consumer lifestyle. While many of the effects of this "campaign" are evident in data concerning their physical and psychological health, there is a paucity of research that recorded young people's direct understanding of their circumstance. Hence, do young people believe they were targeted? Do they feel that being a consumer is a central role in their lives? I decided to use as the primary research question: "How do young people understand and experience consumer culture over the course of their lifetime?" Additional questions (those not identified by the interview script) were spontaneously introduced as the interview process unfolded to help facilitate the dialogue and encourage reflection from each of the participants. The fact that individuals were asked to recall events that took place early in their lives meant that the credibility of the results was heavily dependent upon the participants' ability to access childhood memories. It is possible that the participants had a different recall from how childhood events actually unfolded; however, the bulk of the interview questions were designed to illicit the *feelings* that the participants associated with such events. It appeared that the participants accessed past feelings with relative ease judging by the certainty with which they answered the questions.

QUALITATIVE RESEARCH DESIGN

In the not so distant past, qualitative research was largely criticized for being "unscientific" relative to quantitative research. Some of these attitudes still remain. It may, therefore, be of help to extrapolate on or justify the qualitative process as a bona fide methodology for those skeptics who regard it as inferior. Hence, for readers who are not familiar with a qualitative paradigm or regard it negatively, I have included some of the specific details that should help explain the basis for the study at a concrete level.

Interviews

Typically, the semistructured qualitative research interview involves an informal and interactive process, utilizing open-ended comments and questions. Although a series of questions may be developed in advance of the interviews, these may be varied, altered, or not used at all since each participant's story unfolds through a process that cannot be anticipated.[4] The researcher attempts to obtain unprejudiced descriptions of the "life world"—the world as it is encountered.[5] The interview is considered one of the main methods of data collection in qualitative research as it provides a forum whereby the participants' descriptions can be explored, illuminated, and probed. I attempted to facilitate dialogue by employing questions that probed feeling states such as "How did you feel when that happened?" or "What was that like?" These types of questions help to translate human experience by revealing how it presents itself in real life. The self cannot be understood as well if questions are centered on fact finding through a "what"-type orientation in which the self is treated as a static representation and represents itself," rather than as the "fundamental self."[6] Hence, I followed a descriptive rather than explanatory or analytic format during the process of interviewing, so as to capture as much of the participants' subjective experiences as possible.

Sampling and Recruitment

Because this study focused on a particular issue, the respondents had to be able to speak on that subject. One of the most important aspects of the research is sampling. Students from the University of British Columbia Okanagan Campus (a small university in southern British Columbia) who met the criteria for the research were recruited for the study. The criterion was defined as individuals aged 18 or 19 years (first- or second-year students) who have grown up from birth in either the

United States or Canada, both being representative consumer cultures. These individuals reflect a white, middle- and lower-middle-class stratum. Due to the fact that the sampling did not include a wide range of ethnicity and socioeconomic classes, the results must be understood within the context of the study itself; projections about other sample groups by comparing to the study are limited. Recruitment was carried out by getting permission from professors in various departments and conducting a brief presentation on the research at a number of their classes for first-year students. A stipend of $20 was offered to each participant.

Sample Size

In qualitative research, sample size depends on the research questions, purpose of the study, usefulness of the sample group, credibility, and what can be done with available time and resources. It is up to the researcher to make judgment calls about sample size as there are no hard and fast rules; again, the trade-off between breadth and depth applies.[7] Qualitative research scholars Yvonne Lincoln and Egon Guba believe that the size of the sample is determined by the primary criterion of redundancy, yet, in this study, redundancy played a small role in the valuing and estimation of the data.[8] Repetition, for example, may inform the researcher's analysis of a particular phenomenon by placing more importance on it. Furthermore, for the purposes of this study redundancy bore little relevance as each respondent's perspective was deemed relevant regardless of content. For this study, 20 subjects in total were recruited with equal numbers of males and females.

Data Collection

Data were derived from several sources, including (1) in-depth, semistructured interviews with participants, audiotaped and transcribed; (2) contact summaries or field notes completed shortly after the interviews; and (3) written memos that upon further reflection informed the analysis. Credibility was met through the process of faithful transcription of the interviews.

Data Analyses

In essence, data analysis in qualitative studies involves reading through the transcripts several times; coding, or identifying significant phrases or sentences, working to develop a list of nonrepetitive, nonoverlapping statements; formulating meanings and clustering them into themes common to all respondents' transcripts; and integrating the results into an in-depth, exhaustive description of the phenomenon including verbatim examples.[9] I used MAXQDA qualitative research software for all memos, codes, and textual data analysis from initial coding, conceptualization, and core categories to writing narratives.

Coding

Coding is the first step in taking an analytic stance toward data in qualitative studies.[10] The coding process involves analyzing raw data and elevating it to a conceptual level.[11] Code names were derived either from statements made by the participants (e.g., "shopaholic") or in some cases, subjectively designated based on a careful review of the data, so as to best capture what had been relayed (e.g., "more is not better," "free of fad influence"). In an attempt to contextualize and deepen my understanding of each participant's unique perspective, codes were assigned only after all data had been collected and reviewed. After initial codes (concepts) were identified, deeper analysis, aided by memo writing, highlighted the relationships between concepts and eventually led to the development of categories. Finally, through the process of reviewing and analyzing categories, themes began to emerge (e.g., "Inside the Culture Industry"). Identifying themes is an important step because it guides the researcher in his or her attempts to sift through the data systematically, reduces the data, and eventually combines the data.[12]

Critical Discourse Analysis

The discourse of each interview constituted an important source of evidence of the social structures and processes specific to consumer cultures. Additionally, each interview revealed the political machinations, exertions of social control, and possible ways of resistance and empowerment. It was, therefore, important to deconstruct the social systems revealed in each of the interviews at a structural level, as well as evidence of agency of each participant. I utilized critical discourse analysis in tandem with critical theory to ensure that the wider cultural context was also critiqued in the final analysis of the data. When applying Norman Fairclough's conceptualization of critical discourse analysis, all forms of discourse (written, aural, visual, texts, photographs, brochures, television commercials, cereal boxes, and so forth) are treated as significant active phenomena and not just representations of reality.[13] Language is not a neutral, information-carrying mechanism but rather a site where social meanings are imposed, created, and changed. Hence, the content of a given text is both a representation of various power dynamics of the given culture in which it is situated and, at the same time, produces such dynamics. Through critical analysis, the researcher is able to look beyond the taken-for-granted assumptions and meanings that manifest themselves in language. Critical discourse analysis aims to expose and critique the strategies that individuals use in everyday discourse as a means of revealing political, social, and economic structures:

> Its particular concern is with the radical changes that are taking place in contemporary social life: with how discourse figures within the process of change, and with shifts in the relationship between discourse and more broadly semiosis and other social elements within networks of practices. We cannot take the role of discourse and social practices for granted, it has to be established through analysis.[14]

Thus, social relations, identities, cultural values, and even consciousness itself are all in part discursive. According to Fairclough, discourse figures in three specific ways in social practices: as part of social activity or of producing social life; in representations dependent upon each social actor; and in ways of being or in identities. This three-dimensional analytical framework specifically brings together micro- and macro-level factors in the production and interpretation of discourse. That which is discourse driven is also knowledge driven in that knowledge is generated and circulated as discourse. The process through which discourses become operationalized within societies can be revealed in the dialectics of discourse. It should be noted that discourses not only include representations of how things are and have been but also are representations of how things might or could or should be—which is how new identities or modes of being come to be produced.[15]

TRUSTWORTHINESS

An important task of the qualitative researcher is to establish the "trustworthiness" of the study. Lincoln and Guba suggest that researchers may approach trustworthiness from four differing perspectives, including (1) "truth value"—do the findings reflect the truth(s) of the participants?; (2) applicability—can the findings be applied in other settings?; (3) consistency—would the same findings appear if the study were repeated?; and (4) neutrality—are the findings determined by the participants rather than the biases of the researcher?[16] These four perspectives reflect the respective concepts of validity, reliability, and objectivity in traditional or positivist research. The authors suggest that qualitative researchers revert to the use of the term "credibility" as a means of confirming whether the findings are trustworthy and believable. Furthermore, it is not appropriate to simplify the differences between qualitative and quantitative research by suggesting that one is subjective and the other, objective. "Objectivity" is only ever achieved through the eyes of an observer whose values, beliefs, and expectations pose an element of subjectivity. Indeed, within qualitative research, objectivity is deemed to be a "chimera: a mythological creature that never existed, save in the imaginations of those who believe that knowing can be separated from the knower."[17]

Truth Value (Credibility)

The paradigm of critical theory, in contrast to positivist "standards," regards perceptions of reality as always being influenced by an individual's *subjective* experiencing. The qualitative researcher may strive only to increase the accuracy of individual perceptions, either his or her own and those of the respondents. Thus, the qualitative researcher relies heavily on the credibility of respondents to establish the truth value of findings.[18] Researchers may strengthen credibility during the process of inquiry by rigorous documenting and ensuring that each participant was treated equally and fairly.[19]

Applicability (Generalizability)

In qualitative research the central question often asked is whether or not results in one situation can be used to speak to or help form judgments about other results. Hence, are the results generalizable? Lincoln and Guba used the term "fittingness" rather than generalizability as a means of defining the degree of "congruence" between the context of the research subjects and the context of a comparable population.[20] In other words, do the results of the research reasonably fit with our understanding of the larger picture? One approach is to provide "thick" rich descriptive data that can then be judged as to its merit and applicability with regard to comparable others of the general population.[21] My study was conducted with this in mind such that details about the experiences of each of the participants were fully revealed and expanded upon within the interviews. The comparative analysis that was undertaken here was internal, that is, within the sample. I asked the question: To what extent are the experiences of these students around consumerism similar or different? The findings, not unexpectedly, should reflect common cultural experiences for this group. Nonetheless, considering the homogeneity of the sample, it should be stated that the findings of this study may or may not generalize to a wider population. I leave it up to future research to decide the extent to which the findings are a good fit with the wider population, one that is representative of the general Canadian or U.S. population of 18- or 19-year-olds.

Consistency

Consistency relates to the traditional concept of reliability—can the findings be replicated? The traditional assumption that reality is knowable and independent of time suggests that the "truth" about a given phenomenon can be ascertained. On the contrary, in qualitative research, context and time are important variables and are deemed to alter perception dramatically. A qualitative researcher must, therefore, assume that the existence of an element of uniqueness in a particular study will not necessarily lend itself to replication.[22] The results of this study are, therefore, unique and stand alone as significant in their contribution to enhancing knowledge about the subject. Arguably, it is not necessary to "prove" that a replicated study would arrive at the same results or conclusions.

Neutrality (Confirmability)

Third, neutrality is linked to the traditional concept of objectivity. To determine what is objective, researchers often look for intersubjective agreement. That is, "what a number of individuals experience is objective and what a single individual experiences is subjective."[23] Researchers also assign objectivity using their judgment as to whether an observation or assertion is factual and confirmable, in contrast to biased or opinionated conclusions. Qualitative researchers prefer *confirmability* because the emphasis on what is observed appropriately emphasizes characteristics reflective of the data.[24] Throughout the interviews I attempted to address issues of neutrality by reflecting back to the participants what I had heard and sought clarification accordingly.

VALIDITY

According to Guba and Lincoln, no one method, or collection of methods, can claim to be exclusively valid for any given study as there are a myriad of ways to approach any research question.[25] They also argue that while the concept of validity traditionally rests upon whether or not the researcher's interpretations can be trusted to accurately convey human phenomena, which is difficult to verify. Angen (2000) suggests the following framework as an alternative to more traditional modes of validity: Has the research question been carefully framed to account for the historical timeframe in which it is based? Is the research carried out respectfully? Are the arguments persuasive? Are the results capable of being disseminated widely? Further to this, psychologist Maureen Angen suggests that rather than framing validity within the dyad of truth or falsehood in qualitative analysis, it should speak more "on the moral and practical underpinnings" of the study than on methodology.[26]

Ethical Validation

Ethical validation refers to the process by which all research agendas must answer to underlying moral assumptions. The researcher's application of the methodology reflects his or her political *and* ethical stance. As Angen notes, researchers have argued that qualitative inquiry sustains an ethical level of acceptability when all voices are heard, when no voice is excluded or demeaned.[27] Qualitative research can be seen as ethical when the consumer of research moves beyond his or her understanding of the topic and toward new interpretations. Furthermore, ethical research does not claim to be the final word or authority on a given topic; rather, it should incite exploration in new and more fruitful directions. Thus, if the research study inspires action and leads effectively to foment change, it has achieved ethical validation.

RESULTS

In order to achieve a cross-sectional analysis of the data, each interview script was analyzed and coded. Ten categories arose from the codes and are subsumed under three main themes. The results section follows a top-down hierarchy of "theme, category, code" format. The three themes derived from analysis are as follows: Inside the Culture Industry, Identity, and Media. The themes are distinct but not rigidly so, tending to be somewhat porous, with codes and categories overlapping at times. Additionally, short narratives highlighting the experiences of three of the participants are also included in the results to allow fully for exploring the richness of the data. The purpose of the narratives is to give a composite picture of a participant's background, views, and experiences as they relate to being a young person living in a consumer culture. Additionally, each narrative illustrates how a single individual interprets his or her circumstance as it relates to a specific code(s). For example, the "James" narrative demonstrates this participant's struggle to acquire and retain cool. The "John" narrative is reflective of the struggle to establish values in a consumer culture and what that means to an individual who wishes to go against the norm. The "Ingrid" narrative was selected because it so clearly demonstrates the harm done when adhering to a media-conscious lifestyle with an emphasis on materialism. All of the names found throughout this section, and elsewhere in the dissertation, are pseudonyms.

INSIDE THE CULTURE INDUSTRY (THEME)

Three categories—ownership, brands, and capturing cool—delineate what it is like to be inside the culture industry, to experience mass consumerism. The participants' experiences about acquiring, craving, owning, and losing goods are all relevant to this theme. Additionally, what it means to desire brands, and to have a cool persona, is central to understanding what it is like to be a young consumer in a commodity-driven culture.

Ownership *(Category)*

The first category emerging from the analysis is about how the process and engagement of consuming affects the individual. Each code is representative of the impressions, thoughts, and feelings associated with the process of acquiring consumer products on a personal level.

Endless Desiring *(Code)*

A number of participants felt that their desire for objects, acquisition of those objects, and eventual satiation was experienced as an endless cycle such that "There's never been a time when I've been completely satisfied with everything I have" (Susan). The participants were not able to articulate why the need for more is never satiated, and instead, they were resigned to the fact that this is simply how it is. Susan further stated: "Like it's unfortunate that we always feel that we need stuff, but that's [how] we've been raised I guess." Susan stressed that even small items, like pens, can become an object of desire whether there is a real need or not. As John stated: "Sometimes you see more stuff as you're shopping and just toss it in the cart, but you wish you hadn't when you got home." Visually seeing others with objects of desire incited desiring of the same. For example, Jeff talked about how knowing that his younger brother had a television in his bedroom directly influenced him to wish for the same. Oscar described how he started to notice the presence of iPods more and more, until he was eventually able to acquire one. Tom was able to articulate how elusive the feeling of satisfaction can be in that it appears to cycle endlessly from desiring to satisfaction to craving more:

I definitely feel satisfied. But it's . . . brief like it's not . . . long-lasting so at the same time, I guess . . . I never felt fully satisfied for long, like forever, you know what I mean . . . You constantly want something else, but in the moment you do feel satisfied after you buy something that you needed. That's interesting to think about though because in that moment you have what you want but . . . that moment is fleeting so . . . really you don't.

Intense longing for items was accepted as the norm with little insight as to why:

In the end I didn't even end up really wearing the clothes, so it was really just a waste of money and I shouldn't have bought it. I don't know if it was an advertisement that swayed me or just that moment thinking, "oh, I need this" and I don't really know why. I just know I needed to have it. (Pam)

Ted talked about how he would engage in shopping, even though he felt he had everything that he needed; he said there were times when he could not justify another purchase, but he could not resist looking at new stuff. George explained how meaningless, yet compelling, buying could be, as though he had to follow through on the purchasing process in spite of better judgment:

I went into Value Village . . . I was with my friend. We were just like messing around I guess, he was buying a shirt and then I saw this giant leprechaun hat and I was, like, that's awesome. So, I just took it off the shelf and went to purchase it and it was $14 and I've never seen something so expensive in Value Village, and it was just so meaningless . . . but I'm already at the till so, I can't *not* buy it. So that was the worst, I think, that was the worst purchase I've ever made in my life.

The realization that the object of spontaneous desire brought little, even less, satisfaction than normal was described as a source of anger by more than one of the participants. The anger seemed to be tied to a feeling of having been deceived by someone in authority.

Seeing others with a desired object was said to be a constant reminder of not having, both from within the family, and out. More specifically, wanting to have what one's parents had surfaced quite frequently throughout the interviews. Participants named such items as dirt bikes, cars, boats, and houses as those things that they had grown to enjoy in their parents' household and wished to continue having access.

Interestingly, desiring and craving new objects was not always described as a frustration. James talked about the fact that desiring was exciting and that it was fun to hunt down cool objects while on a shopping spree. At the same time, he acknowledged that being satisfied in consumer culture is somewhat elusive: "You always want more stuff. I'm totally a consumer so I always want more and more. But, like, I don't know, it's pretty tough to be satisfied." While noticing that desires are never replete, most of the participants did not feel that they had been taken in or manipulated by marketers to want more; rather, they felt in charge of their own desires, however frustrating they may have been. Still, one of the male participants, Christopher, noted how external forces, such as the fashion industry, created pressure for young people to believe that without the latest fad they were deficient: "It makes you feel like you need to buy more stuff."

In general, upon reflection of their childhoods, the participants felt their desiring had been relatively intense. They recounted stories where they had desperately wanted certain objects for play, like a Tamagotchi, for example:

When I was little I think I got pretty frustrated when friends had it and I didn't sort of thing. Looking back, like it was really probably like a $10, $15 thing and like it's not that big of a deal, but yeah, at the time, you're a child you're like they have it and I don't understand why I can't. (Alicia)

Similarly, Susan said, "When I was little, Pokéman came out at the time, I didn't have the console I needed for it so I wanted it so badly I even dreamt about getting it."

Having the object of desire out of reach as children was described as a source of frustration (conflict) between some of the participants and their parents.

Shopaholic

Both male and female participants described the feeling of being, at times, almost lured to spend despite their better judgment, whether because they did not have the money, or they simply did not need the purchase. Pam talked about having a closet full of clothes and yet continuing to add to the collection seemingly endlessly. In particular, Nancy admitted to having a "shopping problem" and was distressed about how much of a problem it could become when she had increased financial responsibilities. She reported that she always had to buy, that she had a behavior pattern with no closure: "I always have to buy something, like, if I see something I like, I always have to buy it, for a reasonable price, obviously." Lack of money was apparently no deterrent to spending as she described it—she merely set her sights on lower-priced items. "If I go to a grocery store I'll buy a magazine and stuff that I don't need, I'll still end up buying them." Others talked about how excess spending money was quickly dispensed on goods whether they were needed or not. Ingrid attributed her spending as a child to the commercials that she viewed when she was younger, thus connecting a shopaholic lifestyle, or problem, with advertising itself. As she reflected on her past behavior, she was confused as to why she was so driven to spend and what made the object(s) so desirable. Floyd described how the acquisition of goods always gave him something to look forward to. As he put it:

There's always in the back of your mind you're getting something you want because obviously you purchased it and it's coming at some point. I think you're a little anxious because you want to make sure, for clothing, if it fits or whatever, if it's right. But in the back of your mind, you're a little excited.

Further, Floyd was positive about consumption and felt that he should give into his desires regardless of cost: "Don't let money be an object. If you want something that bad, don't consider the price, just buy it." George talked about how impulsive he was when it came to acquiring things and that he had learned this from his mother, or at the very least, had begun to mimic her. So without labeling it as such, a number of male participants (Christopher, Tom, George) also felt that they had a "shopping problem," in that they too shopped impulsively and purchased items that they came to regret.

High on Acquisition

Throughout the interviews, both male and female participants were able to describe the good feelings that resulted when acquiring something that they wanted, including excitement, "pretty awesome," happiness, "loving it," ecstasy, good, having something special, "really really exciting," feeling great, satisfaction, pride at being able to make a purchase with one's own money, feeling glamorous, confident, feeling more mature and independent (in the case of getting a car), feeling more respected by peers, and feeling accepted. With new technology, in particular, excitement was expressed as one of the prime reactions. In terms of cognition, the participants felt included if they acquired objects that others had. Joyce reiterated: "It makes me feel like I'm part of something." Furthermore, as the participants recalled the events leading up to and actually acquiring the object of desire, their faces often beamed with excitement. There was no insight or understanding expressed as to why such extreme emotions were felt; rather, somewhat simple explanations were provided such as: "If I like something that I like, it makes me happy I guess" (Nancy). It is important to emphasize that the "high" associated with acquisition was difficult for the participants themselves to understand or expand upon. Sam strived to express himself: "I felt good. I felt just happy, I guess. I didn't feel proud or anything about what I did because I didn't accomplish anything. I was just happy to have it." Receiving gifts of desired objects reinforced the participants' feelings that they were receiving out of love, that the giver was expressing love: "I was ecstatic like and really like, I don't know. It was almost like I knew my parents really loved me, like it was just nice. It was a good feeling" (Tom).

Parents and friends were often described as responding positively to the participant's acquisition of goods. Participants described that when they had to wait quite a while before getting the object of desire, the anticipation built and added to the excitement felt when they actually acquired it. Tessa recalled the great happiness she felt when she finally owned an iPhone. Male participants were also awestruck when it came to descriptions about acquiring things. And, with the bigger items like that of a car, the perception that an accomplishment had been achieved was particularly strong. Jeff stated: "It just feels like you fit in and everything like that." Having a car was also associated with "becoming closer to an adult."

Acquisition Stymied

In general, the participants reported a wide range of negative emotions associated with not acquiring the object(s) of desire or when acquisition was stymied. These emotions included the following: disappointment, feeling "pretty bad," "so bad," sadness, depression (even "extreme depression"), frustration, feelings of being punished, cheated, jealousy of others who have the desired object, feeling less than ("I could've been a better snowboarder"), impatient, isolated, anxious, annoyed, and feeling left out. Not having the object also provoked feelings of jealousy of others and disappointment with parents who were seen as sometimes responsible for not purchasing the desired object. For example, James's parents prevented him from purchasing a dirt bike, even though he had the funds to cover the cost. He described how "constricted" he felt as a result. Ted talked about what it was like to not have something that was popular with his friends: "I was definitely jealous and not really mad at my parents, but just kind of disappointed." Sonja recalled a time when her parents refused to buy her a Barbie doll and what that felt like: "Even though I would ask my mom to get it for me, like when she said she said no, I would be sad."

It should be noted that the participants also described their ability to "get over" a particular object, stating that it was, after all, just a pair of sunglasses or just a pair of jeans. For example, Oscar talked about consoling himself when he was unable to acquire a desired object by convincing himself he did not really need it: "At first I was pretty bummed out, but I soon realized afterwards that I didn't need it. It was kind of more of a wanting, not so much of a necessity." However, the participants did not always overcome the desiring per se, but rather were able to shift their focus to another and more easily attainable object.

Social Reinforcement of Acquisition

Social reinforcement from friends and family appeared to be highly salient when it came to buying. Many of the participants mentioned that it was when they were shopping with their friends that they most regretted making purchases. In fact, this theme came up frequently— the feeling of being pressured by friends to buy when an item was more expensive than the budget allowed for—or even in the case of an article of clothing that the participant truly disliked. George summed it up: "My friends were really terrible influences on me. I know that from high school and not having a lot of money in my pocket, yet still buying a lot of things." Additionally, it seemed that friends tended to influence buying that was motivated by fads. Alicia stated that when shopping by herself she could try on numerous articles of clothing and never buy; she added that when she is with her friends, inevitably, something gets purchased. In general, peers were extremely influential in decisions associated with buying for both male and female participants.

Mothers were described as important figures in the buying process in that many participants felt their approval had to be met in order to make or feel good about a purchase. Sonja reported: "When I'm with [my mother], before I buy something, I would ask her before I would actually buy it. Then she would tell me what she thinks of it, I guess, and if she likes it or not." In recalling purchases that were made where mothers did not approve, many of the female participants recollected feeling sad and disappointed. Bonding with mothers over shopping was mentioned several times among the female participants. Additionally, for the female participants, it was rare that a father's approval was sought, except when it involved a purchase of a technological device. Other family members mentioned as being influential in buying decisions included sisters and boyfriends.

A number of the male participants reported that their mothers would buy their clothing, that they relied on their mothers to determine what looked good.

She'd be like the sweater looks nice on you, you should buy it. I'd be like okay, good choice mom. It always went well like there were never really any issues with things I wanted that I couldn't have or her wanting me to buy something that I didn't want. (Ted)

Interestingly, Ted also described how his mother's "excessive" spending influenced him to not spend; this was the only example where social reinforcement was a means of influence to *not* purchase.

For female participants, Facebook was described as influencing a wide variety of purchases. Participants stated that seeing pictures of other people clothed in a particular way fomented desire to do the same: "If someone posted a picture of, for example, like their nails like painted really nicely, I guess, it could affect me too and influence me into buying nail polish and then it would make me want . . . to buy more" (Sonja). According to the male participants, Facebook did not influence any of their purchases.

Seeing others dressed in a particular way or having desirable objects influenced the participants in such a way that it "makes me want to get [them]" (Nancy). Having the same possession as others for the female participants was described as providing a conversation piece, a mutual commonality or bonding that was perceived as highly desirable. The female participants stated that they felt encouraged by their friends to buy technology if they were lagging behind with older devices. Having the right technology was attributed to impressing others, even inciting jealousy, which was considered to be a desirable outcome. Only Tessa indicated that she relied solely on her parents to purchase things and negotiated with them in this regard: "I'll tell them that I want something and they'll tell me if they can get it for me or not. If they say that they can't get it for me right now, I'll wait." Susan, an only child, recalled appealing to her mother to purchase items but was often rebuked to buy with her "own money." As children, the participants remembered wanting what their friends had, as well as recalling how they had influenced their friends to buy.

The male participants reported that their friends thought they were cool and were envious of them when they acquired something that was deemed to be socially desirable. They also reported that their friends were a "terrible influence" and partly responsible for their inability to save money. For example, John recalled buying Nike Shocks because his friend had assured him that they were a superior shoe. Big purchases like cars were highly reinforced by peers, according to both male and female participants; both reported that they were regarded as being "cooler" once they had acquired a car. On the other hand, Floyd felt that his shopping habits were free of influence from friends because he did his shopping online, when alone.

Fanatical about Fads

Predominantly, female participants talked about how badly they desired to keep up with fads, how important it was to them, and that it was a pressure to see new clothing or new fashion because they felt the need to stay current in this regard. Interestingly, Joyce cited a non-clothing example, the Pokémon phenomenon, and how badly she wanted to be part of it. She described it as:

When I was really young, when the whole Pokémon thing just came out, everybody had the cards and I never got [them] because I just never did. But I always wanted them . . . It [made] me feel like I wasn't included in that whole fad, or important time in whatever situations.

The majority of the female participants were aware that they were being influenced by fads, yet they felt it was important to pay attention to the latest trends. Unquestionably, they felt that they would be perceived in a negative light wearing clothing that was out of style. Alicia summed it up as follows:

The worst is when you really like something and it goes out of style but then you've got that confliction of "Oh, I really like these," but I feel so out of place wearing these in public and that's obviously a big problem because you sort of, like you don't want to get rid of it then, but you can't wear it out.

They also expressed strong negative feelings about the unpopularity of out-of-date clothing seen on people outside of what was considered to be the cool group:

Interviewer: How would you describe the feelings associated with that pressure?

Judy: Well I guess just what you would consider that popular stereotype in high school that I think people kind of emulated in high school. They wanted to be like that. They always had new clothes and things. But you see people that you didn't really want to be like and you'd see that they didn't have friends and that they would be wearing this one-piece jumpsuit or I don't know something really strange at the time and you would think I don't really want to look like that. I want to look like these people with all those friends. I guess it was like a social acceptance kind of thing.

As another example, Pam exclaimed: "Yeah, you see people wearing it, like celebrities or whoever, anything that looks really good. I don't know how they do it. They definitely make me want things that are 'faddy.'"

Brands

Brands were described as being extremely important to both male and female participants, though in slightly different ways. Male participants had the impression that because brands were less important to them in terms of clothing (though important when buying sports clothing and equipment or technology), they were not under the influence of brand marketing. Female participants, on the other hand, readily admitted to coveting branded clothing, often lamenting at the price. Neither male nor female participants were able to articulate why brands captured their attention to the degree that they felt compelled to wear or own branded items.

Brand Acquisition: Male Participants

According to Floyd, brands associated with technology were very important to one's social status. "If you don't have an iPhone or BlackBerry, I guess I feel like you get looked down upon in this sense . . . People are condescending towards you if you don't have a brand new phone or whatever." He also felt left out, that those around him all seemed to have the "right" phone. With respect to clothing, Floyd felt that buying and wearing brand names allowed him to wear articles that few others could acquire because of their high price. Hence, such articles were viewed as status symbols. Floyd was adamant that he would not wear certain logos or brands unless they were considered to be "high end." When asked why he was seeking "brand status," he replied: "It's just the exclusivity of it and that 99 of the other 100 people probably won't even know about the brand . . . It makes you unique, original, it's not American Eagle and every other kid's wearing it." Similarly, Jeff, who also admitted to wearing brand-name clothing, seemed to have no real purpose for doing so: "I just think it's normal to wear them." He described how important it was to have expensive equipment for hockey refereeing, including $700 skates, which he described as "totally unnecessary" but for the fact that he was after a certain look of competence and professionalism. He described branded clothing as important to have because "they look nice . . . they're clean clothes . . . I think that's kind of the look I like." Jeff felt strongly that wearing clothes without the right brand meant that one could face negative judgment from others.

Interviewer: How did it feel once you had the Adidas (shoes)?
Jeff: Well it felt good. It felt like, it's like "Oh cool shoes" and it was like, you know . . . I can't really explain the feeling, but you do feel like you fit in.

Interviewer: Fitting in and . . . ?
Jeff: And in getting their approval . . . too.

James was able to articulate the importance of possessing brand-name clothing and believed that owning such items was responsible for his level of confidence. He denied that brand names were nothing more than the sale of a logo and argued instead that they were worth their money, that they were a superior product, and that this was the main motive in buying them. As he stated, "Brands live up to their name." Several other male participants admitted that brand clothing, sunglasses, and so on, while important in high school, were less important now that they had entered university. One of these individuals, Christopher, claimed that he now buys whatever he feels will enhance a "cool" look, brand or not. There appeared to be a desire to be free of brand influence yet, at the same time, admitting that brands "make you feel that you look good" (Christopher).

George raised an interesting dilemma in that he professed to hating brands except when it came to his sport (skiing); it was then that he felt he had to have brand-name clothing. "I really hate how I have to do that, but I don't know why I still feel like I need to do that." He struggled with the fact that brands pose a dilemma in that one feels obligated to conform in order to achieve a particular look, but at the same time, one sacrifices individuality. Ted also bought sport brands, but said he did so not because of the fact that it was a brand, but because he felt that the athletes who endorsed the products and clothing were credible. A second male participant, James, concurred with this sentiment, claiming that he bought brand products, not because they were brands, but because they were functionally superior. John was particularly put off by the price of brand clothing. However, when it came to cars and computers, he felt brands were relevant and important to his choice making. He cited an example about how owning an iPhone, when they were first made available, contributed to feelings of popularity with his friends. Hence, John felt that the branding of technology had as much to do with status as with functionality—status is achieved by being up to date. Sam expressed resentment toward the Apple Corporation, believing that they had deliberately created undue social pressure to purchase an iPod, for example, such that MP3 players were no longer accepted as cool.

Brand Acquisition: Female Participants

The majority of female participants relayed that they paid great attention to brands, particularly clothing, and felt justified in choosing to purchase brand-name items. The participants listed several top brands that they consider to be acceptable and took pride in their ability to pick out clothes deemed to be cool. The attraction to branded clothing was considered to be a matter of good taste: "I have to love it to buy it and . . . brand names, they offer what I love" (Joyce). Alicia described herself as a "brand-name kind of person" in which she professed loyalty to the particular brands that she had bought over many years. And like some of the male participants, she denied that she was blindly taken in by the brand name, but rather, declared she was buying brand-name clothing because of its superior quality. Brands were associated with wearing what was "in" and were seen to guarantee the most current fashion trends. Branded clothing was deemed to enhance how one felt and looked: "I think that brand is considered like to be very in and then I think if I wore that brand I'd feel like 'oh I'm wearing like the latest thing' kind of feeling" (Sonja). Participants recalled how in high school it was very important to them to have brand-name clothing, though they claimed not to know why this was important except that they were excited when they acquired branded items and were keen to "show them off." In particular, Ingrid said she felt better about herself after acquiring a brand-name purse because, as she put it, she would be perceived as "well-off. You were better I guess." Judy talked about how she was so devoted to the brand-name "Roxy" that she did not want to wear any other type of shirt. She related that she felt accepted, confident, and happy as well as excited to be wearing a Roxy article of clothing and talked about how she would often unbutton her coat to show off the brand-name logo T-shirt underneath. In summary, the pressure to adorn with the latest fad, synonymous with brand clothing, was related as extremely powerful to the degree that clothing that was "out of style," even if well liked, was rejected and no longer worn. Ingrid captured this phenomenon with the phrase, "That's so five minutes ago."

Brand-Free

Interestingly, some of the participants contradicted themselves at other points in their interview as to whether or not brands were important to them. For example, Floyd, one of the male participants who had exclaimed how proud he was of his ability to afford high-priced brand clothing, also stated that he was his own person, that he could turn his back on brands if the look did not appeal to him:

I want to stay trendy like I said, but at the end of the day, if you don't like what they're wearing, or how they're wearing it, or the style they're wearing I'm not going to just go buy it because they have it. I'm still going to wear something that I think looks good on me and that I'm comfortable wearing.

The capacity to reject brands that did not appeal was also expressed by Floyd: "[If] I was to find something that wasn't a brand name I would still buy that . . . over a brand-name thing." And from Jeff, who had admitted earlier in his interview to liking the look of brand clothing: "You don't need the best clothes. You can still look the same in other clothes." Only one of the female participants, Ingrid, who had talked about how good she felt in brand-name accessories, later described: "I don't really buy brands. I buy what's efficient for its use, you know, what works is good for me." Both Sara and Susan were adamant that they did not shop with brand names in mind; rather they both felt that they chose clothing based on "whatever fits, whatever's cheap" (Sara). Finally, Tessa considered that she was free of brand influence, yet in the same sentence professed her loyalty to Apple products. Likewise, Pam considered herself above the brand phenomenon, but then recalled that she had bought a "Roger Federer" tennis racket. It is possible that the buying and wearing of brand clothing for a number of participants was never explored prior to the interview and, therefore, was not something that was well understood. Indeed, when asked why he was attracted to brand-name clothing, Floyd exclaimed: "I've never really thought it through as to . . . why I'm buying brand names. You got me thinking."

Can Do Without / Materially Satisfied

There were a few individuals who felt that they had achieved some level of material contentment. However, only a minority of the participants related how unimportant it was to them to accumulate and display to others the things that they owned; they felt that they had achieved some level of material satisfaction, however fleeting. For example, Tom expressed that it was not a hardship to go without desired objects, particularly when his parents provided all his financial support:

It was just kind of out of sight out of mind, like I just knew it was kind of beyond our means. So, it was like once I had like gotten over the concept, like it just won't happen for me, it was like I just kind of stopped thinking about it mostly I think. It wasn't like feeling really sad or like being upset over like I couldn't have it. It was just like that's kind of ridiculous to think like your parents should buy you [something]. So it was like, it was kind of just like yeah, whatever. It's not a big deal.

Two other participants related material satisfaction and how that felt:

John: I'm not in need of anything.
Interviewer: How does that feel?
John: Pretty good. Like I stopped wanting like just random junk, items,
               stuff like that. I don't think I need anything else. I mean I have a good
               family, I'm up here, it's nice. I started my life, I'm set.

and:

Interviewer: How did it feel to have all those possessions that you wanted?
Sonja: I guess I was happy because I felt like "oh, I finally don't have like
               something that I want to get anymore." I finally like feel good with
               . . . what I have.

Capturing Cool

This category developed from codes relating to the participants' experiences and desires to achieve a "cool" status. Three codes were designated to this category: achieving cool through acquisition of goods, adoption of a celebrity look, and what it means to be motivated by cool. This section also includes a narrative about one of the participants who felt he personified cool.

Cool Persona

Cool was generally described as a feeling of comfort and security, as having the things that "you want," those that define others as cool. By having the "right stuff," those items that embody a cool persona, the participants felt they could be "part of something," be cool with others who had achieved this status, and fit in with the "right" group. Tom gave the example of Pokémon cards and how he became more popular with his peers once he acquired them. Cool was then also partly defined as a social phenomenon and was, therefore, greatly dependent on the type of friends one had. Feeling cool derived from the possession of the right technology (iPods, Apple computers, smart phones or iPhones, the Apple brand in particular) was a common theme among female participants. Surprisingly, technology seemed to be more potent with regard to cool than even clothing. Thus, having the latest technology was deemed to increase one's popularity with peers and the potential for achieving a state of cool.

Alicia noted how a lot of the popular television shows aimed at young people (e.g., *One Tree Hill*, *90210*, *Gossip Girl*) have characters that emulate what it means to be cool and popular. As a result, she believed that the popular teens in high school emulated the hairstyles, clothes, mannerisms, and accompanying lifestyles of such characters. There was some lament expressed that keeping up with brands required constant vigilance such that attaining the state of cool required continuous and vigilant effort. Pam recalled how embarrassed she was about not having the right snowboarding pants, that they were definitely "not cool." Judy talked about wearing jeans that were uncomfortable, exorbitant in price, and not to her taste, but because they were deemed cool, she had decided to buy them:

There was this brand of jeans in middle school that everyone always had. They were like these jeans with a one-inch zipper. When I look back on it they were really awful. They also looked terrible on me because they look good on stick thin people, so I don't know why I bought them.

Judy also said she felt cool when wearing a jersey that designated her membership in an athletic team and attributed this to her feelings of confidence. In the opposite direction, one participant, Ingrid, recalled how she often deliberately dressed against the mainstream to stand out and as such, felt cool: "I had these really bright pink shorts, and I love fishnets on arms, and don't ask me [if] it was from the *Wrestler*. They were bright and neon . . . I thought I was just great." Clearly, being cool was associated with feeling popular and being envied by others—both highly desirable states.

Desiring a Celebrity Look

There were certain celebrities whose lifestyles became the object of desire for a number of the female participants. When asked directly if they could describe a time when they admired and maybe even wanted to be like someone portrayed in the media, many of the female participants compared themselves to a particular television character, as this example demonstrates:

One of my TV shows, *90210*, there's one character named Ivy and I just love everything about her, like I actually can admit that I've gone to stores and like I would actually say like would she wear this or you know, like how would she look . . . I definitely compared myself to that one particular character many times . . . It makes me feel good that, like, if I'm able to accomplish the task of being like her. (Joyce)

Joyce also relayed that the desire to emulate this particular television character had a direct impact on the type of shopping that she did: "She looked really good on that one episode so I went to buy something that looks similar, or like maybe not the exact same thing, but like you know, like a similar style of shirt."

Other celebrities were also admired: "I've always kind of really been envious of a famous DJ or a singer, a band, whatever. I always thought that would be kind of cool" (Joyce). Admiring and wishing to emulate singers was reiterated by yet another participant, Sonja: "Someone like Selena Gomez, she's the same age as me and then I kind of admire her because she's already so successful and . . . she's, a good role model for other girls because she's a singer/actor." Joyce reported that she felt good by trying to emulate a particular celebrity because of the fact that so many millions of people pay attention to this person's affairs. The female participants talked extensively about buying clothes with celebrities' styles in mind. For example, Sonja bought perfume specifically because it was a Britney Spears line. Nancy also exclaimed how celebrity worship influenced purchases: "I've seen those shoes in a lot of magazines and like every celebrity is wearing them, and they look good. That's why I've always wanted them and that's when I started wanting them."

Tessa lamented that she wanted to retain her uniqueness as much as she craved the look and lifestyle of Angelina Jolie. Others, Sara and Pam respectively, cited Kate Winslet and Kate Hudson as stars they wished to emulate. Ingrid felt like a failure for not looking more "Latino," in particular, like Jennifer Lopez, including both her ethnicity and physique. A few female participants described the emotions associated with desiring the celebrity look: "Definitely kind of jealous 'cause [there's] a big difference between my lifestyle and their lifestyle so I get a tiny bit jealous about it" (Nancy) and "Maybe envy, not really jealousy because I'm not upset about it, I just envy what she has [and] I don't" (Pam). Susan, on the other hand, exclaimed that she did not ever feel the desire for the celebrity lifestyle or look.

A majority of male participants admitted to being attracted to the celebrity look. For example, Floyd talked about wanting to be like Brad Pitt because "he never seems to be in the media for arguments or fights, or gestures, or anything like that. I guess he seems like a stand-up guy. He seems happy, has kids, he's making millions." And George talked about wanting to be a particular baseball player and went so far as to buy a hat "because the Yankees have them," as well as wishing to purchase Yankee jerseys. George also admired the type of suits that the Yankees wore at press conferences and tried to model that particular look. As another example, Oscar described that he had purchased "old-style Ray-Ban" sunglasses because a lot of "pop stars and rap stars" were wearing them and "they [had] become super popular." Wanting to be like a professional athlete, in general, was also mentioned by Sam: "To be a professional athlete like just having that and playing your sport as your job is pretty appealing to me. So, yeah, I guess I'd like to be one of them." James expressed how he had wanted to emulate a character from the movie *Wall Street*, mainly because he was wealthy. Finally, Tom stated that he was attracted to a musician in a particular band and wished to emulate the band members because they had like-minded values. As he put it, "Like I've always wanted to live like them [Mumford and Sons] . . . They're cool and they have a good style. I think their importance of life and understanding of things seems to be pretty, pretty deep and cool."

Motivated by Cool

The participants talked about how the lure of new trends and fads is so powerful that most attempts to resist are futile, often resulting in capitulation. For example, Christopher described how he had been pressured by peers to replace his running shoes with what was considered to be a more cool "skate" shoe. Tom described the painful realization of not being dressed in a cool article of clothing and how in "the next instant" he felt compelled to rectify the situation. He also talked about how the trend-setting cycle is continuous, that one is subjected to constant fashion change. He described the motivation for conforming to the fad as: "You do want to fit in. As much as I hate saying that, you totally do, and that influences you a lot." Tessa expressed how she felt that "keeping up with trends is like part of your job practically." Another female participant, Pam, talked about how self-conscious she was that her car was not as cool as those of her friends. Only Sara, out of the female participants, described her determination to break away from the cool trend-setting lifestyle; she talked about her ability to rebel against the "central crowd" in high school and find her niche in a group that was more interested in the arts than achieving cool:

At first you definitely recognize that you're being alienated. So, I guess the same feelings of frustration and lack of approval from sort of the greater society, but after some time, spending [time] in that artistic group, it felt fine. We all recognized that this was sort of our place and we were happy, so it was like okay, we'll just stick with it.

The following narrative demonstrates James's background, views, and experiences as they relate to the pressure to adopt a cool persona. This story depicts the struggle to acquire and retain what it means to be "cool" and delineates what benefits, if any, there are in such pursuits.

James's Story: Personifying Cool

James came from an upper-middle-class family that was generous to him throughout his growing-up years, particularly when it came to paying for clothing. He began working when he was 15 and was able to save up enough money to purchase his own car by the time he entered his last year in high school. James stated that the car provided him considerable freedom to attend events and go places with his friends, who were also pleased about him owning a car. James believed that he was the type of person who was totally in control about deciding on purchases and says that he has always been the "businessman" in his family, in that he looked into "get-rich-quick schemes" throughout his growing-up years. He, therefore, felt that he was very responsible with money and, as a result, freely spent money on those things that he desires. James stated that he "thinks about money a lot" and has grown used to having expensive objects: "I want a nice car, I want like toys, like dirt bikes and all this because I've grown up with it." James also liked technological objects and mentioned that he had a $300 set of headphones. He also reiterated that he would "love to be wealthy" and "loves earning money" and plans to become a lawyer to ensure that he is in a middle- or upper-class socioeconomic bracket. James admires a character from the movie *Wall Street* and imagines that it would be "so cool" to be him, work on Wall Street, and own one's own business. He so admired this character that he bought the ringtone for his phone, which was used in the movie. James said that he admires the *Wall Street* character mainly because he is wealthy.

James loves to shop for new clothes because "it's fun" and he enjoys keeping up with fads. He attributed his love for shopping and clothes to his mother, who showered him with new items continuously throughout his childhood and growing-up years. He considers shopping to be a "hobby" of sorts. James believed in brands and felt guaranteed of a good-quality product as compared to a nonbrand item. As he put it: "I think brands live up to their name." James described a time when his mother bought him a $500 pair of jeans and how wearing these jeans gave him a boost in confidence. It was also important to James to be physically fit or "jacked" and reiterated that he is influenced by other "jacked guys" portrayed in the media. James feels fully an individual, "well rounded," athletic, and confident. He stated that he was one of only 25 high school students who were perceived to be in the "cool group," those who were the "popular group of kids" that everyone knew, and "would like to talk to and ask to hang out and, like, get invited to parties." When asked why he thought he had achieved a "cool" status, James replied that it was due to his confidence.

James says of himself that he is "totally a consumer" and always craves more consumable products; he does not in any way feel frustrated by this but finds that it is an exciting process. He wants to be the one "with the latest thing" because "it's kind of cool" and "fun." As a consumer, James stated that he has no values, that he is not motivated by any principles in terms of shopping. When asked about climate change, James thought it was a "natural problem" and that it is not a "huge deal right now." Instead, he stated that he is excited about the future and has no real worries in that regard.

Summary: Inside the Culture Industry

The participants were clear that desiring objects, as well as acquiring and owning them, was a powerful force that significantly shaped their lives. They talked about a perpetual longing, never feeling fully satisfied, and always craving more. Seven of the participants (Pam, Nancy, Ingrid, Floyd, Christopher, Tom, and George) felt they had a "shopping problem" as their need to spend money seemed, at times, overpowering. Acquiring goods was associated with powerful emotions such as excitement and happiness; likewise, when the acquisition of goods was stymied, strong negative emotions prevailed. Interestingly, a minority of participants (Tom, John, Sonja) claimed to have experienced material satisfaction; they described how they had learned to be content in other ways such as appreciating their familial support and environmental surroundings.

Being a consumer was experienced as a social affair, especially as it involved mothers, and that most sought their approval around purchases they made. Technological goods, in particular, were highly coveted and deemed critical to one's overall acceptance and social positioning. Further to this, paying attention to fads was deemed to be very important (more so for female than male participants) and intimately tied to self-esteem. When it came to brands, both male (Floyd, Jeff, James, Christopher, George, John) and female participants (Joyce, Alicia, Ingrid, Judy, Pam, Tessa) stated their desire to acquire branded objects, although there was some confusion as to whether or not brands were really all that important. Nonetheless, brands were associated with establishing a cool persona, as were technological goods, in particular. Sara and Susan claimed to be free of the "brand effect," not based upon any principle, but because brands were experienced as being pricier. A number of participants (Floyd, Jeff, Ingrid, Tessa, and Pam) were conflicted about brands, declaring that they were important, and then in other places in their interview, claiming to be above brand desiring.

Cool was considered a state that was highly desirable, if not necessary, one that required vigilance or constant effort to maintain. This
sentiment was shared by Alicia, Pam, Judy, Tessa, Christopher, and
Tom. Only Sara, out of all the participants, was able to articulate her
rejection of cool as defined by the status quo and how she sought a different niche, one that brought fulfillment. A combined majority of
males and females (including Joyce, Sonja, Nancy, Tessa, Sara, Pam,
Ingrid, Floyd, George, Oscar, Sam, James, and Tom) wished to emulate
the look of the celebrity, in terms of personality and clothing style.
Sentiments related to ownership, brands, and capturing cool are all
important in understanding how the participants perceived their identity and values as consumers.

IDENTITY

Five categories were designated as important to understanding how
identity is shaped and formed in consumer culture. The first, individuality, offers a description of how the participants feel they retain their
individuality in a culture of mass production. The second, conformity,
deals with the pressure to conform and what that means. The third,
nonconformity, outlines the viewpoints expressed by those who felt
they were relatively immune from the influences of consumerism. The
fourth, values, addresses how values influence consuming behaviors
and what it means to have values as a consumer. The fifth, money,
provides a description of the participants' views on the value of money,
including financial security, and how having/not having money influences self-regard.

Individuality

Determining how individuality is expressed and maintained in consumer cultures was a topic of great interest to the participants and one
that they readily discussed. The first code, "I'm My Own Person," addresses these concepts, while the second code, "In Control," has more
to do with how the participants asserted themselves against the forces
of advertising. The final code, "Individuality versus Conformity," has
to do with what it means to be an individual in a culture that rewards
conformity.

I'm My Own Person

The female participants suggested a number of ways or distinguish-
ing characteristics that ensure individuals remain unique despite

owning the same objects as millions of others: personality, sense of self, interests, a voice within, a style within, distinctive articles of clothing (e.g., glasses), character, and imagination. Specifically, Sonja felt that she was able to remain distinctly individual because she felt certain that her choice in clothing articles would be different from what others might choose. She noted that sometimes not having trendy clothing makes one "different from the others." Sara described how she maintains a sense of uniqueness: "As a writer, I put a lot on our imagination and our ability to think, and ways of thinking, and how we express ourselves . . . That's how we keep our independence and our individuality." Tessa expressed that perhaps, in our consumer culture, there is no individuality on the basis of what you own: "I guess there's no individuality. I mean as a person you're an individual but not by the things that you have . . . it's what character you are basically and not by what you possess."

The male participants felt that their possessions did not define them or reflect in any way their true selves. For example, "I don't feel [that] what I decide to buy like says who I am" (Oscar). They stated that it did not matter to them or their friends what clothing they wore. In general, the male participants felt free of media in the sense that they did not turn to media to "understand what I want, I'm like, or what I need" (Sam). Floyd felt that earning money and spending it however he desired was an expression of individuality, of acting on his own impulses, likes, and dislikes. He also talked about how he went against the norm and wore clothes that were clearly not in style; he somehow found the gumption to wear them because "I have the ability to not care about irrelevant people in my life . . . I just don't care what they think." George defiantly stated that he paid no attention to cool, that he could not even define it, and ignored it as much as he could: "I don't really know who is cool and/or what is cool, and what isn't cool." His position was shared by Jeff: "I'm not really striving to be cool. I'm really who I am, and if people think what they think of me, that's fine with me." One's family background was identified as determining uniqueness and individuality with the male participants. In general, the male participants talked about how getting out of high school changed the pressure they felt to conform, to have to fit in. They also equated money and owning a car as a way of establishing independence from the family and, by doing so, gaining a sense of individuality. Having one's parents educated about media motivation was helpful in establishing individuality for Christopher. He stated: "Both my parents, they raised me to not buy into media stuff, not believe everything you see . . . They're not easily persuaded, so that kind of got passed down to me."

In Control

This code captures the beliefs that many of the participants shared—that they are in control about what they decide to purchase because they are able to research, apply discipline, and discern the veracity of advertisements. The underlying supposition about advertising was a rejection of the notion that advertisements are able to influence and sway potential buyers beyond their rational control. The participants believed that having the right knowledge was all one needed to determine whether or not an advertisement had validity. Indeed, Judy insisted that despite seeing advertisements about fashion for women, she was not affected by them because fashion was not important to her, and, therefore, she concluded, advertisements must not be affecting her. Susan felt that she was disciplined about money and, thus, in control of her spending:

I feel like I'm a better person because I have been raised to be so aware of my money, that I don't go on shopping sprees, I don't go with daddy's credit card and go buy lots of stuff . . . I mean the fact that I've been raised to be very conscious of what I'm spending I feel will eventually make me be a better person . . . I feel I have a better . . . .handle [on] my money with purchases, that I don't have to deal with things that I have to have.

As another example of being in control, Tessa said: "According to me, advertisings just exaggerate stuff. Sometimes, like they don't necessarily bring out the exact truth of the product. Of course that's what ads are supposed to do, right? I have a clear understanding of that."

Interestingly, some male participants (Tom, Sam, Christopher, Jeff, and John) saw themselves as in control because they "researched" the quality of a product, and its usefulness, before they shopped. They claimed to not shop impulsively, but, rather, carefully weigh the pros and cons before making a purchase; they were also wary of false advertising. It should be noted that the idea of researching a product thoroughly, before buying, was also important to some of the female participants (Judy, Tessa)—a process they claimed was a deterrent to impulse buying. Research was then seen as mitigating the sort of random shopping that people engage in, that is, shopping without any particular item in mind. Further to this, once they began earning their own money, many of the male participants stated that they were particularly careful about what they spent it on and felt that they had a good grasp of money: "I think that now being a bit older and more educated and more mature, you just think of things in terms of if it's really necessary or not. Is it worth half that last paycheck . . . So definitely [I] try and not do impulse buying" (Oscar).

Individuality versus Conformity

Some of the participants were clearly bothered about their individuality, or lack thereof. As an example, Ingrid described how she liked wearing "outrageous clothes" that were popular in the 1970s and 1980s. She also talked about getting piercings and tattoos as a means of establishing individuality: "I'd love to have different . . . tattoos all over my body, you know express . . . on my body what I am." Additionally, she also talked about dying her hair "different colors of the rainbow" as a means of ensuring her individual expression. On a simpler level, Alicia felt that her uniqueness could be achieved by amalgamating clothing ideas from several people whose styles she wished to emulate. Ted insisted that his decision to have a "mullet" hairstyle was motivated by the desire to break free from conformity of the status quo. As he put it: "I purposely have a dumb haircut just because no one else has one. It's just funny . . . I'm aware that I don't care." Ted also insisted that his group of friends would accept him just as he was and that how he looked was of little importance relative to how he behaved. The male participants seemed to feel that it was relatively easy to create one's own personal style and still be accepted. For example, Christopher felt that he was outside the norm when he and two friends decided to wear "short shorts" all summer because "it was hilarious" and clearly against the norm. Interestingly, some of the participants defined or perceived individuality as it relates to what one is wearing or possessing. James explained: "Like hats, I'm not a hat person so hats like don't look good on me, but they might look good on another dude . . . so I guess, I don't know. Everyone stays pretty different." In another example, Alicia perceived that her uniqueness as an individual was temporarily established because her laptop computer case was pink and no one in her immediate social circle had anything quite like it. She equated individuality with ownership of relatively rare items:

You look around in the room and you see all the laptops and what stands out to you is that that girl has a pink laptop case . . . Laptop cases are becoming more popular, more and more people have them and that's beginning to take away from the individuality . . . As the year went on, I started seeing more and more people with laptop cases like that on their backs. So, yeah, as certain products become more popular that contributes to taking away from the individuality.

In contrast, Susan did not seem to be particularly concerned about a loss of individuality. She defended conformity as a good thing, a type of unifying process in which everyone can communicate under the same language.: "I guess it kind of amasses us like if we all have the same thing, it all brings us together, and it all kind of lumps us together as the same group in a very vague sense."

Conformity

Two codes were used to capture the essence of what it means to conform within consumer culture—both the perceived pressure to conform and the desire to fit in by the adoption of fads.

Pressure to Conform within Consumer Cultures

The participants, in general, related how they are struggling with the concept of individuality and how to achieve a sense of self when the pressure to conform, both self-imposed and external in origin, is such a strong pull. The female participants spoke of how they seek to imitate clothing advertised in the media and fashion trends of all kinds. For example, Ingrid talked about the pressure she was under not to wear pants that were flared at the bottom because of the fad for "skinny jeans." Additionally, many of the female participants also wished to embody the lifestyle, look, and advantages of media characters: "Every step of my life I've wanted to be like someone from the media" (Tessa). Further to this, Pam lamented that despite trying to look different from other people, she failed in her attempts. Perhaps the most dramatic change was Alicia's example of transitioning from homeschooling to attending high school. She found herself watching a particular television show and desiring to adopt the look of one of the characters; as a result, she changed her hair, started wearing makeup, and sported a new look with different eye glasses. Sonja found that she picked out her personal style by reading magazines: "I think when I read them I look at what they have because then it seems like magazines are telling you what's in style and what's the new trend, so maybe [I will] buy something similar to that." The struggle to be perceived as an individual by adorning a look that others do not appear to have was articulated by Pam:

I try to wear things differently than other people do. It's hard, it's really hard because I do put a lot of effort into looking different than other people do, but in the end I don't think you end up looking different at all.

Judy also talked about this same issue, how she felt less of an individual, less original as she struggled to fit in and wear what everyone else had.

George really captured the issues of conformity for young people in consumer cultures. He talked about how he had tried not to pay attention to fashion magazines but ultimately ended up doing so. He struggled with finding his own opinion, that is, whether the latest fad did indeed look good, or whether it was just that he was swayed by marketers to believe that it looked good. He felt that it was almost impossible to maintain an opinion that was not influenced by marketers. In the end, George often felt persuaded to buy advertised clothing in spite of his own sense of taste:

> I remember the summer going into . . . a clothing store and there were . . . all these manikins [that] were wearing sweaters and it was like it was summer and I was like, "Why are you doing this?" and then, but I was like, "Oh they look pretty good actually," so like, I bought one.

George also talked about the dilemma of not knowing his niche within the culture; he was drawn to sports and bought athletic clothing, yet he did not see himself as an athlete. Ultimately, he believed that the media would eventually persuade him to fit into at least one of the styles marketed. Ted noticed that between his two sets of friends—East Coast versus West Coast—their Facebook pages and communication were essentially the same. He felt this was quite a revelation, that despite their desire to be individuals, young people were all sounding the same, adopting the same outlook:

> It's funny . . . it's basically the exact same, like even though I think now of my friends from home, they're not like my friends from here. Like I can't actually think of two people you know that are the same, but they totally are . . . It's all the same . . . even though they're like 3,000 km away. Like, it's all basically the same. I hate saying that about my friends . . . it seems like most people are kind of the same everywhere you go.

Additionally, Oscar talked about how he had given up wearing relatively new clothing because it was seen as out of style. John talked about how he had been influenced by advertisements to buy a certain style of clothing, to be up to date with athletic or outdoor gear, like snowboarding apparel. Even when it came to listening to music, Christopher confessed that he was never comfortable playing music of his choice around others, on the chance that it was not considered cool. He admitted to being influenced by others' opinions of him: "I mean if someone says that looks good on you, like even if it's just a stranger . . . you'd feel more confident wearing it, so it makes you want it, right?" Christopher captured the feeling of *not* conforming as "almost like you stick out now, like because, you know, you're not the one that fits in, so you feel almost like you're separated." The feeling of insecurity about one's preferences as a result of changing fads was reiterated by Sam:

I just worry about if other people will think that it looks nice or that sort of thing, but often times, I don't know what I think. I find it hard to make decisions about even my preference and then, yeah, when I hesitate, and a lot of people hesitate, you kind of think, oh well, so-and-so thinks this looks good, or will my friends think this is a cool shirt?, stuff like that. So, yeah, that makes me hesitate.

He further stated that he had never really felt a loss of individuality because he was dressing like other people: "It didn't occur to me that I was blending in and that I might lose some sense of individuality if I were dressing like other people." Tom talked about how frustrating it was to feel the need to conform. He gave the example of Pokémon cards and how invested he was in that particular game and how, eventually, the cards became "totally worthless."

Pro Fad

Most of the male participants argued that keeping up with fads was, for the most part, a positive process. For example, despite expressing how confusing it was to establish oneself beyond the confines of the latest fad, Tom defended this as enjoyable and, therefore, justifiable:

I don't think that fads are that bad. There's a reason why you enjoy it, so if you enjoy it, then who cares? Like it's kind of probably pretty annoying that like you [can't] have the same thing for that long. So, you'll be spending money again, but it comes down to that you enjoy it and you like to be a part of it, so it's good.

Adhering to fads was justified as a good thing because it involved change and, as Floyd reiterated, "a reason to buy more clothes, to work harder, to get something that's in style." Seeing others adorning themselves in the latest fashion trends leads one to think, according to George, that "it's just like everyone else is doing it and you're like 'oh well, that looks good,' like I should do that as well." Yet another male participant, Tom, explained that he felt fads provided a valuable opportunity: "I think it's just a way of expressing yourself, like it's self-expression."

The female participants, on the other hand, did not reiterate that keeping up with fads was enjoyable; rather, it was seen more as pressure and necessity so as to minimize negative feedback in social situations. Alicia summed it up as follows:

In terms of clothes when I was younger I would buy a lot more things that . . . would go out of style and I think that's kind of frustrating because you spend the money on it and . . . you want it to last a little longer . . . I still have things like that now, but I do a lot less of that . . . because . . . you invest the money and the next season it's out of style. You don't feel comfortable wearing that article out and then it's . . . sitting at the bottom of your drawer and it's sort of like "Well, that was a waste" and you could've bought something that wasn't so season-specific, or like, would've lasted you longer . . . I think definitely disappointment there, frustration. The worst is when you really like something and it goes out of style . . . and that's obviously a big problem because . . . you don't want to get rid of it then, but you can't wear it out.

Susan talked about fads in a positive light; in particular, she described using fads as a gauge to help her determine what clothing would look best for her, specifically: "To see what is . . . socially acceptable for what to wear."

Nonconformity

The nonconformity category was important to identify, as a number of participants were adamant that they were not swayed by the trends or fads within the culture. Indeed, the whole idea of a consumer-oriented lifestyle was questioned, albeit by a minority of participants.

Free of Fad Influence

Those female participants (Sara, Susan) who identified themselves as coming from a "low-income family" stated that they were free of fad influence due to a lack of funds; they discussed their preference to buy clothes off-season so as to secure low, on-sale prices:

When I shop for clothes, I always go to the sale racks right away. I'd much rather buy something that used to be $50 and now is $10 than brag about buying something expensive . . . I'd rather buy winter clothes in summer or spring because I know they're on sale . . . I'm always like one year behind everything, but I mean that's just how I've always shopped because then I can get more for my money. (Susan)

A number of female participants (Sara, Tessa, Susan, Ingrid, Nancy, and Judy) all expressed the desire to be their own person and reject those fads that did not appeal due to aesthetic reasons. Clearly, their desire to look good was expressed, but not at the expense of feeling pressured to adopt a fashion style they were not comfortable with. They talked about not wanting to dress just to impress others, but to do so according to what they sincerely liked. Sara, in particular, described the disconnect she felt with the images of young people in fashion magazines and how this impacted her willingness to adopt a fad: "You'd see images of kids doing these sort of fun activities and realizing that I . . . didn't enjoy those and that, for some reason, what I enjoyed wasn't being portrayed in these magazines." It was with some determination that Ingrid expressed her ability to wear something that she had chosen in the face of a negative reaction from others: "I don't really go with what society [likes]. I usually go for what I like."

Paying attention to fashion was a low priority for a number of the male participants. Some expressed that their selection of clothing was based on whether or not it appealed to them, and not on whether or not it was fashionable. As George defiantly exclaimed: "Everyone needs to be themselves or else like what's the point in even like living? . . . You want to find your own personal style and like everything you like has to be stuff that you actually like, so that's very important." George, Jeff, and Ted all talked about how they deferred to their mothers to choose and buy their clothing, relying on their judgment as to how they should look, as opposed to keeping in style (George clarified that this is less the case now that he is older). Male participants also expressed indifference with respect to fashion, of not caring: "I don't care about fashion. I don't have much fashion sense, so I guess fashion's the lowest priority of things on my list . . . sports and stuff like that is a bigger concern to me" (John). Christopher emphasized that he was more interested in the practicality of clothing, whether it was functional, as opposed to aesthetically pleasing. As with the female participants who identified themselves from low-income families, limited funds were also a factor for some of the male participants insofar as keeping up with the latest trends.

Questioning a Consuming-Oriented Lifestyle

A few male and female participants were opposed to buying and possessing "things." For example, Sara expressed her desire to fill her life with experiences rather than with objects, preferring travel over consuming. She also expressed an interest in acquiring a sailing license and how she felt that experience would be so much more valuable than that of a consumer. Jeff was adamant about not spending money and talked about how he would insist that his mother return items that she had bought for him that in his view were too expensive; put differently, he was passionate about minimizing spending for any reason. Sara was unique in her ability to articulate what she perceived to be the futility of consuming:

We're sort of influenced to buy these . . . things like makeup and CDs and stuff when we really don't need them, but for some reason we're going to buy them . . . It seems odd to me. A lot of the things that people use you notice that they'll throw them out afterwards, or they'll play with them a couple of times and then just put it off to the side. So it really doesn't seem to be much other than sort of instant gratification of just buying.

She also articulated that she had little interest in acquiring commodities and, instead, wanted her life to be full of meaningful experiences. On the topic of ownership, John concluded that it was "stupid to have to have everything that everyone else has." As a final caveat, both John and Jeff talked about how much they hated shopping, though they did not specify a dislike of the process of consuming itself.

Values

This category reveals how the participants at times contradicted themselves. For example, many of them declared that they had no values with respect to consuming and yet, at the same time, wished to declare their concern about the environment.

No Values Related to Consuming

The majority of participants did not hesitate to confess that they had weakly formed values when it came to buying products. They stated that they were motivated by likes and dislikes, convenience, price, and that which was valued, or highly rated. They also indicated that they had little interest in accumulating information that might impact the kinds of products consumed (e.g., animal testing). Alicia talked about how important it was to her to buy the genuine article with respect to brands as opposed to buying a "knockoff"; she considered this a type of value. Hence, it appeared that the absence of obvious values had to do with the desire of wanting an object and disregarding its manufacturing process (e.g., child labor practices). The following statements are examples of the type of responses elicited on the topic of values:

Environmental issues have always been something that I've wanted to care about, but I can honestly say, it's never really been a concern to me. (Floyd)

I know I should be more conscientious about what I do, but I mean I don't do it which is really bad because I feel like . . . a hypocrite. (Susan)

If I bought some like terribly "un-environmental" . . . thing I probably wouldn't feel too good about myself. I still wouldn't care almost to a level where like it's never been like okay . . . I'm not going to buy this because of the environment. I've never gotten there. (George)

I probably should care, but I really don't really look into [environmental issues]. (Jeff)

I don't think [sustainable products] mean a lot to me or people my age, sadly. (Sam)

Choosing to live a less "consumeristic" [life]style . . . I think I would find [that] . . . it would be more difficult, and it would be less enjoyable. (Tom)

I guess also, just like not making the effort to know, like I guess, overall, like I don't care. (Joyce)

Ted recalled that while he was living at home, his mother would not buy Kraft products because of their affiliation with Big Tobacco; he complied with this restriction for about two years until he moved out of the family home. It should be noted that two of the participants, Tessa and Nancy, stated they were not sure if they were lacking in values or whether it was more a question of not knowing or having arrived at a decision as to their personal values.

Socially Conscious with a Caveat

For the majority of the participants, cost was a big motivator when it came down to making purchases; many indicated that if cost was no issue, they would choose a product deemed to be environmentally friendly, but only under those conditions. For example, Christopher and Pam both stated that they would like to support the green movement, but that it would be too cost prohibitive:

[If] you know there's a green product and it's $50 more, say [the product is] $100, or say [it's] a $200 product and the green one is $50 more, then I probably wouldn't buy it. (Christopher)

The greener something is the more expensive it seems to be. Like things made in Canada versus things made in China is a big price difference. And right now, going to school, I don't have a lot of money so I don't have as much of a choice. But I think if I had a choice I would definitely buy the greener things. (Pam)

The fact that the participants were students, the majority of whom were on limited funds, was seen as a legitimate reason not to buy environmentally friendly products. Sam, like Pam, felt that as he got older, he would pay more attention to environmental issues because of the luxury of having more money.

Conscientious about the Environment

Approximately half of the participants stated that they were conscientious about the environment as consumers, although only Tessa and Ingrid were previously involved in any organizations related to environmental causes. None of the participants indicated that they were currently connected to organizations specific to the environment. The others talked about not buying products with unnecessary packaging, buying biodegradable soap, buying products that had been recycled, buying products that did not involve harm to anyone else (this participant could not clearly articulate what was meant by that), not buying products tested on animals, not buying anything produced by child labor, and buying from companies that in some way do good by "giving back" (the example included buying from a shoe store that for every pair bought donates one pair of used shoes to charity). In summary, equal numbers of male and female participants claimed that they were conscientious when it came to the environment. The following is a sample of a few declarations:

I try to get stuff with the least amount of packaging as possible, or if I notice like the box has been made from recycled products, or the paper is from recycled stuff, or it's used from recycled materials, then . . . I would definitely try to lean towards that. (Oscar)

I don't like products that are made in places where child labor is used. I think that's horrible. It's not like I go out of my way to look for things that are child labor-free, I guess that I'll feel a lot better about the product. Like I'll just think about it and I feel happier about the product if I know that in some way they were either thinking about the environment like cruelty to animals or children . . . I love organic food and free-range meat and stuff like that. I just like it better. I just like the idea better. (Tom)

I bought this bag and it made me feel . . . very good about myself because it was like a vegan-made bag. It looked like leather, but it wasn't leather . . . I was doing some sort of good for the world by purchasing this bag that wasn't leather and it was made of plants. (Pam)

Consuming in the Context of Environmental Issues

This is the only category that has its own code. Despite knowing about global warming/climate change and its potential damage to the planet, many of the participants did not feel it was incumbent upon them to make any changes with regard to consumption or even to care about the issues necessarily. The following excerpts capture their varying explanations and points of view:

I just hope nothing happens to me . . . It's inevitably going to happen that some polar ice cap is going to melt, or there's going to be some hurricane or whatever that wipes out humanity, but I don't take it really too seriously . . . I just don't think it's going to happen in my lifetime, that it's going to be like that big of, that important of a deal. Like I need to stop right now or else tomorrow is going to hurt me. (George)

I want a sustainable world for obviously my children, my children's children, and like generations to come and everything, but I honestly really don't think about the environment because it's not really something that I can really deal with myself. Obviously I could go into professions that would do that, but it's obviously, . . . it is a big deal but . . . I don't really think it's a big deal to me but I know I should care about it. (Jeff)

I heard that . . . we need to stop eating fish because they might be like, you know, we're running out of our fish supply, like our wild salmon. I just started eating more fish because I figure we're not going to have that long to eat fish anymore . . . .it doesn't really matter. Like every million years, every billion, like a couple of million years, something terrible happens to the earth and you know everyone dies . . . and it's baked and the whole thing is covered in like volcanoes or whatever, so it kind of makes me just not really care because realistically like in the grand scheme of things on the earth, it doesn't, you know, we can't do anything to it. (Ted)

I'm not like the type of person [who] is like a tree hugger sort of thing . . . I know like for like global warming I know like both sides of the story, like yes, it's happening, but it's happened in the past and . . . I recycle and stuff I mean it's awesome, everyone should, but at the same time I'm not, . . . not going to drive my car somewhere if I want to go somewhere due to greenhouse gas emissions. (James)

I guess I haven't really experienced it yet to know what it's like so I don't really feel like it's going to happen. Like people are saying it's going to happen, but I haven't really experienced it yet. I know there's climate change now, but it's like not really intense change, so I haven't really experienced it really and it just doesn't really affect me. (Nancy)

I'm definitely supportive of all the efforts that are being made like with different companies and stuff trying to move more toward things that are environmentally friendly, but it's not a huge thing in my life. It's not something that I'm really passionate about or anything . . . I'm not sure I want to make huge sacrifices for the cause either . . . I don't think I want to give up my car for the sake of reducing the emissions . . . I wouldn't want to give it up, so there's an extent to which I support the cause. (Judy)

Judy also argued that the very existence of climate change was questionable and that both sides need to be considered before any judgment is made about its veracity:

I'm not convinced about climate change. From what I've heard there's two sides to the story. One side says that humans are causing climate change and the other side says it's part of the natural cycle of the earth. So I'm not convinced. It's not something that I feel concerned about.

Money

Participants discussed money in varying places throughout the interview, particularly with regard to questions about their financial security, both in the present and the future. Additionally, discussions ensued about whether money could guarantee happiness, how much value was placed on money, and the participants' overall relationship to money. This section ends with a narrative about one male participant, who indicated that his values had determined his educational and career choices.

More Is Not Better

One of the important realizations that surfaced on the topic of money was that having more stuff does not necessarily make one feel better, hence the numerous stories of regret from the participants. Ingrid described the disappointment she felt as a child when she had desperately wanted a toy only to find that it gave her little to no fulfillment when she acquired it: "When I finally got it, I didn't really care for it." Many of the participants talked about having wasted money on particular purchases whether it was because they were quickly bored with the desired object or, for whatever reason, never ended up using it. They also recognized the limitations of the desired object and how their expectations could not always be met:

The commercials for Hot Wheels made it look sweet. I mean it was cool, I guess, but like after like two or three days, it kind of just got put away. It took up the living room yeah for like Christmas day and the next day . . . There's not much else you can do until you buy more and more Hot Wheels. So that was kind of kind of a let-down I guess, but we did really want it for like three or four weeks leading up to it, me and my brother both. (Ted)

It appeared that while the participants were able to cite specific examples of when they had regretted buying something, they did not explicitly articulate the notion that "more is not better." Instead, they felt victimized by the flaws inherent in the items they had purchased or received. It should be noted that it was certainly not the majority of participants who expressed "disappointment" as the prime emotion when acquiring a desired object.

Several of the male participants felt they could be content with very little, not a "huge amount," but simply enough to cover their needs. For example, Ted stated, "I have felt a lot of time that I do have all the stuff I need." Christopher also indicated that he had reached saturation points with commodities:

There's always things that are like out of reach, that you realize [are] not really possible, like a brand-new Mercedes . . . As far as things like accessories and clothing . . . there's definitely been times when I've just been happy with what I have.

Relationship to Money

Most of the participants desired to be at least as well off as their parents and preferably, more financially secure. There appeared to be differences in the relationship to money relative to gender. For example, the male participants were far more interested in accumulating money than the female participants. Most of the participants talked about their ambitions to own a house, cars, and even luxury items like boats. Only Floyd confidently believed that he would be "quite wealthy" (in the millions) one day, and that by the time he reached thirty he would be making "seven figures." James expressed hope that material success was in his future: "While I'd love to be wealthy obviously like everyone would love to be wealthy, but who knows." John stated that while he did not expect to be "ridiculously wealthy," he still wanted to have more "stuff" than the average person. He talked about how important money was and expressed his desire for wealth: "[Money] is not the most important thing, but it's one of them, for me at least, as bad as that sounds." A number of male participants were clear that money was not necessarily going to change their lives. For example, Oscar was able to articulate that, while more money might ease the pressures of life, it "wouldn't change the way I make my decisions or change my personality." Two male participants had reservations about the ability of money to increase happiness. Ted believed that "I'd be happy with less money, but [a job] that I liked." Christopher reiterated that money was not of central importance in his life, at least not at the present time: "[Money] is not a huge deal to me compared to some people that I know who, you know, instead of having fun this summer, they worked two or three jobs. So for me it's not a big priority."

In comparison, one of the female participants, Sara, talked about how money was important to her but within the context of providing basic amenities and even the opportunity to be altruistic:

I definitely like money. I've learned that it is a valuable tool in living life to pay for whatever . . . It helps a lot and the more money you have it seems like the more security that you have and the more freedom you have to go traveling or to go to the movies, and even donate, or sort of help out other people.

Female participants held little belief that they would achieve a lifestyle beyond that of middle class. "I hope to be in middle class, like I'm not dying to be in upper class, it would be nice, but I would be happy in middle class, being able to support myself and family" (Sara). When answering the question about whether or not money was important, Ingrid was uniquely different from the others as she replied: "I'm not really big on money as long as I'm happy, I guess." She related how her parents were quite well-off and that she had grown up watching how the wealthy lived, noting that money did not contribute to any lasting happiness; she said she derived happiness from her relationships with friends:

I guess it was just the people I met and they didn't care for money but they cared for life and they showed me a whole different view, or whole different life on how things were and I loved it . . . My fiancé was a major one, he didn't have money . . . he found happiness just in nature. He would take me into the woods and show me different things and talk about different animals. You know, it was nice. It was a different change and I liked that.

A slight majority of the male participants (Floyd, John, James, Christopher, Sam, Tom) believed that they would be free of financial worries when they were older as compared to less than half of the female participants (Joyce, Nancy, Ingrid, Judy). It seemed that the male participants were only slightly less worried about achieving financial success than female participants.

The following narrative provides a picture of what it is like for young people participating in consumer cultures who wish to act in keeping with their values. In particular, John's story covers the struggle to establish values and what it means to challenge existing norms.

John's Story: A Career Path for the Environment

John came from an upper-middle-class family and was well provided for during his childhood with a variety of toys and other possessions. He remembers as a child wanting things and then being disappointed, or bored, even with those that were highly coveted. He remarked, when looking back in time, that many of the objects he acquired with his parents' money or his own were "an awful waste." When he was younger, it was very important to John to have branded clothing; he was very caught up in the skateboard culture between the ages of 10 and 14 and bought clothing specifically designed for this activity and other sports. John describes himself as being one of the "cool" kids in high school and was particularly self-conscious about this "status." He said: "I had the newest phones, all the clothing brands you needed . . . [I was] good at sports, [I] did well in school." Presently, John insists that he no longer cares about clothing styles and says he has not changed his wardrobe in the last ten years. He was convinced that the media intensely targets his age group and that he no longer "buys into it." John believed this change was a result of advice from his parents to be wary of media. Additionally, he worked in retail for a number of years and became disillusioned by what he perceived to be excessive corporate profit. John viewed advertising as a scam and saw it as manipulative to the extent that it preys on people's weaknesses.

John stated that he now buys only what he really needs. He remarked feeling guilty about buying objects from China and tried to only buy those from North America so as to support local economies (while admitting this is difficult to do). John also professed to feeling guilty "a lot of times" when buying things made in the Third World because of the pollution generated from their industries. He felt that the globe is headed in an imminently dangerous direction: "I think there are going to be some major repercussions in the future. And people are going to wish they had listened back 10 years ago when they said, made all those reports, where our earth is going, heading." John proclaimed that he has chosen environmental engineering as a career path in order to participate in the production of "greener energies." While it is important to John to have a job with a good income, he made it clear that he also wants one that is "helping society as well as opposed to going into, like, oil and gas engineering where . . . you'll be a millionaire, but it all comes down to what your ethics are right now."

Summary: Identity

When considering individuality within the context of consumer cultures, many of the participants (Sara, Sonja, Tessa, Oscar, Sam, Floyd, George, Jeff, Christopher) maintained that despite commonality of ownership with thousands, even millions of others, they were distinctly unique. They also declared that character, as well as family background, and not possessions, determined one's identity. Yet, at the same time, a number of participants (Ingrid, Tessa, Alicia, Sonja, George, and John) recalled a time when celebrities and television programs greatly influenced the formation of their identity. They recognized the struggle to be an authentic individual against the forces of wanting to fit in and achieve social acceptance. While a few male participants (Tom, Floyd, George) and one female participant (Susan) believed that adhering to fads was a positive, Alicia, in particular, relayed that she felt it was a negative. She regretted spending on clothing articles that could only be worn briefly because they were no longer in style.

Both sexes described a time when they had adopted an "extreme" fashion as a means of expressing their individuality and going against the norm: dying hair in the "colors of the rainbow" (Ingrid); wearing "short shorts" (Christopher); a "mullet" hairstyle (Ted). Additionally, Alicia felt her uniqueness was expressed in objects that she owned and others did not.

A few participants (Sara, Jeff, and John) reiterated that having material possessions was not necessarily a good thing, nor would they lead to greater happiness. Some expressed how they felt disillusioned after acquiring something that had once been deemed highly desirable. In particular, Oscar articulated that he was not motivated by money, and that having money would not change his personality. Sara and John, in particular, stood out from all other participants in their capacity to understand the futility of buying while expecting happiness.

However, more males (e.g., Floyd, John, James) than females could easily imagine a life of relatively high material comfort; female participants felt that achieving middle class was likely the highest status they would acquire. Overall, the majority of both sexes had trouble envisioning a financially secure future.

With regard to values as a consumer, the majority of participants (Floyd, George, Jeff, Sam, Tom, Ted, James, Joyce, Sonja, Alicia, Sara, Tessa, Susan, Nancy) were more concerned about their ability to acquire an object than about the ethics involved in its manufacture. Furthermore, for Tessa, Susan, and Christopher, cost was *the* factor driving their purchasing decisions. Eight participants (George, Jeff, Ted, James, Floyd, Oscar, Nancy, Judy) expressed indifference or disbelief about the importance of climate change and the connection between consuming and damaging environmental events.

Clearly, the impact of media on identity, willingness to conform or not conform, and values was powerfully felt and was important to self-efficacy. Indeed, how the participants viewed the presence of media, and its relationship to the self, was a theme that kept recurring.

MEDIA

Media plays a powerful role within consumer capitalist societies, impacting individuals on many levels, including self-regard, relationships with others, and how one views the greater global community. Advertising is a major part of media and is, therefore, addressed as a category of its own in order to reveal the participants' views and understanding of the process of advertising.

The Self, Relationships, and Media

All of the participants indicated that they watched media on a regular basis, often as a means of connecting to or bonding with friends and family. Media entertainment was integral to the social lives of the participants. Additionally, some of the participants indicated that they gained vicarious pleasure from imagining themselves as the fictitious or "real" characters (in the case of reality TV) depicted in media. For the majority of male and female participants, comparing oneself to figures portrayed in the media was reported as having a negative impact. This section also includes a code on media effects with regard to relationships with parents and peers. Advertising was given a separate code from media itself because of its critical importance in understanding the self.

Technological Goods

Technological goods were seen as tools that are an extension of the self, or as Alicia described, "it's always with you." Owning technological goods was also regarded as that which "completes" the self, when one has acquired all of the technology deemed necessary to function in the current culture. Each piece of technology was seen as "personalized," so as to be representative of the individual owner; hence, there was a perceived intimacy between the use of technology and the expression of the self, as well as self-image. The acquisition of technology, whether current or during childhood, was seen by the participants, like Jeff, for example, as paramount to their individual social success, ability to entertain themselves, and capacity to "keep up" with the culture generally. "I think it's important to everyone really. I think if you don't move along with technology, you're kind of behind everyone else" (Jeff). Technology was seen as critical to academic performance and being able to connect to friends, as well as the larger global community, through social networking sites like Facebook (which all of the participants were participating in on a regular basis). Old and dated technology was seen to represent a failure in being able to experience the opportunities that others, with newer technology, were more privileged with:

I also had my old old phone for a really long time, so getting a new phone is something new and exciting. And obviously something like an iPhone, that can do so much, go on the Internet, play music . . . call people, text people, so yeah, it was an exciting day. (Joyce)

Further to this, the participants related that if their capacity to connect through technology was interrupted because of loss or malfunctioning, their relationships suffered. Indeed, technological goods were attributed as the glue that held friendships together—the unifying force:

You can talk to other people who have the same phone for free and it kind of creates a bond between you and your other friends, or people who have that phone. With the iPhone you can talk to each other and see each other's faces while you're talking to each other. (Pam)
    I actually lost my cell phone like two weeks ago and I was pretty out of the loop for a while, like I just didn't go out as much, like especially when you don't, I don't have a home phone. I was basically unreachable unless you actually drove to my house and like knocked on the front door, which I guess you could do, but most people just don't answer the phone. I'd say it definitely helps having a cell phone and even where I like got a Blackberry as a new phone . . . which kind of gets me even more, going out more, and stuff. It's like way easier just to invite people to go do stuff and come over. (Ted)

Individuals felt isolated and lost when their technology failed them or was inaccessible. Interestingly, technology was also seen as defining one's social class, particularly for the female participants; owning up-to-date technology presented a means of displaying one's privileged socioeconomic status. This, in turn, was perceived as a way to feel good about oneself:

I have an ex who for his 18th birthday he got an iPhone and then I have a friend that for her 18th birthday she got an iPhone. And I got mine on my 18th birthday and when my ex got his, because he was a year older, so when he got his I was a little jealous at the time. Like it was almost "Oh like I want that" and like he was from a wealthier background, like he's much better off and so I kind of looked at that . . . I would get sort of thoughts that he thought he was a little bit better than me. So when I got that iPhone that was like for me an almost like "Ha! See, like I am as good as you" . . . [My iPhone] was newer by then, the new one had come out so I had something better than him. And that made me feel so much better about myself which is really kind of a weird thing how that is linked. (Alicia)

While it was initially exciting for the participants to acquire new technology, discovering that someone else was in possession of higher-level technology tended to deflate their positive feelings:

You're frustrated because you don't have the same opportunities as other people who have the updated technology and so if you don't keep yourself up-to-date you're almost missing out on something that everyone else has access to. So, that's definitely a frustrating thing. It's hard to keep up with and it's too expensive to have the new thing every single time, but yeah, it's a problem. (Alicia)

I can think of like my cell phone a couple of years ago when everyone was getting iPhones and I just . . . had some clunky cell phone and it's kind of like, like you feel out of the loop a little bit, like everyone's doing something that you can't do. (George)

Technology itself was marvelled at for its speed and capacity, particularly the smart phones; they reflected on how they had desired a cell phone when only a small elite in their age bracket were able to acquire them. The participants also recalled how the capacity to play games was viewed as being cool. For example, a number of participants remembered how important it was to have Game Boy and Nintendo when they were younger. At the same time, there was also defiance expressed toward technology, the ability to live without it, to find other means of entertainment. As Tessa exclaimed, "I'm not like a person who's like without technology I cannot live kind of person, but with technology it makes life easier for me." And Susan: "Everyone's so used to technology that it would be a culture shock not to have it, but I personally don't feel like life would be difficult. I don't feel it would definitely ruin life." Imagining life without technology was viewed as practically inconceivable and tantamount to a type of culture shock for the vast majority of participants (Joyce, Ingrid, Pam, Tessa, Sara, Alicia,

Sonja, Floyd, George, James, Ted, Jeff, and John). Additionally, keeping current with technology was also described as a pressure:

And the big problem with technology is that oftentimes when they come out with new systems or whatever stuff stops working online and on the Web, it won't run on older stuff. And so, you have a problem there because, like, you're frustrated because you can't access the same material, and you don't have the same opportunities as other people who have the updated technology. And so, if you don't keep yourself up-to-date you're almost missing out on something that everyone else has access to. (Alicia)

Alicia also concluded that technology divides people into social classes—the wealthy are far more advantaged by virtue of the fact that they can access up-to-date technology—which is gauged by the ability to communicate and express oneself:

So I think [technology] disadvantages a lot of individuals who can't keep up financially with the changes in technology because I think everyone should have equal opportunity to use the same features on the web. And I remember when I was younger I would run into programs that wouldn't run because we had older computers . . . It creates [a] division almost between classes too because like the newer like technology obviously the wealthier individuals are able to purchase that and always keep updated and have access to that stuff and if you have a little bit less money and like especially the more impoverished people definitely can't have that technology.

Jeff thought it was important to keep up with technology as best one could but did not think having the latest equipment was particularly important to their social positioning: "I think that it's overrated . . . I think like people might look at it like, 'His family's maybe a bit better off,' but I don't think it really affects anything." The majority of male participants regarded technology as an essential but also fun commodity, and as with the female participants, the path through which they could connect with others.

Screen Time versus Down Time

Not all of the female participants were positive about the impact of technological goods on their lives. Specifically, Sara talked about how, as a child, she had been content with very little, often choosing to play outside with her friends until she became an adolescent and was introduced to technology-based toys, particularly video games.

Interviewer: Can you describe a time when you were a child or adolescent when you really wanted to purchase something?

Sara: I can't really think of anything in particular. I don't know. When I was a kid, I didn't really want much. I was content with just sort of playing outside. We lived in a cul-de-sac, so I was really close to all of my friends and we would just go to the park that was there, or we'd play street hockey with some of the older kids' toys and that kind of stuff. But I never really wanted anything.

Interviewer: That's unusual.

Sara: It's sort of weird and how it also changed when I hit adolescence. That's when I started getting introduced to all these gadgets and stuff and that's when my parents were like okay the toys have changed basically, but they're also a little bit more pricey and a little bit more out of reach I guess.

Interviewer: So what do you mean by gadgets? Videogames?

Sara: Yeah, like the videogames, the MP3 players, and those sorts of little things. I guess that they were just starting to get popular.

Additionally, Ingrid described how once she got hooked on the computer she spent less time outside; MySpace and Facebook consumed a considerable amount of her time as well as browsing the Internet. Yet, surprisingly, the participants expressed little regret about how tied to technology their lives had become. Indeed, it was accepted with resignation as though there was nothing that could be done to alleviate this dependence. "We're putting so much into technology and I don't believe in real technology you know . . . It's bad enough that I have a cell phone. But I keep it because I have to" (Nancy). Participants detailed how constant their use of cell phones was and how texting was an ongoing activity throughout the day, even at the objection of family members. As Nancy described: "Maybe when I'm always constantly on my phone during dinner, or going out and stuff in the car ride, like constantly texting, it might have affected [my parents] a little bit." It is noteworthy, that none of the male participants felt that they had sacrificed quality of life or outdoor experiences because of the use of technology. Furthermore, they stated that it was in no way seen as a negative influence, even when family members objected to the way it was monopolizing their lives.

Self-Worth Compromised by Media

Many of the female participants relayed that they negatively compared themselves to girls/women portrayed in the media. Specifically, they talked about "perfect skin" as an example of feeling less than and wanting to look more like those depicted in advertisements, magazines, or movies. As an example, Joyce said: "I like how their skin looks, so I want mine to look like that." Another example included the shape of one's face or eyes not meeting the standard of a typical model (hence, lacking beauty specific to the dominant culture). As a final example, having the right weight, relative to models that were below normal body size, was a big concern. Many of the female participants mentioned how messages from family and friends, those encouraging them to feel good about themselves, came into direct conflict with messages from the media:

You tend to always feel a little less than you should, I guess. You don't really value yourself as much when you're not like [a media model] . . . it's frustrating to know you're supposed to feel one way about yourself and then you see it in the media that you're technically supposed to be this way. (Sara)

Most of the participants indicated that they realized the ideal media image was unattainable. For example, Judy talked about how she used reason and logic to mitigate the impact of the celebrity life; she did this by focusing on the negative aspects of such lifestyles and the tendency to abuse drugs. Pam tried to downplay the role of media and its impact on how she felt about herself. She stated that she did not feel "mentally" altered by media, yet, at the same time, admitted that how she thinks about her body has been impacted. Pam acknowledged feeling pressure from the portrayal of models in the media:

I think you just feel like you should be one of the girls on *America's Next Top Model*, or on the cover of the magazine, or say in those tabloid magazines to see these women that are all done up all the time. And you think . . . "Why can't my hair look like that all the time?" or "Why don't I look that nice or that put together all the time?"

In perhaps the most extreme example, Ingrid recalled being teased in elementary school for being too "big" and looking "manly." She revealed that her negative body image intensified as she got older and began to watch more television shows depicting models. As she put it, she felt like an "outcast" for not being the right size; she felt undesirable, unattractive, and that she stuck out among her peers. She stated that this type of negative thinking still plagues her today: "I have more confidence than I did when I was a kid, but I couldn't say I've reached that point where I could say I am still pretty. Isn't that sad?" Nancy seemed somewhat confused as to whether the media, in its portrayal of the female body, had a negative or motivating effect: "I guess media is always . . . saying how skinny people are pretty and like your body has to be a certain way. And sometimes it makes me want to like go on a diet or eat healthier and work out, exercise, and stuff."

A number of male participants, like the women participants, experienced negative self-image as a result of paying attention to media.

George talked about how he had compared himself to one of the characters in the movie *Super Bad* and recognized what a "loser" he was because he felt he was similar to one of the protagonists in the movie who was portrayed in a negative light. He stated that he had held himself in too high esteem until he had seen the movie and that "it kind of knocked me back down to earth a little bit." Oscar noted that the media tried to portray perfect human beings that are next to impossible to attain, but difficult to disregard; these depictions, he noted, include images of those who are "honest, smart, thoughtful, healthy, physically fit, [and] strong." He was also aware of the link between eating disorders in young people and the media portrayal of 'body beautiful' as ultra-thin. Indeed, Christopher described how he felt pressured to be in shape as a result of observing actors in the media who were "especially buffed." Oscar also felt inadequate because of bad acne as a teen and remembered a particular television show in which an actor portrayed a kid who had acne, and how he was targeted in a negative way. Tom also talked about having had acne in high school and how seeing actors with flawless skin on television made it more difficult. He stated: "So if you feel like you have an imperfection . . . [the media] might make you think about it." In a positive direction, Sam attributed the media as a motivator to staying in shape based on the portrayal of "perfect bodies" that made him "want to keep a healthy body."

Emulating Media

Alicia described how she had modeled her aspirations and goals according to what she saw her favorite characters doing on television. More specifically, she desired having a boyfriend, being able to drink alcohol, and going to parties. While she never considered herself a member of the "super popular crowd," she believed she had come close to living the ideal life as defined by media. She lamented that in the end she had not embodied a fulfilling existence and recalled breaking up with her boyfriend, among other disappointments, as very difficult: "It's ironic because . . . that is sort of the one thing that I wanted out of life. [The lifestyle] was definitely created by media and realizing that's just not how it works was probably one of the hardest things to get over."

Male participants said they were caught up with the celebrity lives of athletes and their brand of clothing and equipment. For example, Jeff talked about how he strived for the fitness level of television actors. James also wanted to emulate images of men's health and fitness: "I probably work out from seeing . . . toned or like 'jacked' guys and being, like, Okay, I want to be like that." He also talked about how he worked to develop muscle mass and maintain a "skinny" body like those of male models. Additionally, James talked about wanting to emulate a character out of a movie or television series. For instance, in the show *How I Met Your Mother*, a character named Barney was idealized by James because "he makes tons of money and he's got great friends and he lives in . . . an awesome apartment with lots of awesome stuff in it . . . That kind of life seems very . . . good to me." The fact that the Barney character wears suits influenced James to want to do the same and has "changed my mind on suits for some reason. I was definitely influenced by it for sure."

Media Wary

Male participants described themselves as media wary in that they believed the media could manipulate; however, they felt they were above this level of influence. Ted observed the negative effects of media on his younger brother: "I see him being manipulated sometimes . . . No one really sees it in themselves." Christopher talked about how his middle school had provided students with information on some of the negative effects of advertising and how this "really opened my eyes." Additionally, he claimed that his mother talked to him about the media targeting of young people, including the practice of "Photoshopping." Ingrid recognized how girls are sexualized in the media: "[The media makes] girls put themselves out there more provocatively . . . I find it very disturbing when you see . . . 13-year-olds, 14-year-olds, 15-year-olds in high school, you know, trying to show their 'booty.'"

Media Effects on Relationships with Parents and Peers

Only Tom, felt that watching media misrepresented his parents and parents in general: "I don't think the media portrays . . . [the] good interest that your parents have at heart. They mostly portray the opposite." George was adamant that watching media had not resulted in any perceptual change with regard to his parents. Joyce, who said she was raised in a one-parent family, stated that she felt somewhat envious of the financial position of two-income families that were portrayed in the media. Alicia felt that watching media had a profound negative effect on how she viewed her parents and that this reinforced her own rebellious behavior:

Watching media, often times parents are sort of portrayed as dumb or naïve or uninformed or whatever it may be, and I think I drew parallels between that and my own parents in some instances. And if you see that one kid on the TV show acting up and rebelling against their parents, then it's almost like, "oh, it's okay" for me to do that, too.

Other female participants, Sara and Susan, said that they had more positive regard toward their parent(s) in terms of appreciating who they were compared to those depicted in media.

Tom stated that watching media impacted how he viewed his peers. He described, in particular, that watching the television show *Friends* led him to try to determine which role he played within his peer group:

You're comparing yourself with different characters on TV, even though they're not real. It's like you could learn something from them. Maybe it's their style of humor or the way they dress . . . I think you're looking for a role to play [within] your group of friends.

A couple of the female participants said watching media resulted in a type of bonding with their peers, "a good way to grow your relationships" (Tessa), as a result of having something in common to talk about. Additionally, Sonja stated that the television show *Pretty Little Liars* reinforced for her how important it was to treat her friends well. Finally, Nancy reiterated that watching the movie *Mean Girls* helped her determine which of her friends were "the mean ones or who, at least, seemed to be the mean ones, and then who are, like, the nicer ones. You can kind of tell the cliques apart after seeing how they [are] portrayed."

Advertising

This category reveals how the participants view and relate to advertising as a ubiquitous presence in consumer culture. As with the category on values, a number of inconsistencies about advertising effects emerged from the data.

The Lure of Advertising

Most of the participants agreed that advertisements persuaded them to buy, although a number of participants, both male and female, were convinced that they were immune from any significant influence. In some cases, the participants stated that they enjoyed advertisements, making a point of watching the ones that they deemed to be "fun." Tessa, for instance, felt that the only advertising that had any influence on her was about technology. Susan noted how advertisements are a significant part of her life and how strange it would feel if they disappeared. Yet Susan also felt that "they influence my values by ending up telling me what to value." Advertisements were also seen as dictating to the individual their underlying choices: "I don't like advertisements just because they ask you to do something or try something, 'do this, do that,' when really I just want to do what I want to do" (Pam). Pam saw the pervasiveness of advertising as intrusive: "I think lots of the time I don't read them and I feel like I don't see them, but they're still there, and I think subconsciously, I know that they're there. They're everywhere." Pam also described how seeing an advertisement that really connected with her was highly reinforcing ("It was nice, it was cool"). Knowing that advertisers are solely interested in making money was acknowledged by Sara, who recognized that advertisements could influence her to buy, even products that she did not need: "Every once in a while I feel like the advertisements have gotten to me, or I shouldn't technically be buying this, but I kind of want it so I'll do it anyway and sort of give up something else in my life." Judy also concurred that she could be persuaded to buy quite easily: "They're getting what they want by getting me to buy something that I don't necessarily need or because I think it's a good deal. So I guess I feel dumb."

Floyd felt that advertisements could be informative and that "you might see something in a commercial that you end up going and buying, and if it weren't for [the ad] you wouldn't have bought it." He felt strongly that taking offense to an advertisement was to be narrow-minded:

I am not religious at all, so it might be one-sided saying this, but I honestly find if someone . . . takes . . . offense to an advertisement, I feel like they are too strong in one belief and they need to realize that there's more than one view on life and not one way is a hundred percent correct. So I think it's fair game for them to advertise whatever.

Floyd was also sympathetic with corporate advertising because of the risk involved in getting their products sold. Pam agreed that advertisements provided a valuable and educative role about products that one would otherwise not know about.

Jeff believed that advertisements influenced beyond our cognitive awareness, at a level that cannot be felt or detected though, surprisingly, he also felt that advertisements were "genuine." He viewed corporations as doing good deeds by making money and stimulating the economy ("It's what makes the world go around"), and that it is rare that advertisers are "inappropriate." And while he stated that the media largely targets young people in his age group, he insisted that he did not feel any pressure as a result of this phenomenon. Ted volunteered that he pays attention to snowboarding sport advertisements and that he has been persuaded to buy from corporations that sponsor athletes he admires. At the same time, he acknowledged that advertisers know how to get young people to buy their products and that sponsoring an athlete may be one of those tactics: "I mean it's good for us the ads are so relevant, but it's probably bad because they really do know exactly how to make us buy their product." Christopher stated he was influenced by advertisements and that repeated exposure to such advertisements would definitely contribute to the possibility of him purchasing the advertised product. Additionally, he remembered viewing an advertisement about McDonald's as a child and how disappointed he was with the real product once he had acquired it. He said that as an adult he is still swayed by food advertisements: "If I see a Subway commercial or something, I'm hungry. I want to go out there and buy a Subway." Like other participants, he felt strongly that advertisements influenced, whether consciously or unconsciously, causing us to act in certain ways that benefit the advertiser. Christopher also mentioned that advertisements for videogames were particularly enticing and held a powerful sway over him. Finally, Tom relayed that, "Most of the time I believe [the advertisement] and have no issue with advertisement." He also expressed the opinion that advertisements "can't really lie" because the public will keep them honest. He felt that individual consumer research would ultimately mitigate the effects of false information advertising and protect the consumer from any intentional deceit.

Confused about Advertising

It appeared that some of the participants believed that they had some control around advertising and were even immune from its effect—advertisements were annoying at worst and, at best, informative. Susan felt that she was not influenced by advertisements because most of them were for products that she could not afford, those she called "big-ticket items." She seemed confused as to whether or not advertisements for, say, movies could influence her in any way. Further to this, Susan questioned whether advertisers could wrongfully portray information in order to sway people to buy their products: "They could get in trouble for that, right?" She also felt that advertising was a fair system, that the "whole point of consumerism" is to manipulate people to buy whatever it is that a corporation is selling. She elaborated that the choice to buy or not is up to the consumer, that the consumer has full control. Ingrid also felt that advertisers would not lie, but then amended her answer by declaring that "maybe" they do. So, while advertisements may be an exaggeration of the truth, she believed that "what they're telling you is pretty much true." Ingrid distinguished between those advertisements that were "genuine" and disingenuous. Again, the theme as to whether an advertisement is truthful or not seemed to be a point of confusion. Having the "right" information from family and friends would, according to Alicia, greatly determine whether or not she would buy an item whereas she would be less influenced by what the advertisement claimed. Additionally, George seemed confused about advertising; first, he stated that one cannot really trust anything advertised on television, but then went on to say that he could trust because "they're not going to totally make [it] up." Overall, he felt the system of advertising in consumer societies was "pretty fair" and a viable means of selling products.

James admitted that he is more easily swayed by car advertisements because "I love cars" but concluded that because he does not have the money to purchase a car, the advertisements are, therefore, of no influence. James also felt that advertising was fair and that it was up to the individual to take responsibility as to whether or not they believed the advertisement, that is, "if they're smart enough." Christopher also agreed that it was up to the consumer to determine whether or not he or she is swayed by advertisements and felt the onus was on the consumer to research a product before purchasing, as an antidote to false advertising. Again, there seemed to be some confusion in ascertaining the veracity of advertisements with regard to consumer responsibility.

Negative on Advertising

Some male participants found fault with advertisements. To begin with, Floyd thought that a large percentage of advertisers lie, but he then reworded his comment to say "just false information, maybe not lying." John believed that advertisements were an "unacceptable waste of time" and that advertisements with respect to food were particularly deceiving. He eventually concluded by taking exception with advertising as a whole, indicating that "it's kind of manipulating a lot of people. I guess targeting age groups where a lot of people haven't had the ability to mature and get out of the advertising cycle." John also felt that the billions spent on advertising could be put to better use toward countries that "have so little." Ted was so opposed to advertisements that he installed an "ad blocker" to screen out all advertisements from his computer. James zeroed in on men's health magazines and noted that half their content was made up of advertisements, which he described as a negative. He also objected to the content of the advertisements in that they were not in the best interest of the consumer and had more to do with selling the product than providing sound advice on how to become healthy. According to Christopher, advertisements override the consumer's better judgment: "It's saying, like, I can't decide for myself." He went on to say that he resented how advertisements are able to sway one into buying a particular product, that they have this degree of power over the consumer. George found advertisements "annoying" because of the subtle and overt pressure elicited from advertisements to spend money. He also talked about how advertisers use sexual content to sell their products and how they portray women as "stupid."

Few female participants objected to advertisements in any significant way. Sonja took exception with the skewed way in which advertisements are designed, that all people who use the advertised product will experience the same thing. Sara was less vocal and noted that a lot of products advertised seem to be so unnecessary. She believed that a lot of these advertisements are based on becoming a certain type of person, or having a certain image, rather than "just being yourself." Only Ingrid believed that advertisers deliberately manipulate and that the majority of people taken in are young people. As for the male participants, again only one male participant, Oscar, felt that corporations were manipulative, though not necessarily in a pejorative sense: "I'm not saying it's manipulative in a positive and I'm not saying it's manipulative in a negative way . . . Whatever is best for a specific company . . . they'll just try to manipulate you to buy."

Self-Worth and Advertising

A number of female participants (Susan, Pam, Nancy, and Ingrid) talked about how they compared themselves to models portrayed in advertisements. Some male participants (Oscar, Christopher, and Sam) also claimed to do this. A few of the female participants felt that advertisements led to feeling incomplete as a person. Nancy had trouble articulating how this incompleteness manifested except to say that while other people in their lives would tell them that they were "whole and should appreciate themselves," this was opposite to the media messages. Sara reiterated that "[Advertisements] all seem to say you're not complete without this kind of a product, so it's sort of a downer." Susan relayed that the effects of the portrayal of women in media, while somewhat negative, did not overly impact her: "It's not like I feel like my day is ruined from seeing that." Pam felt that the portrayal of people advertised in the media leads to desiring that look and lifestyle: "Advertisements for the clothing companies like Crew and stuff do influence you to be the kind of people that they put in their ads." Pam also suggested that advertising detracts from individuality because advertisers are trying to convince all of us to buy the same products, their products: "I would rather not see any advertising at all and just pick for myself what I want." Conversely, Judy declared that she felt good about herself, specifically her normal-sized weight, when viewing advertisements depicting obese women for weight-loss clinics.

The following narrative offers a more detailed look at what it means, at a personal level, to be impacted by media depictions of the "ideal" body. Ingrid's story reveals the harm incurred when engaged as a consumer adhering to a media-driven lifestyle and cultural norms.

Ingrid's Story: Despair and Media

Ingrid stated that she grew up in a poor family that eventually became "rich." She remembers longing for particular objects and then quickly casting them aside, accumulating a "basement full of toys." By the time she was seven, Ingrid remembered wanting to be like particular actresses and models because of their body type. As she grew into adolescence, these desires increased such that she became obsessed with the actress Jennifer Lopez because of her Latino look, one that was shared by members of her family, particularly her sister. She described that when comparing herself to Jennifer Lopez she would feel "really bad, really bad." While growing up, Ingrid was a plus-size body type and, as such, was criticized by her parents and sister for being too big. She was clear in laying blame for her negative self-image with the media, however, because she believed that her sister, in particular, was influenced by media and had adopted media standards of beauty:

[Watching media] made me feel gross . . . kind of outcast for not being that [ideal] size. You know you'd feel a little depressed inside because you're not . . . that desirable. You don't feel like you're pretty or . . . You just feel like you're that ogre I guess you could say. You stick out.

Ingrid said that one of the outcomes of having body dysphoria was the decision to wear "baggy clothes" so that "no one could see my figure." She stated that she tried to please her family and friends by wearing clothing that was considered to be "in," even wearing "skinny jeans" to the point of developing a rash on her legs. She noted that other acquaintances were also struggling with acceptance of their physical appearance. In particular, Ingrid recalled an incident in which her friend's sister committed suicide apparently because she felt physically inadequate. Ingrid shared that she had also attempted suicide on multiple occasions for the same reasons, that she felt deeply depressed about her physical appearance. When asked if she felt the media held some responsibility, she replied: "They hold a huge responsibility . . . If it wasn't for my sister getting into the media and then putting that on me, I wouldn't have even thought about [my physical appearance]. I never cared . . . I was more of a free spirit when I was a lot younger." Ingrid went on to say that she felt the media sexualized young girls and that it "has a lot of influence on children because they're like clay, you know you mold them . . . It's childhood [that] makes up the person and what you're doing is making them into really bad people."

Ingrid said that she eventually arrived at a point in which "I wear what I want [now]." She declared that she arrived at a decision to not follow the status quo: "I don't really go with what society [says], I usually go for what I like." She attributed her ability to express her individuality to an accepting group of friends, including a boyfriend. She described the feeling of individual expression as: "I was happy for once . . . wearing clothes . . . where people liked it and you felt good and so you were like 'Hooray.'" As a means of self-expression, Ingrid wished that she could have multiple piercings and tattoos, despite anticipated disapproval from her mother.

Ingrid stated that she is "annoyed" by advertisements, that many of them are false, but admitted that they still influence her to some degree. She said that she feels in control only "sometimes" when shopping and that "if I have spending money it's gone." Yet Ingrid was clear that she was not ambitious about striving to be wealthy as an adult and felt that money was not the answer to her happiness: "If you have [money] for the moment, it doesn't make you happy for a long span of time."

Despite feeling compelled to shop, Ingrid was quick to point out that she adhered to a number of values when shopping, including no animal testing, no child labor, or "anything that was made that harms anything else." She was very positive about the green movement and had done some volunteer work with one such organization. Ingrid was clear that she accepted the global environmental crisis as real: "We've done a lot of damage to this earth. People are so ignorant . . . they just reject this global warming . . . They can reject it for now but then they are going to damn themselves when it happens. That's my worst fear."

Summary: Media

About half of the participants expressed how important technology was to their day-to-day functioning, how it had come to be an extension of the self (Alicia), or a completion of the self (Ted, Pam, Joyce). Furthermore, technology was described as a means of establishing one's good standing socially. For Alicia, in particular, technological goods were regarded as a way of determining and expressing socio-economic status. Sara, Ingrid, and Nancy lamented the way technology, as an activity, seemed to detract from time spent on nonscreen endeavors. The participants talked about how texting and phoning was somewhat of an obsession, even in the face of family members' objections.

With respect to use of and exposure to media, many of the female participants (Joyce, Sara, Pam, Ingrid, and Nancy) said that they were bothered by their physical appearance, comparing themselves to media figures. Additionally, some male participants (George, Oscar, Christopher, and Tom) stated that their self-image had been compromised by media portrayals of men. These participants were of the mind that media watching had led to negative self-worth. Alicia, Jeff, and James also felt they were impacted by the behavior and values of media figures (characters on television shows), but in a different way, as they strived to emulate them. Further to this, Joyce, Sara, Susan, Alicia, Sonja, Nancy, and Tom looked to media as a kind of measuring stick with which to analyze and compare the quality of their relationships with family and friends.

Many of the participants (Tessa, Susan, Pam, Sara, Judy, Ted, and Christopher) indicated that advertisements were effective in getting them to consider and perhaps, even purchase, consumable goods. Susan, Ingrid, George, James, and Christopher, in particular, were conflicted about advertising, specifically its helpfulness, authenticity, coerciveness, and ability to persuade. The pervasiveness and pressure felt from advertisements were viewed in a negative context by some participants (John, Ted, James, Christopher, George, Sonja, Sara, Ingrid). At the same time, the participants talked about advertisements as "genuine" and felt it was the rare occasion when advertisers falsified information about products. Indeed, Susan believed that the forces of the free market would keep advertisers honest. Christopher felt that consumers were responsible for their individual purchases and that this had little to do with corporate manipulation. A number of female participants (Susan, Pam, Nancy, Ingrid, and Sara) and male participants (Oscar, Christopher, and Sam) felt that their self-worth was compromised by exposure to advertising of various genres. Furthermore, advertising was seen as detracting from individuality in that consumers were treated all the same and, ultimately, behaved in unison.

8

Primed to Consume

The findings from the "Deconstructing Consumerism" study suggest that consumer culture mediated by technology dictates, to a significant extent, consumer-oriented attitudes and behaviors of today's children and young people. As Barber noted, consumer culture is ubiquitous, omnipresent, addicting, and, hence, "totalizing" in its capacity to infiltrate the lives of its citizens. Furthermore, consumption is an aspect of culture that plays a significant role in the construction of contemporary identities. Specifically, consumer culture acts as a force that molds and shapes identity and accompanying lifestyles in sync with the role of a consumer. Coveted commodities are in constant flux and at the whim of marketers' economic agendas. The identities of children are similarly subject to continuous change as fads come and go, thus destabilizing the self so that conforming to such trends becomes a powerful means of appeasement. The participants in the study demonstrated, to a high degree, a "conforming persona" with respect to a buy-and-consume modality, media use, and a belief in consumerism as a viable lifestyle.

In contrast, some positive elements of understanding and resistance to consumerism were evident. A minority of participants considered themselves different from the status quo and believed that individuality was determined by the qualities we emulate, rather than strictly on appearances. A number of participants each *rejected* other aspects of consumerism such as "more is better" (Ted, Christopher), "being cool is a good thing" (George, Jeff, Christopher), "fads express who we are" (Sara, Susan, Ingrid, Nancy, Judy, Tessa), and "money leads to happiness" (Ingrid). Two participants (Sara and John) stood out as nonconformists because of their overall capacity to question consumerism and to seek fulfillment through alternative means. Considering the age of the participants, the data suggest hope for those who are able to mitigate the harms of consumer culture, perhaps not in its entirety, but enough to minimize some of the ill effects.

INSIDE THE CULTURE INDUSTRY

One of the themes that strongly emerged from the data was the sheer power of the process of consumption, the way in which the participants described being influenced to buy and acquire material possessions. They talked about how they felt compelled to acquire things for which they had no need. Capitalism, in the modern era, has steadily shifted from serving society's real needs to fomenting false needs. Ultimately, the market dictates in a top-down fashion. The participants recognized, to a degree, that they were buying commodities for which there was no discernible need. Central to this is the notion of desiring and the sense that one can never feel satiated, or fulfilled to satisfaction. There is an accompanying emptiness and frustration that goes hand in hand with desiring. The participants' lack of insight about why we seem to engage in a continuous stream of purchasing is reflective of the fact that acquiring objects of desire seems to make logical sense. The letdown afterward, the feelings of a hollow fleeting contentment, were somewhat confusing to the participants. This confusion is tied to feelings of dissatisfaction, feelings that seem to defy all logic, since commodities are touted as having the capacity to fulfill deep psychological and social needs. And when commodities fail to satisfy, the consumer often assumes the self to be somehow deficient.

The desiring of consumer culture is part of what Barber meant by the "ethos of infantalization," the way in which individuals regress and fall victim to market dictates about what it is that they need. It is in this regard that the participants rationalized unjustifiable consumerism to normalize a "shopaholic" lifestyle. Being impulsive about spending in the pursuit of more goods, and even feeling incomplete, is also part of Barber's infantalist ethos. When Nancy stated that "I always have to buy," she was expressing how the phenomenon of consuming had taken over many aspects of her life, that it was dominant. Bauman believed that the addiction to shop has associations with the freedom to *create* an identity. It is insecurity that drives the modern citizen to cling to objects that are tangible, even if unfulfilling in the long term. Hence, the quest for the desired identity becomes a full-time occupation.

Adorno warned about the culture industry's capacity to erode critical thinking and control the social-psychological process related to the wishes and desires of the ordinary citizen. It appears that the participants' behaviors with regard to consumption are just that—rote responses wielded by those benefiting the most from consumer capitalism. Indeed, the culture industry discourages reflective cognition and critical analysis, as Adorno noted, to ensure that mass-produced commodities remain enticing. It is important that we learn about the dehumanizing aspect of capitalism and begin to evaluate critically its impact on the self, society, and broader environment. Hence, what Marx referred to as "commodity fetishism" occurs, in which the social relationship to objects becomes more important than the use value of the object; in consumer culture this seems to be a primary condition. The participants showed such intense liking and longing for objects, while seemingly oblivious to their practical value, or lack thereof, for the sake of their symbolic value. Furthermore, it seems that material possessions come to be regarded as part of the extended self and thus have implications for self regard. Objects are often used to compensate for perceived personal inadequacies and so temporarily boost self-efficacy. This may explain why the participants described deep disappointment when the acquisition of an object was somehow thwarted and, ironically, disappointment once the object had been acquired.

In Chapter Seven, I described the participants as being "high," using an addiction metaphor because of the intense emotions associated with acquiring the desired object and the seeming endless appetite for material possessions. Again, I found a noted lack of insight among them. The feelings associated with acquiring were not analyzed; rather, they were normalized and treated, at least initially, before the reward of the purchase dissipates and the craving begins again, as positive experiences. There appeared to be a strong sense of denial about the illusory gains associated with the acquisition of commodities. Furthermore, receiving gifts was equated with a transfer of love; exchange of commodities was considered central to expressions of caring. The participants rationalized their need to "have" when acquiring objects of desire because the drive to possess is so salient, as Fromm noted. They talked about how important it was to shift from one object to another in order to satisfy their desires. It is the momentum of desiring that drives the consumer toward a state of heightened vigilance about choosing the "right" commodities to feel fulfilled. In consumer culture, this is an endless process, one that drives the cycle of craving and acquiring objects. Each commodity can be replaced by something even "better," so that cravings operate in a cyclical fashion. Rather than questioning this process, it becomes easier to find fault with oneself ("I don't really need this") or the desired object ("It's not really necessary").

The participants were able to articulate some of their feelings as they recalled acquiring objects that disappointed. However, they had little insight as to the cause of those feelings. There was an element of confusion as to why the coveted object could reap such little reward. Ted and Christopher stood out by their declaration of satisfaction with the amount of "stuff" owned, that they needed little else; this attitude is contrary to the cultural propaganda that desiring can only be appeased through more consuming. It is ironic that the quest for and purchase of commodities is oftentimes more rewarding than the object of desire itself—hence the noted expression, "buyer's regret."

Questioning the consumer system comes with great risk. There would be too much at stake because our lives are so inextricably connected to acquiring, consuming, and even selling (eBay) commodities—it would require rethinking one's values, beliefs, ambitions, identity, and social relationships. As Marcuse noted, "one-dimensional man" is incapable of ever knowing his true needs because they are not his own and are, instead, largely "administered" in a top-down fashion. Rejecting aspects of consumer culture is representative of a complex conversion of many factors, including self-esteem, identity, social status, and even religious or spiritual orientation. Furthermore, participation in consumer culture means conforming to the status quo. Since we favor in-groups over out-groups,[1] shopping, as a norm, comes to represent far more than a recreational pastime. As Joyce described when buying objects that others already had: "I feel like I'm part of something."

Consuming is a process that ties and reinforces social connections or relationships, as evidenced by the extent to which the participants received support from friends and family regarding consumption. It is a highly social activity that can unite individuals who might otherwise have little to converse about. Indeed, social conformity, or the process by which we are influenced by others, accounts for quite a large piece of consuming behaviors. Since consuming is both a societal norm (macro) and group norm (mezzo), the compulsion to participate (micro) is powerful. We only have to think back to the Asch experiment to recognize that the desire to fit in, even at the expense of one's integrity, overrides other behaviors. Commodities thus impart connectivity in terms of creating, maintaining, and changing relations among people. John's dialogue about being influenced by his friends to buy Nike Shocks is reminiscent of the Elliot and Leonard study in which children described their desire to be part of a brand community.

The heavy reliance on mothers' opinions and approval suggests that within family dynamics, women are seen as having expertise when it comes to buying. Mothers may wield more influence than fathers in this regard because the management of the household and care for children are still predominantly left to women. When their children grow into teenagers, mothers are still regarded as having the capability of choosing what is best to buy and wear. Hence, the process of shopping, acquiring, and seeking mothers' approval was perceived as a type of bonding, especially by the female participants. Mutual regard for commodities and a shared interest in acquiring such commodities is a way of connecting with others in consumer cultures. Another important aspect of the reliance on mothers is the way in which commodities have become symbols of love and affection.[2] At the same time, corporations wish to be perceived as purveyors of love through the sale of their products, as Ewen explained.

The whole notion of fads is a reflection of how corporations successfully market their goods in an ever-changing new style that works upon our insecurities about acceptance. Marketers steer the individual into recognizing and acknowledging the body and self as intrinsically flawed, inadequate, or at the very least, incomplete, thereby needing commodities for self-transformation. Maintaining or managing the self with a correct array of commodities becomes an ongoing, laborious process for shoppers evaluating, acquiring, and consuming. Fads are associated with social success and acceptance, being at the forefront of a changing world. By not adhering to fads, one runs the risk of social rejection and accompanying loss of attention. As Judy explained, "I want to look like those people with all those friends." We also saw how the participants showed great affinity with subcultures defined through fads and brands, as Stephen Miles discovered in his study of teenagers. In both cases, the participants were quick to adopt the "in" fads, rather than going off in a direction truly unique. It should be noted that receiving attention is one of the most powerful drives we have, and this plays a vital role in everything that we do. Indeed, Bloom states that "attention is the oxygen of the human soul . . . Without attention our immune system shuts down and brain cells in our hippocampus kill themselves off. So we all compete for a space in the eyes, minds, and hearts of others."[3]

The participants associated brands with an elevation of social success, social acceptance, and status in general. The brand, highly visible, is a safeguard from becoming a social outcast or experiencing incidences of rejection. Brand purchases are associated with positive attributes like confidence, just as they are advertised. Further to this, the purchaser seems to forge a bond between the brand label and his or her own sense of self. Barber stated that an individual's consuming persona is *the* dominant self in consumer capitalism. The visibility of the brand becomes a measuring stick with which to judge and know others. Indeed, brands are a prominent way of demonstrating compliance, especially in cultures obsessed with appearances. The results from the study, similar to those found by Elliot and Leonard, and sociologist Jane Pilcher,[4] all point to the fact that children, from younger to older, use branded fashion items as a way to judge others and establish their own identity "markers." As Dittmar found, our physical presentation, including fashion style, in large part determines how we are judged, and which attributes we are believed to possess.[5] Adorno noted how conformity to fashion styles is a requirement for survival in the culture industry based on this very notion of judgment. The other important aspect of brands is the way in which they are incorporated with self-concepts or, as Chaplin and John described, "self-brand connections."[6] In other words, the brand is attributed with characteristics that we wish to integrate with our perception of the self.

Female participants in the study were more adamant about the importance of brands than males, possibly because images associated with femininity remain more prominent than those of the masculine male. This concurs with what sociologist Rachel Russell and professor of work and organizational studies Melissa Tyler found in their research, namely, that young girls define their femininity primarily through their role as consumers, taking their cue from marketers as to the feminine ideal.[7] Additionally, socialization is strengthened by group dynamics: conformity is socially reinforced, while deviation from the norm can lead to exclusion or banishment. The male participants, not surprisingly, were more apt to acknowledge the importance of brands when it came to sports and technology and less so with clothing, though it was not entirely absent. Brands have been introduced in consumer culture as necessary if one wishes to maintain a level of status deemed to be socially and psychologically desirable. It is also important to note that because the participants have grown up with brand culture from birth, it likely feels quite natural to imbibe brands of all kinds. Since brands are less strongly associated with the quality of products they represent, but are instead affiliated with deep symbolic meaning and sentiments as well as emotional attachments, it is little wonder that their appeal to youth is so powerful.

The defiance expressed from both male and female participants concerning brand influence seemed more like a reaction to feeling a loss of individuality than rebelliousness against external pressures or the system of capitalism itself. The conflicted emotions they expressed about brands, wanting to be trendy but at the same time wanting to be true to the self, appear to be an important aspect of the branding phenomenon for some. Rejecting brands that do not capture one's personal style is a form of nonconformity; specifically, social psychologists Edward Deci and Richard Ryan refer to this as a construct that is not in agreement with the inner self.[8]

Despite the forces of consuming so characteristic of their culture, four of the participants (Tom, John, Sara, and Sonja) were able to articulate their dissatisfaction with the lifestyle, indicating that their level of well-being was not tied to consumption. It is not clear whether they were motivated more by a desire to not conform or whether they simply recognized the limited fulfillment of coveted objects. Sonja captured it best when she described the relief that "*not* wanting" brought. All four participants seemed to recognize the futility of always wanting more, that it could never lead to high levels of contentment. It should be noted that none of these individuals stood out from the others in an obvious way other than their ability to critically evaluate their experiences.

Being perceived as cool, wearing the right brand, following the fads, was seen as elevating social status and increasing the likelihood of acceptance. Cool promotes one to a position envied by others; this is deemed to be an achievement in consumer culture. Cool is not defined in terms of personality or character traits but in terms of what one possesses (the correct array of commodities), according to the participants. The possessions deemed to enhance cool are not necessary for survival; rather, they are all superfluous; again, reflecting the notion of false needs that Barber described. Marketers have constructed cool to be that which personifies the quintessential consumer—someone who has it "all." In other words, cool is a function of superficial appearances. As with wearing the right brand, being cool is associated with a feeling of confidence that can only be found in the objects one possesses and the confidence that supposedly brings. It seems, therefore, that material goods are anthropomorphized and endowed with the emotions associated with success, intimately extending from the self.

Craving the lifestyle, look, and characteristics of a celebrity suggests that the participants feel a deficit in their lives and have become dissatisfied, all the while fantasizing about "what can be." This deficit could reference physical appearance, financial status, fame, and success (however defined) in general, all of which reverberate with identity construction. Hence, we may attempt to imitate the personality and character of the celebrity as a means of aligning with his or her identity. Additionally, wishing for a celebrity life has become far more common than in the past and is an indicator of narcissistic trends in young people, as noted by Twenge and Campbell. The denigration of the "poorly commodified" self is a powerful tactic that marketers use to keep one forever desiring a makeover—what better than to be rich, famous, and beautiful?

Sara and John were the only participants who talked in depth about breaking away from consumer culture, rejecting a life tied to the ups and downs of acquiring commodities, rejecting the norms and finding their own niche. Sara communicated that she had an epiphany about the shallowness of consumer culture while still in high school. John contemplated the futility of materialism and the harm that consuming does to the planet in later high school and early days of university. It is in this sense, in the ability to assert oneself in social interactions and shape one's immediate experiences, that Sara and John demonstrated individual agency. They defied the strata of the surrounding culture in an effort to express individuality, true to form and, on some level, contrary to the status quo. In a more minor way, Jeff also expressed dissatisfaction with the endless spending that consumerism demands.

IDENTITY

Despite wishing to be cool, having the latest brand, and dressing according to the latest fad, the participants seemed to believe that, for the most part, they were true to themselves. They vehemently defended their individuality, certain of their uniqueness and autonomy. They did not equate consuming with a surrender of individuality; even if they did, it was probably far too threatening to entertain at a conscious level. In working on their appearances, young people must negotiate the competing demands of forging an identity to fit in and be accepted, but at the same time wishing to stand out as an individual. Horkheimer, Adorno, Marcuse, and Barber all stated that the "captains" (to borrow a term from Ewen) of consumer culture must convince us of our uniqueness as a means of keeping mass consumption alive. Indeed, individuation, as well as the the belief we are free to choose commodities on demand, is central to the workings of the culture industry. In other words, it involves selecting a "unique" configuration of mass-produced commodities to express our "unique" individuality. Being in control is tied to notions of being true to oneself, being an individual, not being pulled and swayed by advertisements. Many of the participants were adamant that their decisions around consuming were methodically and carefully calculated, that they were in control and wilfully choosing. Adorno characterized the notion of "informational" advertising as an attempt to manipulate potential buyers by having them believe they are in control of their decisions. The participants showed a degree of naiveté by believing that they were immune from advertisements as a result of engaging in research. Cialdini's investigation of the "six weapons of influence" clearly demonstrates that marketers use effective and relatively simple tools to persuade us to buy their products. He wisely cautioned that unless we understand and recognize persuasion tactics, it is highly likely to experience manipulation by those applying the "influence principles."

For the most part, the participants felt that individuality is largely achieved or represented through appearance, rather than through attitudes and behaviors. Specifically, they felt that hairstyle, clothes, eye glasses, and tattoos (to name a few) were all ways to distinguish the self. What was notably absent from the majority of participants' responses was the means by which personality and values contribute to one's uniqueness. Consistent with Giddens's theory, the participants seemed to experience identity as a construct that is closely aligned to the body, likely because of the high degree of importance placed upon the physical in consumer cultures. According to professors Jennifer Maguire and Kim Stanway, attention to appearances is inseparable from the process of identity production in modernity and begins to take on the characteristics of a "do-it-yourself project."[9] In consumer cultures one develops a tacit (and sometimes verbalized) understanding that the body, and hence the self, is flawed, inadequate, or at least incomplete. Maintaining the body has become intimately tied to corporate agendas in which the latest corporeal fads and fashions dictate identity and physical construction (desirable body types to go with the wardrobe). Of significance is the fact that the participants seemed confused as to how their identity manifested and which components of their lives shaped identity. Indeed, one of the greatest challenges to identity formation within modernity is keeping pace with the rapidly changing images, sound bites, and styles of self-expression.[10] The development of identity means doing the work required to "pull the self together" by recognizing areas for transformation and the practices necessary to maintain the body as if it was a commodity. Sociologist Zygmunt Bauman suggests that confusion around identity occurs in consumer cultures because of our attempts to escape a feeling of insecurity that goes hand in hand with a strong identification with objects—thus, leaving the self fragile, vulnerable, and in constant flux. It would appear that consumer culture requires a continuous reinventing of the self as the desired standard is never stationary. This may explain why the participants felt no qualms about keeping up with changing fads. They viewed keeping up with fads as both an opportunity and pressure for reconfiguring their identity. Keeping up with fads was a more enjoyable task for the males. Females, on the other hand, described feeling plagued by the media beauty myth, which is substantiated by many other researchers.[11] Additionally, the participants, though not articulating it as such, clearly felt a pressure to establish an identity that was "current," to keep ahead of the fads, to stay cool. As media researcher Hillevi Ganetz noted, children have never been under such scrutiny when it comes to identity formation—shopping for the "right" look has become a full-time occupation.[12]

Sara and Tessa both declared that imagination, self-expression, and character define individuality, not possessions. In this regard, both these women stood out from the others in their ability to articulate and understand that identity comprises more than physicality. However, it is important to note that Tessa, at various points during her interview, admitted that she was strongly influenced by the media, that media characters helped define her identity. As she described it, "Every step of my life I've wanted to be like someone from the media." Sara, on the other hand, consistently articulated her ability to exercise individual agency through creative expression and determinism. She stated that she was not interested so much in amassing commodities as she was in acquiring meaningful experiences through travel or sailing. Sara seemed to be true to her own convictions, having engaged in some form of critical analysis of the dominant culture. It is also significant that Sara perused the media in an attempt to find her niche, and eventually, came to the conclusion that she was different, choosing to be a nonconformist. George, Jeff, and Christopher articulated that once they left high school there was less pressure to define their identity based on others' expectations or to uphold cool. It is possible that their capacity to reject restricting beliefs, norms, and customs was gained through maturation and a different environment (university versus high school). It is also noteworthy that a number of participants, including females, stated that they were not able to array themselves in the latest fashion due to limited funds.

Both males and females justified conformity as a bonding process with others, as a means of sharing experiences, not as a detraction from autonomy. Both descriptive norms (how to act) and injunctive norms (rules or beliefs), ubiquitously present in media, had an impact on the participants. For example, when George talked about desiring an athletic persona, this was an example of a descriptive norm, related to what Pollack described as the "boy code." Christopher never felt confident enough to play music that was not considered cool, an example of an injunctive norm. Adorno observed that the "real" world is attributed to the realm of movies, television, and other forms of media. This was evident for Alicia, who attempted to model her life after a character on a television show. At the same time, everyone was somewhat disturbed by the level of conformity surrounding them, keen to cite examples that demonstrated a break from the status quo. Many of these examples had to do with the style of one's hair or clothing; putting such emphasis on outward appearance to appear unique or distinct can, in actuality, reflect conformist convictions. In consumer cultures, conformity includes adopting a persona different from oneself and that which reflects the "ideal" lifestyle as defined by marketers. Hence, there is a constant pressure to conform, to fit in and adopt the behaviors of the norm. This poses a dilemma for the individual who seeks to maintain autonomy. We force ourselves to identify with the "other" so that conformity is seamlessly achieved, as though a normal process of maturation. Yet conformity provides a false sense of individualism, ironically offering protection from the fear of becoming invisible. As Adorno and Horkheimer theorized, not to conform is to be rendered powerless on many levels, including physical, emotional, even spiritual. Thus, breaking free comes at a heavy price. Susan's exclamation that conformity unifies and brings people together speaks to what Marcuse meant by social control in capitalist cultures. As capitalism dictates our needs and wants, it simultaneously wields power over the very minutia of our lives.

The fear of not fitting in was palpable for the participants. They appeared to have some recognition at a conscious level that diversity or dissonance, if executed in the wrong way, was risky. This may explain why fads were exonerated, justified, and framed in a positive light as though they inherently magnify self-esteem. Sonja spoke about taking cues from magazines in a positive light, not unlike the teen girls in sociologist Dawn Currie's 1999 study on youths' interpretations of "teenzines."[13] In both cases, the teens identified strongly with stereotypic depictions, despite their inherent sexism and emphasis on the body. Confusing the latest fad with self-expression is a ploy used by marketers over and over—it is that which keeps the culture industry alive. Adorno suggested that the identification with mass-produced products negates critical thinking and imagination. Individuals come to believe that with every new object there will be an exciting new experience, forgetting the banality associated with the acquisition of objects. The participants were quick to say that new technology, new clothing styles, new sports equipment, and so on all elevated their sense of self. They did not seem to recognize the intrinsic falsity, the buying and selling of their very identities.

Being free of fad influences seemed less a genuine desire to rebel from and reject the culture industry, and more about limited funds. For some of the participants, monetary constraints may have led them to rationalize that branded goods and fads were not that important. At the same time, the process of breaking from the constraints of consumer culture is fraught with risk, anxiety, and opportunities for personal failure. There is also the risk that a longing to express *genuine* individuality is nothing more than the reinvention of the self based on a celebrity blueprint, as Niedzviecki pointed out. Indeed, the majority of the participants admitted to adopting some aspect of the look of a celebrity and desiring to become someone even *more* famous and successful. The vast majority of participants shared very little that seemed to be truly creative about their lives, somewhat consistent with the findings by Hee Kim that children's capacity for creativity is in decline.

The majority of the participants were frank in declaring that they had few values, or weakly formed values, related to the process of consumption, such as refraining from purchasing products that had been animal tested, made by child labor, or were deemed harmful to the environment. Since values are intimately tied to identity, it is possible that a lack of values in the face of consuming is yet another sign of how we are swallowed whole when up against the tide of consumer culture. This "lack-of-values predicament" had to be rationalized in some way, and often was, by pointing to a lack of spending money. Only a few participants wished to appear to be cognizant and concerned about the importance of the environment, to express an identity of caring in this regard. When questioned more extensively on the topic of climate change and environmental devastation as a result of consuming, most of the participants demonstrated a high degree of narcissism. For example, Judy felt that because global warming did not impact her directly it was likely not a reality. Twenge and Campbell's research on the rise of narcissism, particularly among today's youth, may explain the data on values.

Convictions that one is not bound to others, as well as feelings of entitlement, are both symptoms of narcissism. Many of the participants described their "bottom line" as being motivated solely by money. They felt somewhat appeased by insisting that having access to greater funds would result in a demonstrable concern for the environment. Yet, when it came to talking about environmental issues specifically, they provided all sorts of justifications to deny the existence of climate change. Furthermore, some of the participants blatantly stated that they had little concern about the issue—that they should care—but could not bring themselves to do so. Indeed, consumerism fosters a self-indulgence and encouragement of materialistic and superficial lifestyles, as evident in the participants' answers. As a caveat, most of them were new to the idea of articulating their values, which may have significance for the ways in which they answered questions on this topic. They may also have been intimidated by the specter of, or felt incapable of, dramatic transformation in their consumptive habits.

Considering the criticality of issues such as global warming and unfair labor practices in the developing world and China, it is particularly confounding that the participants held such little concern. They also denied that the global environmental crisis is real and has relevance for their lives today. Again, these types of attitudes are fostered not only out of ignorance about the facts, but likely because of a narcissistic desire to see the world as fitting with our personal agendas. It appears that relating to an "Other" in the face of desiring is a difficult task, challenging the very core of one's identity, especially when identity has become an extension of the things we own. Social psychologist Michael Billig regards the routines of consumer capitalism as practices that require a form of repression; as disconcerting thoughts about developing world labor practices, for example, enter our consciousness, we must find a way to distance ourselves from connecting them with our commodities and, thus, with our sense of self.[14] It was heartening to note that many of the participants stated that if confronted with two items of the same price, they would select the "green-friendly" commodity. So, on some level, participants articulated a sense of responsibility, possibly so as not to appear or feel hypocritical. This is what Barber referred to as a conflicted "sense of liberty" in which one is torn between satisfying one's conscience and living out the "good" life. Indeed, on some level, the participants were frightened about the impending doom of the planet, but somehow they were not able to internalize responsibility for this possibility. Not all of them showed evidence of narcissistic personality traits; three (Oscar, Tom, and Pam) could identify with the global environmental crisis to the degree that they felt implicated. It is also significant to note that "green consumerism" has become quite popular—participating as a responsible consumer and abiding by such values is no longer about taking a nonconformist stance. Ironically, buying eco-friendly products has appeased the average buyer into believing that the global environmental crisis can be mitigated.[15] It is not clear why some participants, and not others, accepted personal responsibility to the extent that John, for example, wished to devote his entire career to the green movement.

Identity in consumer cultures is closely tied to monetary worth based on standards dictated by the market. Indeed, much of self-esteem is evaluated on the basis of monetary and subsequent material success. The participants' yearning for a middle-class or upper-middle-class future was an aspiration that the majority shared, seemingly oblivious to all that such lifestyles entail. Not surprisingly, the males were far more confident about their monetary future than the females, likely as a result of the fact that men have greater earning power than women. Additionally, there is a societal expectation that men, more than women, should provide the bulk of earnings for the family. Hence, the male participants were able to imagine themselves

achieving an upper-middle-class status, whereas the female participants could not.

Marcuse recognized the drive for money perpetuates conformity and
is binding to a way of life that restricts freedom of mind. Yet the participants seemed conflicted about "more is not better," somehow perceiving
this is true, but at the same time wanting to imagine their future with
above-the-norm material wealth. At some level, they felt it was right not
to place too much emphasis on money, yet at the same time, they craved
all that financial success brings. Like the findings from Twenge and
Campbell's research in which children cited "being rich" as one of their
top ambitions, some of the participants concurred, demonstrating an element of narcissism or sense of entitlement. Additionally, having unrealistic goals about their salaries as working individuals was somewhat
consistent with the Charles Schwab 2011 survey on U.S. teens who expect to earn three times the national household average.[16] Still, four participants (Tom, John, Sonja, and Ingrid) felt that they could build their
lives and be satisfied without having to hanker after material goods.
Ingrid, in particular, stated that the need for money had little to do with
her happiness; rather, it was relationships with others that gave her joy.

MEDIA

The participants described their lives as intimately connected to media. The use of media and its influence did not appear to be well understood, likely because of its ubiquity, familiarity, and taken-for-granted
presence. Indeed, all of the participants had grown up with unprecedented media presence which possibly limited their capacity for deep
reflection in this regard. Additionally, in their development as children,
the participants were surrounded by an object world of technology and
because of this may have experienced a loss of emotional intimacy, as
Turkle described. At some level, media have come to replace aspects of
community and family. Never before has it been possible to get in touch
with so many people over so much distance in such a rapid manner.
The threshold between the public and private space has never been so
low. This explains the fondness that the participants exuded as they
talked about their media experiences, attributing technology with the
power to connect. Yet often, "intimacy" of the type established through
technology is, paradoxically, always at arm's length, illusory, never tangible enough to make for "real" experiences. And as Horkheimer and
Adorno noted, the world mediated through technology begins to take
on a "real" experience; the outside world comes to be seen as a continuation of that presented on the movie screen, television screen, or computer screen. This explains the intense identification the participants

showed with media figures, whether real or not, including celebrities, actors, musicians, and sports stars, cartoon characters, and so on. Reality television feeds on this illusion and, as a result, has become wildly popular—the audience begins to see themselves as an active part of the experience.

The participants were all very familiar with popular culture and adept at using media's tools—smart phones, computers, DVRs, iPads, iPods—which the majority exalted. It appeared that technology was a somewhat seamless extension of the self, forming a basis of self-image. Owning and manipulating an "intelligent" object was regarded as evidence of a level of superiority. The participants' descriptions of what it felt like to either lose technology, or face deprivation through other means, revealed a sense of desperation and great loss accompanied by fear. For some of them, technology was also considered a marker of status, thus making it extremely attractive to own the latest gadgets. Ownership of technological goods, like luxury items, has become a marker of success both financially and socially. It is interesting that as students with limited funds, the participants felt that technology was indispensable and a top priority for purchase. Here again, branding plays a role—the corporate name with any given piece of technology is significant, and more than just for appearance's sake. Owning an Apple iPhone, for example, induces a sense of belonging in the "Apple community," being a member of the fast track.

Aptitude with technology was considered more than just an acquired skill; rather, it was seen as fundamental knowledge and a lifeline with which to access or navigate. All of the participants understood this and while they wished to be perceived in control, their dependency was evident. For example, some of them fondly remembered their sudden rise in popularity upon acquiring an iPhone or iPad and how powerful this reinforcement felt. At the same time, anxiety is part of the new connectivity, though rarely acknowledged as part of the communication revolution—falling "behind" is representative of failure. In our obsession with technological media, we repeat one-way communication with such frequency that unmediated relationships become foreign and, worse, difficult to manage. The use of technology instills a feeling of omnipotence that undermines ordinary give-and-take patterns of relating. Ultimately, behind the compulsion to derive satisfaction from virtual experiences is a longing for fulfillment and acceptance that is not hinged on technology. This was recognized by some of the participants who lamented losses due to technology. For example, Sara described that life before technology was meaningful, that she had been satisfied with playing outdoors with friends until she became fascinated with video games. Ingrid regretted the time she had spent on the computer, missing important moments with her family as a result.

Despite knowing that their lives will never mirror those of celebrities, many of the participants still longed for a chance to be like one. Why does the celebrity seemingly embody all that we desire? In a consumer culture, we are forever faced with an inadequate self in need of more—more money, more things, and more physical beauty, all of which are embodied in the celebrity. The celebrity has become a branded commodity, a cultural product, epitomizing the "successful" citizen-consumer, one who has achieved, even excelled, beyond the cultural ideal. Because celebrities are highly visible in the media, it is no surprise that many of the participants were seduced by images of their lifestyles. The culture industry keeps us entertained with the celebrity in the forefront as a means of defusing the latent dissatisfaction from that part of the self that recognizes we have become objectified. Consumer culture "rewards" those who conform to whatever images are being marketed. The self is thus perpetually unstable, vigilant in its quest for a perfection that is not attainable and in constant need of a makeover. Sociologist Sharon Boden also found in her study that children identify with the celebrity (both entertainment and sports celebrities) in the same way they would with a brand, becoming so enmeshed with celebrity worship as to reconfigure their identity. Like the participants in the Deconstructing Consumerism study, Boden's participants (though much younger) were skilled at interpreting modes of fashion as a means of communication about their personality.[17] While the participants in my study showed a degree of awareness that media can have a negative effect on the self, this was downplayed and seen as that which could easily be mitigated.

Many of the participants felt that their self-regard had been compromised by media. The story of Ingrid speaks loudly to this phenomenon. None of the other participants interviewed made any significant mention of the ways in which girls are sexualized in the media. Like the pressure to conform to a buy-and-consume modality, the 24/7 presence of media with its depiction of the "perfectly" sculpted human being was felt as an enormous pressure by both male and female participants. This again relates to Pollack's "boy code" and the beauty myth that haunts girls and women alike. Furthermore, the desire to emulate media characters shows the extent to which identity formation is often dictated by marketers. While four of the women (Sara, Susan, Ingrid, and Nancy) felt they were free of fad influence and dressed according to their own choosing, all of them admitted to having their self-worth minimized by media. Their pull in two directions demonstrates how confusing a process it is to establish autonomy in consumer culture. Rejecting consumer culture is a complex, nuanced road—it takes a level of maturity, insight, and courage to question one's culture and refuse participation.

Advertising, a powerful facet of media, also contributes to feelings of inadequacy, or as one participant noted, being "incomplete." The ubiquity and power of advertising as a means of getting people to do what marketers map out were only partially understood by the participants. There is a desire to believe that we are in control, that advertisements have not gotten the better of us, and that at worst, they are simply an inconvenience of the modern world. The participants showed a certain degree of naïveté about the intent of advertisements and their ability to side-step advertising influence. Furthermore, there was little awareness of neuro-marketing and how corporations are able to manipulate at the subconscious level despite how prevalent such practices are. This became evident when analyzing answers to the interview question: "Can you describe a time when you felt persuaded by media to be a certain type of person, or to look a certain way?" The participants generally mimicked the attitude that marketers wish us to assume, namely, that advertisements are informative, truthful representations of reality and serve a useful purpose. Understanding that advertisements themselves have the power to dictate the type of person one should be is an important insight that few of them grasped.

No doubt, resisting the culture industry is a monumental task, one that requires more than just knowing. It requires a vigilance and commitment to the autonomous self, to make and act on decisions as a free moral agent that few seem capable of internalizing, let alone desire. While some of the participants agreed that they were influenced by advertisements to some degree, they in no way felt victimized or believed that they were being coerced. Any reference to media persuasion was given a far more innocent context and generally dismissed with little concern. None of them realized the extent to which advertisers went full bore in their targeting of children, particularly at the time when they were born. It is interesting that several of the participants generally felt that the consumer was, in large part, responsible for any sway by advertisements. This may be due to the fact that they wished to be viewed as in control—oblivious to the harms caused by advertising. The fact that they had grown up during the largest advertising campaign in human history would make dissenting that much more difficult. In other words, advertisements were familiar, part of the popular culture, and, therefore, unassuming in a sense. While some participants felt that the media presented images to strive for, they were reticent to accept they could be deceived. Part of the research question was to determine whether or not young people are aware of market manipulation, and it appears they are not to any great degree. Adorno believed that most of society, once under the spell of the culture industry, has little capacity for critical thinking and this was true for many of the participants.

For the majority, media was the backdrop that facilitated peer and family communication. A few were aware that media tends to undermine the protective role of adults, sidestepping them altogether, to form a tight bond with children. Through a process of reflection, Alicia came to realize media was largely responsible for the pejorative views that she held of her parents. She also believed that media was, in large part, to blame for her "rebellious" behavior. However puerile or ridiculous their favorite television programs, the participants saw benefit, enjoying the commonality they had with others who viewed the same programs. Thus, failure to participate in key aspects of popular culture potentially leads to isolation and social abandonment. It leaves one bereft of the details concerning the "stories" of popular culture, trivial as they may be. Keeping abreast of popular culture becomes almost a requirement, an acquiescence that appears to be self-motivated.

APPLICATION OF THE RESULTS AND
PREVIOUS RESEARCH

The results from the Deconstructing Consumerism study provide some insight as to why Schor's 2004 study so strongly indicated that consumerism has a negative effect on physical and psychological health. Based on the participants' statements, it appears that relatively high consumer involvement is associated with a pervasive dissatisfaction, shallowness, and negative comparison. This could explain why high consumer involvement leads to depression, anxiety, and low self-esteem, as Schor found. For example, chronic dissatisfaction can lead to anxious and depressive states, as can feelings of inadequacy. The denigration of the self is a common experience in consumer culture, one that can undermine positive psychological states, as Kilbourne discussed. Furthermore, the participants in the study were short on principles when it came to consuming, which could also enhance negative self-image, leading to anxiety and depression. Finally, consuming was so prominent in the lives of the participants that other more beneficial activities and behaviors may have had little opportunity to offset negative emotive states. This predicament seems to hold true for the children that Schor surveyed. It is important to note that in her study there were no significant differences between males and females, a general finding of this study as well, with the exception of fad pressure, which was reported more acutely by females. It appears that fashion may still be more important to females than males due to sex-role orientation around standardized views of femininity.

When compared to studies by Kasser and Ryan, this research also suggests that individuals high in extrinsic materialistic values, which many of the participants demonstrated, may lead to a detraction of well-being. For example, Ingrid, who shared her suicide attempts, stated that focus on media and desire for a particular look greatly contributed to her negative self-image and feelings of worthlessness.

IMPLICATIONS OF THE RESULTS

The results here suggest that children in consumer cultures face insurmountable odds about how to fulfill the self, establish an identity centered on contentment, and express their creativity. Keeping in mind that the intent of the study was not to establish that consumer culture is harmful to children, I have presented numerous details as to *how* consumer culture imposes on children in the way that it does and why they may feel anxious or depressed or have unfulfilling relationships. We have seen, for example, how branding and attending to fads is a pressure, how desiring the life of a celebrity can be disappointing, and how the endless cycle of desiring or consuming leads to a general lack of fulfillment. We also have a better understanding as to why children conform to cultural standards that detract from their well-being and believe in consumerism as a viable way of life. Finally, we have further evidence that young people, while acknowledging that consumerism is harmful, have little motivation to change their consumptive habits.

Of great importance in understanding the effects of consumer culture with respect to children is "an emerging science, which integrates genetics, epigenetic, neuroscience and developmental science . . . that will *transform* our knowledge of early development" (italics added).[18] It is the environments of childhood that are critically important with regard to brain development and outcomes later in life. As previously stated, it is also becoming clear that more of our daily activities, thoughts and assessments, beliefs and behaviors, throughout life, are directed by subconscious processes of the brain—largely structured by childhood experiences.[19] The deeply embedded neural connections of childhood contribute to worldviews that are resistant to change.[20] Marketers, having recognized the many opportunities (present and future) that childhood represents, are using various tactics to stimulate children's subconscious desires, fomenting cravings for whatever is being marketed. This then raises a moral dilemma as to whether or not advertising to children is ever, as often argued, just an engagement in the articulation of free will. Adults have some capacity to analyze their thoughts, feelings, and behaviors, to uncover subconscious motivations in a way that children cannot—their brains are simply underdeveloped. Thus, the subconscious clearly plays a significant role in all activities associated with consuming and needs to be carefully considered in future research, both in terms of methodology and analysis, particularly as it relates to decision making, likes, dislikes, and desiring. The present study was no exception. For example, it seemed evident that subconscious maneuverings contributed to some of the ambivalence that the participants expressed about advertising and their ability to resist persuasion. The strong emotions associated with buying and "not getting" are likely driven by experiences stored in subconscious memories. Furthermore, seeking a cool persona, celebrity emulation, adoption of fads, and conforming to the status quo by attuning to media all imply elements of subconscious processes associated with social acceptance and the desire to be liked. Revealing an individual's subconscious motivations is an involved process, one that would require an in-depth analysis of attitudes and beliefs as an adult *and* childhood experiences.

WHAT CAN BE DONE FOR CHILDREN?

The battle for children's rights can take on many forms, the most prominent first step being a nation-wide ban on advertising to children. This action, which needs to be implemented at a public policy level, one backed by governmental law, would be a significant start in protecting children from corporate predators. Bans have been recognized and implemented in Sweden, Norway, Finland, and the province of Quebec in Canada. A number of European countries have restricted junk-food marketing, banned advertisements for toys between 7 a.m. and 10 p.m., and banned advertising of any kind within five minutes of a children's program on television.[21] It is clear that without government intervention in the form of policies, regulatory bodies, and laws to enforce certain measures, marketing to children will continue on its current accelerating path. Remarkably, since 2004—a watershed year in the recognition of harms sustained by children—there have been no federal laws passed in the United States or Canada that restrict corporations in their marketing campaigns. The commercialization of childhood has been largely absent from government's agenda.

Efforts to implement regulatory measures, while valuable, will simply not be enough to stave off the ill effects of consumerism. In order to fully understand the problem of consumer culture and the ways it has dominated the lives of children, we must consider the larger context of global capitalism. The free market and neoclassical economics are ideologically preeminent, yet structurally (and theoretically) un-sound and increasingly destructive.[22] The lack of regulation concern-ing the child consumer is arguably a result of the same political forces driving the lack of regulation of global finance, global warming, and rising income inequality. For example, anthropogenic climate disrup-tion (climate change caused by humans) poses a significant threat to the planet and all of its inhabitants—many believe a global systems failure will occur.[23] In Naomi Klein's latest book *This Changes Everything: Capitalism vs. The Climate*, she made it clear that the profit-seeking drive of modern capitalism can only be sustained at great peril to the planet's ecosystems.[24] Modern capitalism is, in many respects, a bro-ken system in its unregulated and unfettered state, depleting resources at an alarming rate. Yet, after years of promoting free-market ideology, plutocrats have successfully convinced government that they must give corporations a carte blanche, even at the expense of public health and well-being. Discourse about democracy is inextricably linked to that of capitalism and thus discourages prudent examination. Klein puts it that "changing the earth's climate in ways that will be chaotic and disastrous is easier to accept than the prospect of changing the fundamental, growth-based, profit-seeking logic of capitalism."[25]

Hence, the child consumerism "problem" is another symptom of a failing global economic system—unsolvable, unless underlying causes are addressed. According to journalist and politician Chrystia Freeland, democracies have become increasingly influenced and controlled by corporate plutocrats and oligarchs at the peril of all other earthly in-habitants.[26] This is in sync with Wolin's theory of how inverted totali-tarianism characterizes U.S. politics. Some activists believe, as does Chris Hedges, a Pulitzer Prize–winning writer, that despite all the ef-fort on behalf of social justice, the battle has been lost—all that is left as a measure of resistance is open revolt against the establishment.[27] Paul Hawken argues that the only way to manage social change will be through the "intermingling," of the millions of social justice and envi-ronmental groups, worldwide, as a unified force.[28] Regardless, in the global context, children *in* consumerism might be considered a modern version of canaries *in* the coal mine. This makes any discussion about consumerism and children not only highly relevant but extremely divi-sive. Indeed, even the middle and lower classes are reticent to criticize capitalism in any form, lest it be viewed as heretical thinking.

FUTURE CITIZENS?

A puppet is free as long as he loves his strings.[29]

—Sam Harris

The commodification process in consumer capitalism is more than just repressive in its endless promotion of the same message repackaged. It is more than just an affront to one's aesthetic sense and loss of individuality. At the time they were writing, Horkheimer and Adorno believed we had reached a point of voluntary participation in the culture industry, fully aware of its insidious effects. They made it clear that people are not dupes per se, but somehow knowingly contribute to their unsatisfactory condition. But what of children, those who have known nothing but the realities of the culture industry from birth? And what then of adults whose childhoods have been steeped in consumerism? We must remember that the authority of the family shifted to industry, from the parents to the advertisers who claimed to have the best understanding of the needs of children, as Ewen pointed out. It seems unlikely that children, even grown-up children, perceive the mendacity, manipulation, and control that surround them. It is certainly possible to develop critical thinking capacities and attain a level of freedom, but as we have heard from the participants, it is the rare individual who is able to separate himself from the culture, to preserve a strong sense of autonomy.

The culture industry has gone beyond the imagining of Horkheimer and Adorno to the extent that it has targeted children. The developing brain has become its new territory. Jerry Mander, activist and media critic, coined the term "privatization of consciousness," meaning that media have now infiltrated to the core of our thought processes, that there is nowhere to escape from the billion-dollar campaign to capture our brain waves: "The combination of television and astronomical advertising spending has effectively reshaped the consciousness of the United States and the entire planet: our self-image, the way we aspire to live, our habits, our thoughts, our references, desires, memories."[30] There is no need to hide the deceit when it cannot be detected. The ultimate success of the culture industry is to create citizens oblivious to its molding capacities and, instead, have them believe they have arrived on their own merit as an expression of their "creativity." Wolin's theory about inverted totalitarianism seems to hold true—corporations are in large part ruling our lives at an intimate level, not just inside our homes, but also penetrating our very being, our identity.

The reification of culture is generated through corporations, those who endlessly market culture as a commodity. The participants in this study, while believing that corporations seem to "get" their age group, perceive it in the most benign and innocent way. They had little to no recognition that corporations strongly influence the way they dress, the technology they use, their relationships, their family dynamics, their views of climate change and how they see themselves, right down to the very core of their identity. None of the participants believed they were pawns in the hands of corporate control. As we know from the Milgram and Zimbardo experiments, it is very difficult to resist instruction from authority figures, a position assumed by media in various forms. Democracy has in great part been eroded beyond recognition in consumer culture so that citizens have been replaced with respondents, objects of manipulation rather than autonomous free-thinking persons. The participants in the study vehemently believed their individuality was wholly maintained despite the phenomenon of mass consumption, seemingly unaware that from birth they have been molded, primed, and enticed into accepting a way of life that has been largely dictated by the culture industry.

Corporations have infiltrated into the most intimate of spaces, including within the family, day care, schools, and leisure time, pounding out their messages over and over, subtly demanding conformity and compliance. Sadly, any possibility of genuine fulfillment slips away as we desperately seek to find happiness from a system that forever stokes, even manufactures, discontent. The majority of participants in the study had an inkling of this, yet seemed to see no way out, somehow knowing that those who choose their own path of self-realization are faced with a loss of security and anxiety as they systematically deviate from the status quo. It is not that the struggle between individuality and generality is new to the human condition. What is new is the inculcation of children from birth by a system so powerful that few can resist or even understand their predicament—what has become the sine qua non of modern existence. According to neuroscientist Susan Greenfield, the plasticity of the brain in children is such that they are "exquisitely sensitive to [their] environment."[31] We now know that much of our worldview or beliefs, as well as the limits on what thoughts we are capable of, are established during early and middle childhood, deeply embedded in the neural circuitry.[32] The culture industry understands and utilizes the extensive knowledge now available on childhood development to inculcate its ideology into children. Greenfield warns that the delicate and critical dynamism and plasticity of the human brain in children presents both "wonderful benefits and terrifying threats" in the construction of identity in the twenty-first century.[33]

Bloom talks about the dangers that can occur when the balance between "conformity enforcers" and "diversity generators" begins to erode.[34] By conformity enforcers, he is referring to the ways in which some of us are driven to enforce group identity and a common worldview that ultimately "shapes the wiring of a baby's brain and literally changes the way that adults see, a collective perception which makes one group's reality another's mass insanity."[35] If conformity enforcers amass too much power, they deter those who might have infused new perspectives or series of ideas/behaviors previously not exhibited within the culture. Hence, the nonconformist, the creative spirit of the diversity generator, can be squelched to the detriment of a culture's evolution. Bloom's theory is apropos to the corporate control versus "child-freedom-of-mind" crisis. The language of the corporation, the memes that corporate culture generates, have become so dominant that many of us accept them without struggle and find ourselves believing due to their ubiquitous presence. Today's children are particularly easy to ply with memes (i.e., advertising) considering their insatiable appetite for technology. The result: guaranteed proliferation of increasing numbers of conformity enforcers.

From what we know of the workings of memes and the outcomes of the study, what kind of person is being raised within the confines of consumer cultures, to keep it operating en masse? We have an understanding that consumer culture fosters and encourages a set of values based in self-interest, a strong desire for financial success, high levels of consumption, and interpersonal styles based on competition.[36] Within consumer cultures significant effort will be needed to foment and sustain attitudes of selflessness, valuing intimate relationships, and feelings of self-worth and autonomy. As Kasser et al. note: ". . . universalism, benevolence, and self-direction oppose [American Corporate Capitalism's] aims of power and achievement."[37] We now know that people oriented toward materialistic values are less empathic and less cooperative, all of which interfere with quality relationships and positive self-image.[38] Self-esteem, which is closely tied to identity, is often undermined by aspects of consumer culture since self-worth is so largely equated with financial success. Sense of self under consumer cultures involves a belief that one is in constant character deficit, fulfilled solely through consumption. Indeed, the values of consumer culture oppose those for self-direction and self-acceptance. Further to this, consumer culture requires us to remain vigilant and competitive, to view others' successes as a threat, inciting our desires. The fundamental tenet of consumer culture is that it is normal and good to act in one's own self-interest with little to no concern for others. Three of the beliefs central to consumerism—materialism, competition, and self-interest—are antithetical to healthy families and sustaining societies in the long term. It has already been widely established that good relationships are a key factor to psychological health. Yet consumer culture values oppose the emotional ingredients that make relationships successful, including being helpful, honest, forgiving, and loyal.[39] The corporation must remain vigilant in fostering the belief that happiness is attained through the satisfaction of material needs if they are to continue reaping the level of profits and power to which they have become accustomed. Children are raised within the culture industry knowing little else, striving to succeed within its confines and suffering baneful psychological consequences.

It would appear that we are currently facing some of the most ferocious and crucial meme "wars" ever: the planet versus neoclassical economics, the people versus unregulated capitalism, freedom of mind versus unfettered corporate advertising, and democracy versus inverted totalitarianism. Indeed, our future is at a critical juncture. It is incumbent upon us to provide children with opportunities to enhance their lives in meaningful ways, to value more than the mere acquisition of goods and consumer-oriented lifestyles. We must also strive to ensure that children experience a true democracy, one ruled by citizens rather than corporations. It will require active disengagement from our current conditioning, a counterrevolution to reclaim and resurrect meaningful human interaction and consciousness dictated by more than "having" and "not having." Ultimately, we must model for our children the human capacity to achieve true contentment through the nurturing of compassion, empathy, and joy.

Appendix: Interview Questionnaire

1. Can you tell me about a time when you really wanted something? How did you feel when you got it? How did your friends react to this? Your parents?

2. Can you describe a time when you wanted something and could not purchase it for whatever reason? How did it feel? How did it affect what you did with your friends?

3. Can you tell me about a time when you decided to start watching a particular TV show or movie? Did this decision involve family or friends? If so, how?

4. How do you feel about watching advertisements? Do they influence you in any way? Do you feel in control about what you decide to purchase? How do you decide whether to believe an advertisement?

5. Can you describe a time when you were a child or adolescent when you really wanted to purchase something? How is it different from today?

6. Do you worry about having enough money to buy things when you're older? How do you decide how much money you'll need? What does it mean to you to have enough money for purchases?

7. Can you describe a time when you decided you wanted to purchase technology? How did it feel to not have this? What changed in your life once you made this purchase?

8. Can you describe a time when you had to wait quite a while before you acquired something? How did it make you feel to have to wait? How did waiting affect your relationships with parents? Friends?

9. Can you describe a time when you admired and maybe even wanted to be like someone portrayed in the media? How did this make you feel? How did this influence purchases that you made?

10. Can you describe a time when watching media changed how you felt about yourself?

11. Can you describe a time when watching media changed how you felt toward your parents? Peers? How did this happen? How did it make you feel?

12. Can you tell me about a time when you regretted purchasing something?

13. How does it make you feel when experiencing changing fads? Do you feel pressured by this?

14. Can you describe a time when purchasing something made you feel more popular with your peers?

15. Can you describe a time when you felt persuaded by media to be a certain type of person or to look a certain way?

16. What does it feel like when you purchase the same things as those around you? How do you maintain your individuality?

17. Has using Facebook influenced the kinds of purchases that you make? Does it make you want to have things?

18. Can you tell me how it felt when you didn't have something that others did?

19. Can you give me an example in your life when how you felt about yourself changed because of something you acquired or purchased?

20. What does it feel like to have purchased something and realize that it is no longer in style? How does having something 'out of style' make you feel about yourself?

21. As a consumer, what beliefs do you hold about yourself that affect what you buy or what you shop for?

22. Can you give me an example of when you hesitated before buying something? What sorts of influences made you second-guess your decision?

23. Can you tell me about a time when you felt the media understood or captured what you needed? How did that make you feel?

24. Can you tell me about a time when you felt you had captured what it is to be 'cool'? How did that feel? Why was that important to you?

25. Can you tell me about a time when you felt you had everything you needed in terms of possessions?

26. Can you tell me about a time when having a lot of money was important to you?

27. Can you describe a time when purchasing something with a particular brand name was critical?

28. How would you describe the values that you ascribe to as a consumer? Do you shop with particular values in mind?

29. In general, does advertising as a whole clash with your values or beliefs? In what way or why doesn't it?

30. Can you tell me about a time when you went shopping with your parents? How did you negotiate what to buy? How does it feel when your parents object to something you want to purchase?

31. How do your parents feel about the goods that you purchase? How does shopping and acquiring things affect your relationship with your parents?

32. How do your parents feel about the time you spend with media? Does this ever create conflict for you? How do you try to resolve this?

33. How have you been influenced by purchases and the purchasing habits of your parents?

34. Do you aspire to your parents' level of success financially, socially?

35. Can you describe a situation when you decided to purchase something because your peers had it? How did it feel once you acquired it?

36. What is it like to shop with a friend? Are you influenced by your friends?

37. Can you describe a time when you felt pressured by your peers to purchase something? How did this feel?

38. As a consumer, what do you think about "green" issues? Are you involved in any organizations in your community? Do these issues impact your consumption habits?

39. How do you feel about our future as consumers in North America?

40. Have you been influenced by the purchases that others make at your school? Are there certain people in particular that have influenced you? What does it feel like to pay attention in this way?

41. As a global citizen, what are your thoughts, fears, and hope for the future considering climate change/global warming?

Notes

CHAPTER 1

1. M. Weilbacher, "Last Child in the Woods," *Adbusters Journal of the Mental Environment* 18, July/August (2010).

2. Gail Dines, "Childified Women: How the Mainstream Porn Industry Sells Child Pornography to Men," in *The Sexualization of Childhood*, ed. Sharna Olfman (Westport, Conn.: Praeger, 2005).

3. Kalle Lasn, *Culture Jam: The Uncooling of America* (New York: Morrow, 1999), p. xi.

4. I completed a "graduating essay" as a requirement for the MSW at UBC in 2002. This essay formed the basis for the nonprofit Who Minds the Child? Media Education Society. The essay in its entirety can be found at www.whomindsthechild .org

5. Juli B. Kramer, "Ethical Analysis and Recommended Action in Response to the Dangers associated with Youth Consumerism," *Ethics & Behavior* 16, no. 4 (2006): p. 293.

6. "Children" is used as an inclusive term for individuals between 0 and 17 years with the following subgroups: young children are 0–7; tweens are 8–12; youth are 12–18; young people are individuals aged 18–19.

7. T. Kasser, R. M. Ryan, C. E. Couchman, and K. M. Sheldon, "Materialistic Values: Their Causes and Consequences," in *Psychology and Consumer Culture: The Struggle for a Good Life in a Materialistic World*, ed. Tim Kasser and Allen D. Kanner (Washington, D.C.: American Psychological Association, 2004).

8. Joel Bakan, *Childhood under Siege: How Big Business Callously Targets Children* (Toronto: Allen Lane Canada, 2011); Helga Dittmar, "The Cost of Consumers and the 'Cage Within': The Impact of the Material 'Good Life' and 'Body Perfect' Ideals on Individuals' Identity and Well-Being," *Psychological Inquiry* 18, no. 1 (2007); Kramer, "Ethical Analysis and Recommended Action in Response to the Dangers

Associated with Youth Consumerism" Susan Linn, *Consuming Kids: The Hostile Takeover of Childhood* (New York: New Press; distributed by W. W. Norton & Co., 2004); Juliet Schor, *Born to Buy* (New York: Scribner, 2004).

9. L. Rowell Huesmann et al., "Longitudinal Relations between Children's Exposure to TV Violence and Their Aggressive and Violent Behavior in Young Adulthood: 1977–1992," *Developmental Psychology* 39, no. 2 (2003); Mark I. Singer et al., "Viewing Preferences, Symptoms of Psychological Trauma, and Violent Behaviors among Children Who Watch Television," *Journal of the American Academy of Child & Adolescent Psychiatry* 37, no. 10 (1998).

10. Tim Kasser, *The High Price of Materialism* (Cambridge, Mass.: MIT Press, 2002).

11. Juliet Schor, "Work, Family, and Children's Consumer Culture," in *Unfinished Work: Building Equality and Democracy in an Era of Working Families*, ed. Jody Heymann and Christopher Beem (New York: New Press; distributed by W. W. Norton & Co., 2005).

12. S. Shellenbarger, "A Box? Or a Spaceship? What Makes Kids Creative," *The Wall Street Journal*, Dec. 15, 2010.

13. M. Morris, "Contradiction of Post-Modern Consumerism and Resistance," *Studies in Political Economy* 64 (2001).

14. Jean Kilbourne, *Deadly Persuasion: Why Women and Girls Must Fight the Addictive Power of Advertising* (New York: Free Press, 1999).

15. B. Wilcox et al., "Report of the APA Task Force on Advertising and Children" (American Psychological Association, 2004).

16. David Buckingham, *Media Education: Literacy, Learning and Contemporary Culture* (Cambridge, UK: Polity Press; Distributed in the United States by Blackwell, 2003).

17. Hal Niedzviecki, *Hello, I'm Special: How Individuality became the New Conformity* (Toronto: Penguin Canada, 2004).

18. Herbert Marcuse, *One Dimensional Man: Studies in the Ideology of Advanced Industrial Society* (Boston: Beacon Press, 1964).

19. Allen D. Kanner and Mary E. Gomes, "The All-Consuming Self," *Adbusters Journal of the Mental Environment* 3, no. 4 (1995).

20. Schor, *Born to Buy*.

21. Moniek Buijzen and Patti M. Valkenburg, "The Unintended Effects of Television Advertising," *Communication Research* 30, no. 5 (2003).

22. Tim Kasser and Richard M. Ryan, "A Dark Side of the American Dream: Correlates of Financial Success as a Central Life Aspiration," *Journal of Personality and Social Psychology* 65, no. 2 (1993); "Further Examining the American Dream: Differential Correlates of Intrinsic and Extrinsic Goals," *Personality and Social Psychology Bulletin* 22, no. 3 (1996); "Be Careful What You Wish For: Optimal Functioning and the Relative Attainment of Intrinsic and Extrinsic Goals," in *Life Goals and Well-Being: Towards a Positive Psychology of Human Striving*, ed. Peter Schmuck and Kennon M. Sheldon (Seattle: Hogrefe & Huber, 2001).

23. R. Elliot and C. Leonard, "Peer Pressure and Poverty: Exploring Fashion Brands and Consumption Symbolism among Children of the 'British Poor'," *Journal of Consumer Behaviour* 3, no. 4 (2004).

24. Liz Frost, "Theorizing the Young Woman in the Body," *Body & Society* 11, no. 1 (2005).

25. Tim Kasser and Allen D. Kanner, "Where Is the Psychology of Consumer Culture?," in *Psychology and Consumer Culture: The Struggle for a Good Life in a Materialistic World*, ed. Tim Kasser and Allen D. Kanner (Washington, D.C.: American Psychological Association, 2004).

26. Daniel Thomas Cook, "The Missing Child in Consumption Theory," *Journal of Consumer Culture* 8, no. 2 (2008).

27. David Buckingham, *After the Death of Childhood: Growing Up in the Age of Electronic Media* (Cambridge: Blackwell, 2000).

28. Henry A. Giroux, "Left Behind? American Youth and the Global Fight for Democracy," *Truthout* (2011), http://www.truth-out.org/left-behind-american-youth-and-global-fight-democracy68042.

29. Schor, *Born to Buy*.

30. Linn, *Consuming Kids: The Hostile Takeover of Childhood*.

31. Tim Kasser and Allen D. Kanner, *Psychology and Consumer Culture: The Struggle for a Good Life in a Materialistic World*, 1st ed. (Washington, D.C.: American Psychological Association, 2004).

32. Joel Bakan, *The Corporation: The Pathological Pursuit of Profit and Power* (New York: Free Press, 2004).

33. Helga Dittmar, "The Role of Self-Image in Excessive Buying," in *I Shop, Therefore I Am: Compulsive Buying and the Search for Self*, ed. April Lane Benson (Northvale, N.J.: Jason Aronson, 2000); "Are You What You Have?," *The Psychologist* 17, no. 4 (2004); Helga Dittmar and John Drury, "Self-Image—Is It in the Bag? A Qualitative Comparison between 'Ordinary' and 'Excessive' Consumers," *Journal of Economic Psychology* 21, no. 2 (2000); Helga Dittmar, Emma Halliwell, and Suzanne Ive, "Does Barbie Make Girls Want to Be Thin? The Effect of Experimental Exposure to Images of Dolls on the Body Image of 5- to 8-Year-Old Girls," *Developmental Psychology* 42, no. 2 (2006); Helga Dittmar and Sarah Howard, "Professional Hazards? The Impact of Models' Body Size on Advertising Effectiveness and Women's Body-Focused Anxiety in Professions That Do and Do Not Emphasize the Cultural Ideal of Thinness," *British Journal of Social Psychology* 43, no. 4 (2004).

34. Kathy Hirsh-Pasek, Roberta Michnick Golinkoff, and Diane E. Eyer, *Einstein Never Used Flash Cards: How Our Children Really Learn—and Why They Need to Play More and Memorize Less* (Emmaus, Penn.: Rodale by St. Martin's Press, 2003).

35. Alissa Quart, *Branded: The Buying and Selling of Teenagers* (Cambridge, Mass.: Perseus, 2003).

36. Sharna Olfman, *Childhood Lost: How American Culture Is Failing Our Kids*, Childhood in America (Westport, Conn.: Praeger, 2005).

37. Sharna Olfman, *The Sexualization of Childhood*, Childhood in America (Westport, Conn.: Praeger, 2009).

38. Meenakshi Gigi Durham, *The Lolita Effect: The Media Sexualization of Young Girls and What We Can Do About It* (Woodstock, N.Y.: Overlook Press, 2008).

39. Theodor W. Adorno, "On the Fetish-Character in Music and the Regression of Listening," in *The Essential Frankfurt School Reader*, ed. Andrew Arato and Eike Gerhardt (Oxford: Basil Blackwell, 1978); *The Culture Industry: Selected Essays on Mass Culture* (London: Routledge, 1990); *Critical Models: Interventions and Catchwords* (New York: Columbia University Press, 2005).

40. Max Horkheimer and Theodor W. Adorno, *Dialectic of Enlightenment* (London: Allen Lane, 1973).

41. Adorno, *The Culture Industry: Selected Essays on Mass Culture.*

42. Marcuse, *One Dimensional Man: Studies in the Ideology of Advanced Industrial Society.*

43. Stuart Ewen, *Captains of Consciousness: Advertising and the Social Roots of the Consumer Culture* (New York: McGraw-Hill, 1976).

44. Benjamin R. Barber, *Consumed: How Markets Corrupt Children, Infantilize Adults, and Swallow Citizens Whole*, 1st ed. (New York: W. W. Norton & Co., 2007).

45. Sheldon S. Wolin, *Democracy Incorporated: Managed Democracy and the Specter of Inverted Totalitarianism* (Princeton, N.J.: Princeton University Press, 2008).

46. Jerry Mander, "Privatization of Consciousness," *Monthly Review* 64 (2012): p. 1.

47. Durham, *The Lolita Effect: The Media Sexualization of Young Girls and What We Can Do About It*; Olfman, *Childhood Lost: How American Culture Is Failing Our Kids*; Linn, *Consuming Kids: The Hostile Takeover of Childhood*; Schor, *Born to Buy.*

48. Bill McKibben, "Cult of the Weird," *Adbusters Journal of the Mental Environment* 9, no. 1 (2001).

CHAPTER 2

1. Anthony R. Pratkanis and Elliot Aronson, *Age of Propaganda: The Everyday Use and Abuse of Persuasion* (New York: W. H. Freeman, 2001).

2. Kalle Lasn, "Advertising Is Brain Damage," *Adbusters Journal of the Mental Environment* 15, no. 5 (2007).

3. Mary Celeste Kearney, *Girls Make Media* (New York: Routledge, 2006); Steven Miles, *Youth Lifestyles in a Changing World* (Buckingham: Open University Press, 2000).

4. D. S. Acuff and R. H. Reiher, *Kidnapped: How Irresponsible Marketers Are Stealing the Minds of Your Children* (Chicago: Dearborn Publishing, 2005); Tim Kasser and Allen D. Kanner, *Psychology and Consumer Culture: The Struggle for a Good Life in a Materialistic World*, 1st ed. (Washington, D.C.: American Psychological Association, 2004); Susan Linn, *Consuming Kids: The Hostile Takeover of Childhood* (New York: New Press; distributed by W. W. Norton & Co., 2004); Alissa Quart, *Branded: The Buying and Selling of Teenagers* (Cambridge, Mass.: Perseus, 2003); Juliet Schor, *Born to Buy* (New York: Scribner, 2004); Susan Gregory Thomas, *Buy, Buy Baby: How Consumer Culture Manipulates Parents and Harms Young Minds* (Boston: Houghton Mifflin, 2007).

5. Allison J. Pugh, *Longing and Belonging: Parents, Children, and Consumer Culture* (Berkeley: University of California Press, 2009).

6. Juliet Schor, "Work, Family, and Children's Consumer Culture," in *Unfinished Work: Building Equality and Democracy in an Era of Working Families*, ed. Jody Heymann and Christopher Beem (New York: New Press; distributed by W. W. Norton & Co., 2005).

7. Christine L. Williams, *Inside Toyland: Working, Shopping, and Social Inequality* (Berkeley, Calif.: University of California Press, 2006).

8. E. Aird, "Advertising and Marketing to Children in the United States," in *Rethinking Childhood*, ed. Peter B. Pufall and Richard P. Unsworth (New Brunswick, N.J.: Rutgers University Press, 2004).

9. Sandra L. Calvert, "Children as Consumers: Advertising and Marketing," *The Future of Children* 18, no. 1 (2008).

10. Williams, *Inside Toyland: Working, Shopping, and Social Inequality.*

11. Schor, "Work, Family, and Children's Consumer Culture."

12. Williams, *Inside Toyland: Working, Shopping, and Social Inequality.*

13. Aird, "Advertising and Marketing to Children in the United States," p. 143.

14. Jane Kenway and Elizabeth Bullen, "Consuming Skin: Dermographies of Female Subjection and Abjection," in *Critical Pedagogies of Consumption: Living and Learning in the Shadow of The "Shopocalypse,"* ed. J. A. Sandlin and P. McLaren (New York: Routledge, 2010).

15. J. Stearns, J. A. Sandlin, and J. Burdick, "Exploring the Big Curriculum of Consumption and the (Im)Possibility of Resistance in John Updike's 'A&P,'" *Curriculum Inquiry* 41 (2011).

16. Pugh, *Longing and Belonging: Parents, Children, and Consumer Culture.*

17. "Daily Media Use among Children and Teens up Dramatically from Five Years Ago," Kaiser Family Foundation (2010), http://kff.org/disparities-policy /press-release/daily-media-use-among-children-and-teens-up-dramatically-from -five-years-ago/.

18. Judy S. DeLoache and Cynthia Chiong, "Babies and Baby Media," *American Behavioral Scientist* 52, no. 8 (2009).

19. Todd Gitlin, *Media Unlimited: How the Torrent of Images and Sounds Overwhelms Our Lives,* 1st ed. (New York: Metropolitan Books, 2001).

20. Pugh, *Longing and Belonging: Parents, Children, and Consumer Culture.*

21. D. Kindlon, *Too Much of a Good Thing* (New York: Hyperion, 2001).

22. Victoria J. Rideout, Elizabeth A. Vandewater, and Ellen A. Wartella, "Zero to Six: Electronic Media in the Lives of Infants, Toddlers and Preschoolers" Kaiser Family Foundation (2003), http://www.kff.org. For full text: http://www.kff.org /entmedia/loader.cfm?url=/commonspot/security/getfile.cfm&PageID=22754; Donald F. Roberts, Ulla G. Foehr, and Victoria J. Rideout, "Generation M: Media in the Lives of 8–18 Year-Olds," Kaiser Family Foundation (2005).

23. Rideout, Vandewater, and Wartella, "Zero to Six: Electronic Media in the Lives of Infants, Toddlers and Preschoolers."

24. Stephen Kline, *Out of the Garden: Toys, TV, and Children's Culture in the Age of Marketing,* Pbk. ed. (London; New York: Verso, 1995); Sharna Olfman, *Childhood Lost: How American Culture Is Failing Our Kids,* Childhood in America (Westport, Conn.: Praeger Publishers, 2005); Neil Postman, *The Disappearance of Childhood,* 1st Vintage Books ed. (New York: Vintage Books, 1994); Shirley R. Steinberg and Joe L. Kincheloe, *Kinderculture: The Corporate Construction of Childhood* (Boulder, Colo.: Westview Press, 1997).

25. Penelope Leach, *Children First: What Our Society Must Do—and Is Not Doing—for Our Children Today* (London: Michael Joseph, 1994); Linn, *Consuming Kids: The Hostile Takeover of Childhood.*

26. Kline, *Out of the Garden: Toys, TV, and Children's Culture in the Age of Marketing,* p. 74.

27. Kathy Hirsh-Pasek, Roberta Michnick Golinkoff, and Diane E. Eyer, *Einstein Never Used Flash Cards: How Our Children Really Learn—and Why They Need to Play More and Memorize Less* (Emmaus, Penn.: Rodale by St. Martin's Press, 2003).

28. Kline, *Out of the Garden: Toys, TV, and Children's Culture in the Age of Marketing.*

29. Postman, *The Disappearance of Childhood.*

30. Acuff and Reiher, *Kidnapped: How Irresponsible Marketers Are Stealing the Minds of Your Children;* Schor, *Born to Buy.*

31. Calvert, "Children as Consumers: Advertising and Marketing."

32. Schor, "Work, Family, and Children's Consumer Culture."

33. Dina L. G. Borzekowski and Thomas N. Robinson, "The 30-Second Effect: An Experiment Revealing the Impact of Television Commercials on Food Preferences of Preschoolers (Statistical Data Included)," *Journal of the American Dietetic Association* 101, no. 1 (2001).

34. James McNeal, "Marketing to Trillion-Dollar Kids," *The Economist* (2006), http://www.economist.com/node/8355035?story_id=8355035&fsrc=RSS.

35. Ibid.

36. Thomas, *Buy, Buy Baby: How Consumer Culture Manipulates Parents and Harms Young Minds.*

37. Aird, "Advertising and Marketing to Children in the United States," pp. 145–146.

38. Thomas, *Buy, Buy Baby: How Consumer Culture Manipulates Parents and Harms Young Minds.*

39. Adriana Barbaro and Jeremy Earp, "Consuming Kids: The Commercialization of Childhood" (2005), http://www.mediaed.org/assets/products/134/studyguide_134.pdf.

40. Ibid, p. 12.

41. Campaign for a Commercial-Free Childhood (CCFC), "Annual Report," 2012. Retrieved December 12, 2012 (http://salsa.democracyinaction.org/dia/track.jsp?v=2&c=e3MjHtuUnIP4E2UKYIxvruw6z5wB0Wdq).

42. "CCFC Urges Fisher-Price to Pull the Plug on Its Newborn-to-Toddler Apptivity™ Seat for Ipad® Device," Campaign for a Commercial-Free Childhood (2013), http://www.commercialfreechildhood.org/ccfc-urges-fisher-price-pull-plug-its-newborn-toddler-apptivity%E2%84%A2-seat-ipad%C2%AE-device.

43. DeLoache and Chiong, "Babies and Baby Media."

44. Thomas, *Buy, Buy Baby: How Consumer Culture Manipulates Parents and Harms Young Minds.*

45. Daniel R. Anderson and Tiffany A. Pempek, "Television and Very Young Children," *American Behavioral Scientist* 48, no. 5 (2005).

46. Daniel Thomas Cook and Susan B. Kaiser, "Betwixt and Be Tween: Age Ambiguity and the Sexualization of the Female Consuming Subject," *Journal of Consumer Culture* 4, no. 2 (2004).

47. Quart, *Branded: The Buying and Selling of Teenagers.*

48. Rebecca Leung, "Tweens: A Billion Dollar Market" (2009), http://www.cbsnews.com/2100-500164_162-660978.html.

49. Faye Rice, "'Superstars' of Spending," in *Advertising Age* (Crain Communications Inc., Mich., 2001).

50. Schor, "Work, Family, and Children's Consumer Culture."

51. Ross Hammond, "Tobacco Advertising & Promotion: The Need for a Coordinated Global Response, 2000," in *World Health Organization* (New Delhi, 2000).

52. Kearney, *Girls Make Media.*

53. "'Tween' Television Programming Promotes Some Stereotypical Conceptions of Gender Roles," *Medical Press* (2014), http://medicalxpress.com/news/2014-04-tween-television-stereotypical-conceptions-gender.html.

54. Media Awareness Network, "Special Issues for Tweens and Teens," Media Awareness Network, http://www.media-awareness.ca/english/parents/marketing/issues_teens_marketing.cfm.

55. UNICEF, "An Overview of Child Well-Being in Rich Countries" (2007), http://www.unicef-irc.org/files/documents/d-3249-In-rich-countries-children .pdf.

56. CBC, "31% of Canadian Kids Are Overweight or Obese" (2012), http://www.cbc.ca/news/health/story/2012/09/20/child-obesity-statscan.html.

57. "Childhood Obesity Facts," Centers for Disease Control and Prevention (2014), http://www.cdc.gov/healthyyouth/obesity/facts.htm.

58. "Child Obesity Facts," Centers for Disease Control and Prevention (2012), http://www.cdc.gov/healthyyouth/obesity/facts.htm.

59. Frank M. Biro et al., "Pubertal Assessment Method and Baseline Characteristics in a Mixed Longitudinal Study of Girls," *Pediatrics* (2010).

60. Sonia Livingstone and Ellen J. Helsper, "Does Advertising Literacy Mediate the Effects of Advertising on Children? A Critical Examination of Two Linked Research Literatures in Relation to Obesity and Food Choice," *Journal of Communication* 56, no. 3 (2006).

61. Julie A. Zuppa, Heather Morton, and Kaye P. Mehta, "Television Food Advertising: Counterproductive to Children's Health," *Nutrition & Dietetics* 60, no. 2 (2003).

62. Ibid.

63. Ibid.

64. D. Levin and S. Linn, "The Commercialization of Childhood: Understanding the Problem and Finding Solutions," in *Psychology and Consumer Culture: The Struggle for a Good Life in a Materialistic World*, ed. Tim Kasser and Allen D. Kanner (Washington, D.C.: American Psychological Association, 2004).

65. Ibid.

66. Moniek Buijzen, Joris Schuurman, and Elise Bomhof, "Associations between Children's Television Advertising Exposure and Their Food Consumption Patterns: A Household Diary-Survey Study," *Appetite* 50, no. 2–3 (2008).

67. R. Craig Endicott, "100 Leading National Advertisers," *Advertising Age* 74, no. 25 (2003).

68. Marion Nestle, *Food Politics: How the Food Industry Influences Nutrition and Health*, Rev. and expanded ed., California Studies in Food and Culture (Berkeley, Calif.: University of California Press, 2007).

69. Kaye P. Mehta, Heather Morton, and Julie A. Zuppa, "Television Food Advertising: Counterproductive to Children's Health? A Content Analysis Using the Australian Guide to Healthy Eating (Original Research)," *Nutrition & Dietetics: The Journal of the Dietitians Association of Australia* 60 (2003).

70. W. Gantz et al., "Food for Thought: Television Food Advertising to Children in the United States" (Kaiser Family Foundation, 2007).

71. W. Neuman, "U.S. Seeks New Limits on Food Ads for Children," in *New York Times*, April 28, 2011.

72. Monique Kent, L. Dubois, and A. Wanless, "Self-Regulation by Industry of Food Marketing Is Having Little Impact during Children's Preferred Television," *International Journal of Pediatric Obesity* 6, no. 5–6 (2011).

73. Ibid.

74. Dasha E. Nicholls, Richard Lynn, and Russell M. Viner, "Childhood Eating Disorders: British National Surveillance Study," *The British Journal of Psychiatry* 198, no. 4 (2011).

75. Jacinta Lowes and Marika Tiggemann, "Body Dissatisfaction, Dieting Awareness and the Impact of Parental Influence in Young Children," *British Journal of Health Psychology* 8, no. 2 (2003).

76. Gemma Lopez-Guimera et al., "Influence of Mass Media on Body Image and Eating Disordered Attitudes and Behaviors in Females: A Review of Effects and Processes," *Media Psychology* 13, no. 4 (2010).

77. Jennifer Siebel Newsom and Regina Kulik Scully, *Miss Representation* (Sausalito, Calif; San Francisco, Calif: Ro*co Films Educational; Girls Club Entertainment, 2010), video recording.

78. Ibid.

79. Jenny Uechi, "An Evolving Sense of Beauty," *Adbusters Journal of the Mental Environment* 16, no. 3 (2008).

80. Marita P. McCabe and Lina A. Ricciardelli, "Body Image Dissatisfaction among Males across the Lifespan: A Review of Past Literature," *Journal of Psychosomatic Research* 56, no. 6 (2004).

81. Ibid.

82. C. Weeks, "More Teens Becoming Regular Smokers, Survey Finds," *The Globe and Mail*, June 1, 2010.

83. "Youth and Tobacco Use," Centers for Disease Control and Prevention (2014), http://www.cdc.gov/tobacco/data_statistics/fact_sheets/youth_data/tobacco_use/.

84. "The Surgeon General's Call to Action to Prevent and Reduce Underage Drinking: A Guide to Action for Families," U.S. Department of Health and Human Services (2007), http://www.ncbi.nlm.nih.gov/books/NBK44360/.

85. Madeline Levine, *The Price of Privilege: How Parental Pressure and Material Advantage Are Creating a Generation of Disconnected and Unhappy Kids*, 1st ed. (New York: HarperCollins, 2006).

86. Kelly J. Kelleher et al., "Increasing Identification of Psychosocial Problems: 1979–1996," *Pediatrics* 105, no. 6 (2000).

87. Mark Olfson et al., "Outpatient Treatment of Child and Adolescent Depression in the United States," *Arch Gen Psychiatry* 60, no. 12 (2003).

88. Tal Ben-Shahar, "Happier: Learn the Secrets to Daily Joy and Lasting Fulfillment" (2007).

89. Jean M. Twenge, *Generation Me* (New York: Free Press, 2006).

90. Ibid.

91. Ibid, p. 107.

92. Cassandra Rutledge Newsom et al., "Changes in Adolescent Response Patterns on the MMPI—across Four Decades," *Journal of Personality Assessment* 81, no. 1 (2003).

93. Daniel Goleman, *Emotional Intelligence* (New York: Bantam Books, 1995).

94. Donald E. Greydanus, "Suicide in Children and Adolescents," Michigan State University College of Human Medicine, http://www2.sap.org.ar/docs/congresos/2011/centenario_sh/greydanus_suicidio.pdf.

95. Levine, *The Price of Privilege: How Parental Pressure and Material Advantage Are Creating a Generation of Disconnected and Unhappy Kids*.

96. "Youth Online: High School YRBS," Centers for Disease Control and Prevention (2013), http://nccd.cdc.gov/YouthOnline/App/Results.aspx.

97. Greydanus, "Suicide in Children and Adolescents."

98. Michael D. Yapko, "The Art of Avoiding Depression," *Psychology Today* 30, no. 3 (1997).

99. Levine, *The Price of Privilege: How Parental Pressure and Material Advantage Are Creating a Generation of Disconnected and Unhappy Kids.*

100. Oliver James, "In George Orwell's 1984," *Adbusters Journal of the Mental Environment* 11, no. 3 (2003).

101. S. Jhally, "The Dialectic of Technology and Magic," in *Cultural Politics in Contemporary America*, ed. Ian H. Angus and Sut Jhally (New York: Routledge, 1989), p. 225.

102. Jane Wakefield, "Children on Screens Six Hours a Day," *BBC News* (2015), http://www.bbc.com/news/technology-32067158.

103. F. J. Zimmerman, D. A. Christakis, and A. N. Meltzoff, "Television and DVD/Video Viewing in Children Younger Than 2 Years," *Archives in Pediatric and Adolescent Medicine* 161, no. 5 (2007).

104. Miriam E. Bar-on, "Current Topic: The Effects of Television on Child Health: Implications and Recommendations," *Archives of Disease in Childhood* 83, no. 4 (2000).

105. Ibid.

106. Communications Committee on "Children, Adolescents, and Advertising," *Pediatrics* 118, no. 6 (2006).

107. Ellen Neuborne, "For Kids on the Web, It's an Ad, Ad, Ad, Ad World," *Business Week* 3475, Aug. 13 (2001).

108. Xiaomei Cai and Xiaoquan Zhao, "Click Here, Kids!," *Journal of Children and Media* 4, no. 2 (2010).

109. B. Wilcox et al., "Report of the APA Task Force on Advertising and Children" (American Psychological Association, 2004).

110. D. L. Mumme and A. Fernald, "The Infant as Onlooker: Learning from Emotional Reactions Observed in a Television Scenario," *Child Development* 74, no. 1 (2003).

111. Marina Krcmar, "Assessing the Research on Media, Cognitive Development, and Infants," *Journal of Children and Media* 4, no. 2 (2010).

112. Makini Brice, "Interview: Dr. Dimitri Christakis Explains Why Television Is Bad for Babies' Brains," *Medical Daily* (2012), http://www.medicaldaily.com/interview-dr-dimitri-christakis-explains-why-television-bad-babies-brains-241578.

113. Aird, "Advertising and Marketing to Children in the United States."

114. Peter Barnes, *Capitalism 3.0: A Guide to Reclaiming the Commons*, 1st ed. (San Francisco: Berrett-Koehler, 2006).

115. Deborah Roedder John, "Consumer Socialization of Children: A Retrospective Look at Twenty-Five Years of Research," *Journal of Consumer Research* 26, no. 3 (1999).

116. Gwen Bachmann Achenreiner and Deborah Roedder John, "The Meaning of Brand Names to Children: A Developmental Investigation," *Journal of Consumer Psychology* 13, no. 3 (2003).

117. C. Oates, M. Blades, and B. Gunter, "Children and Television Advertising: When Do They Understand Persuasive Intent?," *Journal of Consumer Behaviour* 1, no. 3 (2002).

118. Schor, "Work, Family, and Children's Consumer Culture."

119. Andrew Hampp, "Product Placement Dipped Last Year for First Time," *Advertising Age*, June edition (2010).

120. Daniel Thomas Cook, "The Other 'Child Study': Figuring Children as Consumers in Market Research, 1910s–1990s," *The Sociological Quarterly* 41, no. 3 (2000).

121. Mark I. Singer et al., "Viewing Preferences, Symptoms of Psychological Trauma, and Violent Behaviors among Children Who Watch Television," *Journal of the American Academy of Child & Adolescent Psychiatry* 37, no. 10 (1998).

122. L. Rowell Huesmann et al., "Longitudinal Relations between Children's Exposure to TV Violence and Their Aggressive and Violent Behavior in Young Adulthood: 1977–1992," *Developmental Psychology* 39, no. 2 (2003).

123. Marie-Louise Mares and Emory Woodard, "Positive Effects of Television on Children's Social Interactions: A Meta-Analysis," *Media Psychology* 7, no. 3 (2005).

124. Victoria J. Rideout and Elizabeth Hamel, "The Media Family: Electronic Media in the Lives of Infants, Toddlers, Preschoolers and Their Parents," Kaiser Family Foundation (2006).

125. Edward L. Swing et al., "Television and Video Game Exposure and the Development of Attention Problems," *Pediatrics* 126, no. 2 (2010).

126. Rhonda Clements, "An Investigation of the Status of Outdoor Play," *Contemporary Issues in Early Childhood* 5, no. 1 (2004).

127. Holly K. M. Henry and Dina L. G. Borzekowski, "'The Nag Factor.'" *Journal for Children and Media* 5 (2011).

128. Buijzen, Schuurman, and Bomhof, "Associations between Children's Television Advertising Exposure and Their Food Consumption Patterns: A Household Diary-Survey Study."

129. Henry and Borzekowski, "'The Nag Factor.'"

130. Aird, "Advertising and Marketing to Children in the United States."

131. Henry and Borzekowski, "'The Nag Factor.'"

132. Howard K. Bloom, *The God Problem: How a Godless Cosmos Creates* (Amherst, N.Y.: Prometheus Books, 2012).

133. Lynne Ciochetto, "The Meme Machine," *Adbusters Journal of the Mental Environment* 14, no. 5 (2006).

134. S. Kline, "Limits to the Imagination: Marketing and Children's Culture," in *Cultural Politics in Contemporary America*, ed. Ian H. Angus and Sut Jhally (New York: Routledge, 1989), p. 311.

135. Otto Weininger, *Play and Education: The Basic Tool for Early Childhood Learning* (Springfield, Ill.: Thomas, 1979).

136. Jane M. Healy, *Failure to Connect: How Computers Affect Our Children's Minds—for Better and Worse* (New York: Simon & Schuster, 1998), p. 223.

137. Valerie Polakow Suransky, *The Erosion of Childhood* (Chicago: University of Chicago Press, 1982).

138. Healy, *Failure to Connect: How Computers Affect Our Children's Minds—for Better and Worse.*

139. Sharna Olfman, "Where Do the Children Play?," in *Childhood Lost: How American Culture Is Failing Our Kids*, ed. Sharna Olfman (Westport, Conn.: Praeger, 2005).

140. Leach, *Children First: What Our Society Must Do—and Is Not Doing—for Our Children Today.*

141. Kline, *Out of the Garden: Toys, TV, and Children's Culture in the Age of Marketing*, p. 327.

142. Diane Carver Sekeres, "The Market Child and Branded Fiction: A Synergism of Children's Literature, Consumer Culture, and New Literacies," *Reading Research Quarterly* 44, no. 4 (2009).

143. Ibid.

144. Alex Molnar et al., "Schools Inundated in a Marketing-Saturated World," in *Critical Pedagogies of Consumption*, ed. J. A. Sandlin and P. McLaren (2010).

145. Jean Kilbourne, *Deadly Persuasion: Why Women and Girls Must Fight the Addictive Power of Advertising* (New York, N.Y.: Free Press, 1999); Linn, *Consuming Kids: The Hostile Takeover of Childhood*; Schor, *Born to Buy*.

146. Kalle Lasn, *Culture Jam: The Uncooling of America* (New York: Morrow, 1999).

147. John P. Murray, "Media Violence: The Effects Are Both Real and Strong," *American Behavioral Scientist* 51, no. 8 (2008).

148. Craig A. Anderson et al., "The Influence of Media Violence on Youth," *Psychological Science in the Public Interest* 4, no. 3 (2003).

149. Dominique Ritter, "Killer Entertainment," *Adbusters Journal of the Mental Environment* 8, no. 4 (2000).

150. Gloria DeGaetano, "The Impact of Media Violence on Developing Minds and Hearts," in *Childhood Lost*, ed. Sharna Olfman (Westport, Conn.: Praeger, 2005).

151. Sarah M. Coyne and Emily Whitehead, "Indirect Aggression in Animated Disney Films," *Journal of Communication* 58, no. 2 (2008).

152. Murray, "Media Violence: The Effects Are Both Real and Strong."

153. DeGaetano, "The Impact of Media Violence on Developing Minds and Hearts," p. 90.

154. Keilah A. Worth et al., "Exposure of US Adolescents to Extremely Violent Movies," *Pediatrics* 122, no. 2 (2008).

155. Richard M. Restak, *The Naked Brain: How the Emerging Neurosociety Is Changing How We Live, Work, and Love*, 1st ed. (New York: Harmony Books, 2006).

156. AAP, "Policy Statement—Media Violence," *Pediatrics* 124, no. 5 (2009a).

157. Joanne Cantor et al., "Descriptions of Media-Induced Fright Reactions in a Sample of US Elementary School Children," *Journal of Children and Media* 4, no. 1 (2010).

158. Ibid.

159. Newsom and Scully, *Miss Representation*.

160. Ibid.

161. "Youth Violence: Risk and Protective Factors," Centers for Disease Control and Prevention (2004), http://www.cdc.gov/violenceprevention/youthviolence /riskprotectivefactors.html.

162. Levin and Linn, "The Commercialization of Childhood: Understanding the Problem and Finding Solutions."

163. AAP, "Policy Statement—Media Violence," p. 145.

164. Coyne and Whitehead, "Indirect Aggression in Animated Disney Films."

165. Jamie M. Ostrov, Douglas A. Gentile, and Nicki R. Crick, "Media Exposure, Aggression and Prosocial Behavior during Early Childhood: A Longitudinal Study," *Social Development* 15, no. 4 (2006).

166. Coyne and Whitehead, "Indirect Aggression in Animated Disney Films."

167. AAP, "Policy Statement—Media Violence."

168. Keilah A. Worth et al., "Exposure of US Adolescents to Extremely Violent Movies," *Pediatrics* 122, no. 2 (2008).

169. Ibid.

170. AAP, "Policy Statement—Media Violence."

171. Coyne and Whitehead, "Indirect Aggression in Animated Disney Films."

172. Ibid.

173. Brian A. Primack et al., "Degrading and Non-Degrading Sex in Popular Music: A Content Analysis," *Public Health Reports* 123, no. 5 (2008).

174. AAP, "Policy Statement—Impact of Music, Music Lyrics, and Music Videos on Children and Youth," *Pediatrics* 124, no. 5 (2009b).

175. Ibid.

176. Ibid.

177. Ibid.

178. Jean M. Twenge and W. Keith Campbell, *The Narcissism Epidemic: Living in the Age of Entitlement*, 1st Free Press hardcover ed. (New York: Free Press, 2009).

179. Matthew J. Bernthal and Frederick J. Medway, "An Initial Exploration into the Psychological Implications of Adolescents' Involvement with Professional Wrestling," *School Psychology International* 26, no. 2 (2005).

180. Ibid.

181. Ibid.

182. Matthew B. Ezzell, "Pornography, Lad Mags, Video Games, and Boys," in *The Sexualization of Childhood*, ed. Sharna Olfman (Westport, Conn.: Praeger, 2009); Jean Kilbourne, "'The More You Subtract, the More You Add': Cutting Girls Down to Size," in *Psychology and Consumer Culture: The Struggle for a Good Life in a Materialistic World*, ed. Tim Kasser and Allen D. Kanner (Washington, D.C.: American Psychological Association, 2004); Linn, *Consuming Kids: The Hostile Takeover of Childhood*.

183. Katherine K. Wallman, "America's Children in Brief: Key National Indicators of Well-Being, 2008" (Federal Interagency Forum on Child and Family Statistics, 2008).

184. Stacey J. T. Hust, Jane D. Brown, and Kelly Ladin L'Engle, "Boys Will Be Boys and Girls Better Be Prepared: An Analysis of the Rare Sexual Health Messages in Young Adolescents' Media," *Mass Communication & Society* 11, no. 1 (2008).

185. "Preventing Teen Pregnancy 2012–2015," National Center for Chronic Disease Prevention and Health Promotion Division of Reproductive Health (2014), http://www.cdc.gov/TeenPregnancy/PDF/TeenPregnancy_AAG.pdf.

186. Brooke E. Wells and Jean M. Twenge, "Changes in Young People's Sexual Behavior and Attitudes, 1943–1999: A Cross-Temporal Meta-Analysis," *Review of General Psychology* 9, no. 3 (2005).

187. Newsom and Scully, *Miss Representation*.

188. "Preventing Teen Pregnancy 2012–2015."

189. Hust, Brown, and L'Engle, "Boys Will Be Boys and Girls Better Be Prepared: An Analysis of the Rare Sexual Health Messages in Young Adolescents' Media."

190. "Sexually Transmitted Disease Surveillance, 2003," U.S. Department of Health and Human Services, Centers for Disease Control and Prevention (2004).

191. C. Sabina, J. Wolak, and D. Finkelhor, "The Nature and Dynamics of Internet Pornography Exposure for Youth," *Cyberpsychology Behavior and Social Networking* 11, no. 6 (2008).

192. Ezzell, "Pornography, Lad Mags, Video Games, and Boys."

193. Rebecca L. Collins et al., "Watching Sex on Television Predicts Adolescent Initiation of Sexual Behavior," *Pediatrics* 114, no. 3 (2004).

194. "Sex, Kids and the Family Hour a Three-Part Study of Sexual Content on Television," *Kaiser Family Foundation* (1996) http://kff.org/hivaids/report/sex-kids-and-the-family-hour-a/.

195. Rebecca L. Collins, "Sex on Television and Its Impact on American Youth: Background and Results from the Rand Television and Adolescent Sexuality Study," *Child and Adolescent Psychiatric Clinics of North America* 14, no. 3 (2005).

196. Primack et al., "Degrading and Non-Degrading Sex in Popular Music: A Content Analysis."

197. Ibid.

198. Ibid.

199. Ibid.

200. E. Zurbriggen et al., "Report of the APA Task Force on the Sexualization of Girls" (APA, 2007).

201. Sean Condon, "Hot Tots," *Adbusters Journal of the Mental Environment* 15, no. 4 (2007).

202. Ibid.

203. Twenge and Campbell, *The Narcissism Epidemic: Living in the Age of Entitlement.*

204. Meenakshi Gigi Durham, *The Lolita Effect: The Media Sexualization of Young Girls and What We Can Do About It* (Woodstock, N.Y.: Overlook Press, 2008).

205. Twenge and Campbell, *The Narcissism Epidemic: Living in the Age of Entitlement.*

206. Douglas Quenqua, "Graduating from Lip Smackers," *The New York Times*, April 28, 2010.

207. "Tweens' Use of Beauty Products Rises," *MMR* 29, no. 3 (2012).

208. Quenqua, "Graduating from Lip Smackers."

209. Durham, *The Lolita Effect: The Media Sexualization of Young Girls and What We Can Do About It.*

210. Newsom and Scully, *Miss Representation.*

211. Ibid.

212. Victor C. Strasburger and Barbara J. Wilson, *Children, Adolescents, & the Media* (Thousand Oaks, Calif.: Sage Publications, 2002).

213. Calvert, "Children as Consumers: Advertising and Marketing."

214. Ibid.

215. James D. Sargent et al., "Effect of Seeing Tobacco Use in Films on Trying Smoking among Adolescents: Cross Sectional Study," *BMJ: British Medical Journal* 323, no. 7326 (2001).

216. Stacy L. Smith, Marc Choueiti, and Katherine Pieper, "Race/Ethnicity in 600 Popular Films: Examining on Screen Portrayals and Behind the Camera Diversity" (Annenberg School for Communication & Journalism, University of Southern California, 2014).

217. Diane E. Levin, "So Sexy, So Soon: The Sexualization of Childhood," in *The Sexualization of Childhood*, ed. Sharna Olfman (Westport, Conn.: Praeger, 2005).

218. Sarah M. Coyne and John Archer, "Indirect Aggression in the Media: A Content Analysis of British Television Programs," *Aggressive Behavior* 30, no. 3 (2004).

219. Shirley R. Steinberg and Joe L. Kincheloe, "Introduction: No More Secrets—Kinderculture, Information Saturation, and the Postmodern Childhood,"

in *Kinderculture: The Corporate Construction of Childhood*, ed. Shirley R. Steinberg and Joe L. Kincheloe (Boulder, Colo.: Westview Press, 1997).

220. Sharon Bramlett-Solomon and Yvette Roeder, "Looking at Race in Children's Television," *Journal of Children and Media* 2, no. 1 (2008).

221. Henry A. Giroux, "Are Disney Movies Good for Your Kids?," in *Kinderculture: The Corporate Construction of Childhood*, ed. Shirley R. Steinberg and Joe L. Kincheloe (Boulder, Colo.: Westview Press, 1997).

222. E. Seiter, "Children's Desires/Mothers Dilemmas," in *The Children's Culture Reader*, ed. Henry Jenkins (New York: New York University Press, 1998).

223. Nancy Signorielli and Aaron Bacue, "Recognition and Respect: A Content Analysis of Prime-Time Television Characters across Three Decades," *Sex Roles* 40, no. 7 (1999).

224. A. D. Gresson III, "Professional Wrestling and Youth Culture: Teasing, Taunting and the Containment of Civility," in *Kinderculture: The Corporate Construction of Childhood*, ed. Shirley R. Steinberg and Joe L. Kincheloe (Boulder, Colo.: Westview Press, 1997).

225. Jane Kenway and Elizabeth Bullen, *Consuming Children: Education, Entertainment, Advertising* (Buckingham [England]; Philadelphia: Open University Press, 2001).

226. Ibid.

227. Ibid.

228. Schor, *Born to Buy*.

229. Moniek Buijzen and Patti M. Valkenburg, "The Unintended Effects of Television Advertising," *Communication Research* 30, no. 5 (2003); Lan Nguyen Chaplin and Deborah Roedder John, "Growing up in a Material World: Age Differences in Materialism in Children and Adolescents," *Journal of Consumer Research* 34, no. 4 (2007); George P. Moschis and Roy L. Moore, "A Longitudinal Study of Television Advertising Effects," *Journal of Consumer Research* 9, no. 3 (1982); Vanessa Vega and Donald F. Roberts, "Linkages between Materialism and Young People's Television and Advertising Exposure in a US Sample," *Journal of Children and Media* 5, no. 2 (2011).

230. Vega and Roberts, "Linkages between Materialism and Young People's Television and Advertising Exposure in a US Sample."

231. Russell W. Belk, "Materialism: Trait Aspects of Living in the Material World," *Journal of Consumer Research* 12, no. 3 (1985): p. 265.

232. Tim Kasser and Richard M. Ryan, "A Dark Side of the American Dream: Correlates of Financial Success as a Central Life Aspiration," *Journal of Personality and Social Psychology* 65, no. 2 (1993); "Further Examining the American Dream: Differential Correlates of Intrinsic and Extrinsic Goals," *Personality and Social Psychology Bulletin* 22, no. 3 (1996); "Be Careful What You Wish For: Optimal Functioning and the Relative Attainment of Intrinsic and Extrinsic Goals," in *Life Goals and Well-Being: Towards a Positive Psychology of Human Striving*, ed. Peter Schmuck and Kennon M. Sheldon (Seattle: Hogrefe & Huber, 2001).

233. Matthew J. Easterbrook et al., "Consumer Culture Ideals, Extrinsic Motivations, and Well-Being in Children," *European Journal of Social Psychology* 44, no. 4 (2014).

234. Patricia Cohen and Jacob Cohen, *Life Values and Adolescent Mental Health*, Research Monographs in Adolescence (Mahwah, N.J.: L. Erlbaum Associates, 1996).

235. Kennon M. Sheldon and Tim Kasser, "Coherence and Congruence: Two Aspects of Personality Integration," *Journal of Personality and Social Psychology* 68, no. 3 (1995).

236. Tim Kasser, *The High Price of Materialism* (Cambridge, Mass.: MIT Press, 2002).

237. Lara B. Aknin, Michael I. Norton, and Elizabeth W. Dunn, "From Wealth to Well-Being? Money Matters, but Less Than People Think," *The Journal of Positive Psychology* 4, no. 6 (2009); P. R. G. Layard, *Happiness: Lessons from a New Science* (New York: Penguin Press, 2005).

238. Tim Kasser, "Frugality, Generosity, and Materialism in Children and Adolescents," in *What Do Children Need to Flourish?: Conceptualizing and Measuring Indicators of Positive Development*, ed. Kristin A. Moore and Laura Lippman (New York: Springer Science+Business Media, 2005).

239. Ibid.

240. Kasser, *The High Price of Materialism*.

241. Ibid.

242. Ian Bullock, "Happiness," *Adbusters Journal of the Mental Environment* 17, no. 5 (2009).

243. Jean M. Twenge et al., "Birth Cohort Increases in Psychopathology among Young Americans, 1938–2007: A Cross-Temporal Meta-Analysis of the MMPI," *Clinical Psychology Review* 30, no. 2 (2010).

244. Ibid.

245. Buijzen and Valkenburg, "The Unintended Effects of Television Advertising."

246. Ibid.

CHAPTER 3

1. Zygmunt Bauman, "Collateral Casualties of Consumerism," *Journal of Consumer Culture* 7, no. 1 (2007).

2. Kalle Lasn, *Culture Jam: The Uncooling of America* (New York: Morrow, 1999).

3. Zygmunt Bauman, *Liquid Modernity* (Cambridge, UK: Polity Press, 2000); Anthony Giddens, *Modernity and Self-Identity: Self and Society in the Late Modern Age* (Cambridge, UK: Polity Press, 1991).

4. Mervyn F. Bendle, "The Crisis of 'Identity' in High Modernity," *British Journal of Sociology* 53, no. 1 (2002).

5. Vivian L. Vignoles et al., "Beyond Self-Esteem: Influence of Multiple Motives on Identity Construction," *Journal of Personality and Social Psychology* 90, no. 2 (2006).

6. Peter J. Burke and Jan E. Stets, *Identity Theory* (Oxford: Oxford University Press, 2009), p. 3.

7. Ibid.

8. Giddens, *Modernity and Self-Identity: Self and Society in the Late Modern Age*.

9. Ibid.

10. Burke and Stets, *Identity Theory*.

11. Johan Fornäs, "Youth, Culture and Modernity," in *Youth Culture in Late Modernity*, ed. Johan Fornäs and Göran Bolin (London: Thousand Oaks, Calif.: Sage Publications, 1995).

12. Giddens, *Modernity and Self-Identity: Self and Society in the Late Modern Age*, p. 172.

13. Bauman, *Liquid Modernity*.

14. Ibid., p. 81.

15. Ibid.

16. Simon J. Williams and Gillian Bendelow, *The Lived Body: Sociological Themes, Embodied Issues* (London: Routledge, 1998).

17. Erich Fromm, *Man for Himself: An Inquiry into the Psychology of Ethics* (New York: Fawcett Premier, 1947).

18. Madeline Levine, *The Price of Privilege: How Parental Pressure and Material Advantage Are Creating a Generation of Disconnected and Unhappy Kids*, 1st ed. (New York: HarperCollins, 2006).

19. Ali Rattansi and Ann Phoenix, "Rethinking Youth Identities: Modernist and Postmodernist Frameworks," *Identity* 5, no. 2 (2005).

20. Hillevi Ganetz, "Youth, Culture and Modernity," in *Youth Culture in Late Modernity*, ed. Johan Fornäs and Göran Bolin (Thousand Oaks, Calif.: Sage Publications, 1995).

21. AHKC, "It's Time to Unplug Our Kids: Canada's Report Card on Physical Activity on Children and Youth," Active Healthy Kids Canada, http://dvqdas9jt y7g6.cloudfront.net/reportcard2008/AHKCShortFormEN.pdf.

22. Stephanie Pappas, "As Schools Cut Recess, Kid's Learning Will Suffer, Experts Say," *Livescience* (2011), http://www.livescience.com/15555-schools-cut -recess-learning-suffers.html.

23. "Physical Activity and Sedentary Behaviour in Children and Youth," *Canadian Paediatric Society* (2014), http://www.cps.ca/active/AKHK_Guide _Physicians.pdf.

24. "Media and Children," *American Academy of Pediatrics* (2014), http:// www.aap.org/en-us/advocacy-and-policy/aap-health-initiatives/Pages/Media -and-Children.aspx.

25. Michael Ermann, "On Medial Identity," *International Forum of Psychoanalysis* 13, no. 4 (2004); Shayla Thiel Stern, *Instant Identity: Adolescent Girls and the World of Instant Messaging*, Mediated Youth (New York: Peter Lang, 2007).

26. Sharon R. Mazzarella, *Girl Wide Web: Girls, the Internet, and the Negotiation of Identity*, Intersections in Communications and Culture (New York: Peter Lang, 2005).

27. Sherry Turkle, *Alone Together: Why We Expect More from Technology and Less from Each Other* (New York: Basic Books, 2010).

28. Lowell Monke, "Computers in Schools: Moving Education out of the Child into the Machine," *The Internet and Higher Education* 1, no. 2 (1998).

29. Jean M. Twenge and W. Keith Campbell, *The Narcissism Epidemic: Living in the Age of Entitlement*, 1st Free Press hardcover ed. (New York: Free Press, 2009).

30. Ibid., p. 70.

31. Jason J. Washburn et al., "Narcissistic Features in Young Adolescents: Relations to Aggression and Internalizing Symptoms," *Journal of Youth and Adolescence* 33, no. 3 (2004).

32. Allen D. Kanner and Mary E. Gomes, "The All-Consuming Self," *Adbusters Journal of the Mental Environment* 3, no. 4 (1995).

33. Twenge and Campbell, *The Narcissism Epidemic: Living in the Age of Entitlement*.

34. Bill McKibben, "Environmental Movement of the Mind," *Adbusters Journal of the Mental Environment* 18, no. 4 (2010).

35. Ibid., p. 93.

36. Ibid., p. 93.

37. TLC, "Toddlers & Tiaras," http://www.tlc.com/tv-shows/toddlers-tiaras.

38. Joel Bakan, *Childhood under Siege: How Big Business Callously Targets Children* (Toronto: Allen Lane Canada, 2011).

39. Kanner and Gomes, "The All-Consuming Self."

40. Ibid.

41. Gwen Bachmann Achenreiner and Deborah Roedder John, "The Meaning of Brand Names to Children: A Developmental Investigation," *Journal of Consumer Psychology* 13, no. 3 (2003).

42. M. Morris, "Contradiction of Post-Modern Consumerism and Resistance," *Studies in Political Economy* 64 (2001).

43. Lan Nguyen Chaplin and Deborah Roedder John, "The Development of Self-Brand Connections in Children and Adolescents," *Journal of Consumer Research* 32, no. 1 (2005).

44. Beryl Langer, "The Business of Branded Enchantment: Ambivalence and Disjuncture in the Global Children's Culture Industry," *Journal of Consumer Culture* 4, no. 2 (2004): p. 263.

45. Naomi Klein, *No Logo: Taking Aim at the Brand Bullies*, 1st ed. (Toronto: Knopf Canada, 2000).

46. Ibid., p. 21.

47. Achenreiner and John, "The Meaning of Brand Names to Children: A Developmental Investigation"; Stephen Kline, "Countering Children's Sedentary Lifestyles: An Evaluative Study of a Media-Risk Education Approach," *Childhood* 12, no. 2 (2005).

48. Achenreiner and John, "The Meaning of Brand Names to Children: A Developmental Investigation."

49. J. Ross and R. Harradine, "I'm Not Wearing That! Branding and Young Children," *Journal of Fashion Marketing and Management* 8, no. 1 (2004).

50. Achenreiner and John, "The Meaning of Brand Names to Children: A Developmental Investigation."

51. Alissa Quart, *Branded: The Buying and Selling of Teenagers* (Cambridge, Mass.: Perseus, 2003), p. 124.

52. D. Kelly, "Teens Undergo Cosmetic Surgery in Record Numbers," *The Globe and Mail*, June 18, 2010.

53. E. Zurbriggen et al., "Report of the APA Task Force on the Sexualization of Girls" (American Psychological Association, 2007).

54. Marla E. Eisenberg, Melanie Wall, and Dianne Neumark-Sztainer, "Muscle-Enhancing Behaviors among Adolescent Girls and Boys," *Pediatrics* 130, no. 6 (2012).

55. Sharon Boden, "Dedicated Followers of Fashion? The Influence of Popular Culture on Children's Social Identities," *Media, Culture & Society* 28, no. 2 (2006).

56. MTV, "I Want a Famous Face," http://www.mtv.com/shows/i_want_a_famous_face-2/series.jhtml#moreinfo.

57. Boden, "Dedicated Followers of Fashion? The Influence of Popular Culture on Children's Social Identities."

58. R. Elliot and C. Leonard, "Peer Pressure and Poverty: Exploring Fashion Brands and Consumption Symbolism among Children of the 'British Poor'," *Journal of Consumer Behaviour* 3, no. 4 (2004).

59. Grant McCracken, *Culture and Consumption: New Approaches to the Symbolic Character of Consumer Goods and Activities* (Bloomington: Indiana University Press, 1988).

60. Elliot and Leonard, "Peer Pressure and Poverty: Exploring Fashion Brands and Consumption Symbolism among Children of the 'British Poor,'" p. 357.

61. Liz Frost, "Theorizing the Young Woman in the Body," *Body & Society* 11, no. 1 (2005).

62. Ibid.

63. Jane Pilcher, "No Logo? Children's Consumption of Fashion," *Childhood* 18, no. 1 (2011).

64. Russell Belk, "Are We What We Own?," in *I Shop, Therefore I Am: Compulsive Buying and the Search for Self*, ed. April Lane Benson (Northvale, N.J.: Jason Aronson, 2000).

65. Helga Dittmar, "Are You What You Have?," *The Psychologist* 17, no. 4 (2004).

66. Ibid.

67. Helga Dittmar and Lucy Pepper, "To Have Is to Be: Materialism and Person Perception in Working-Class and Middle-Class British Adolescents," *Journal of Economic Psychology* 15, no. 2 (1994).

68. Ibid.

69. Dittmar, "Are You What You Have?"

70. Lan Nguyen Chaplin and Deborah Roedder John, "Growing Up in a Material World: Age Differences in Materialism in Children and Adolescents," *Journal of Consumer Research* 34, no. 4 (2007).

71. T. Kasser, R. M. Ryan, C. E. Couchman, and K. M. Sheldon "Materialistic Values: Their Causes and Consequences," in *Psychology and Consumer Culture: The Struggle for a Good Life in a Materialistic World*, ed. Tim Kasser and Allen D. Kanner (Washington, D.C.: American Psychological Association, 2004), p. 14.

72. Ibid.

73. Helga Dittmar, *The Social Psychology of Material Possessions: To Have Is to Be* (New York: St. Martin's Press, 1992).

74. P. R. G. Layard, *Happiness: Lessons from a New Science* (New York: Penguin Press, 2005).

75. J. Walker Smith, Ann Clurman, and Yankelovich Partners, *Rocking the Ages: The Yankelovich Report on Generational Marketing*, 1st ed. (New York: HarperBusiness, 1997).

76. D. Kindlon, *Too Much of a Good Thing* (New York: Hyperion, 2001).

77. Susan Mitchell, *The Official Guide to the Generations: Who They Are, How They Live, What They Think*, 1st ed. (Ithaca, N.Y.: New Strategist Publications, 1995).

78. "2011 Teens and Money Survey," *Charles Schwab & Co. Inc.* (2011), http://www.aboutschwab.com/images/press/teensmoneyfactsheet.pdf.

79. Twenge and Campbell, *The Narcissism Epidemic: Living in the Age of Entitlement*, p. 172.

80. Antonella Delle Fave et al., "The Eudaimonic and Hedonic Components of Happiness: Qualitative and Quantitative Findings," *Social Indicators Research* 100, no. 2 (2011).

81. Suniya S. Luthar and Shawn J. Latendresse, "Children of the Affluent," *Current Directions in Psychological Science* 14, no. 1 (2005).

82. Levine, *The Price of Privilege: How Parental Pressure and Material Advantage Are Creating a Generation of Disconnected and Unhappy Kids.*

83. Steven Miles, "The Cultural Capital of Consumption: Understanding 'Postmodern' Identities in a Cultural Context," *Culture & Psychology* 2, no. 2 (1996).

84. Frost, "Theorizing the Young Woman in the Body."

85. Ibid., p. 67.

86. Jean Kilbourne, "'The More You Subtract, the More You Add': Cutting Girls Down to Size," in *Psychology and Consumer Culture: The Struggle for a Good Life in a Materialistic World*, ed. Tim Kasser and Allen D. Kanner (Washington, D.C.: American Psychological Association, 2004).

87. Helga Dittmar and Sarah Howard, "Professional Hazards? The Impact of Models' Body Size on Advertising Effectiveness and Women's Body-Focused Anxiety in Professions That Do and Do Not Emphasize the Cultural Ideal of Thinness," *British Journal of Social Psychology* 43, no. 4 (2004).

88. Helga Dittmar, Emma Halliwell, and Suzanne Ive, "Does Barbie Make Girls Want to Be Thin? The Effect of Experimental Exposure to Images of Dolls on the Body Image of 5- to 8-Year-Old Girls," *Developmental Psychology* 42, no. 2 (2006).

89. Ibid.

90. Shelly Grabe, L. Monique Ward, and Janet Shibley Hyde, "The Role of the Media in Body Image Concerns among Women: A Meta-Analysis of Experimental and Correlational Studies," *Psychological Bulletin* 134, no. 3 (2008).

91. Temple Northup and Carol M. Liebler, "The Good, the Bad, and the Beautiful," *Journal of Children and Media* 4, no. 3 (2010).

92. Frost, "Theorizing the Young Woman in the Body."

93. J. Nicole Little and Marie L. Hoskins, "'It's an Acceptable Identity': Constructing 'Girl' at the Intersections of Health, Media, and Meaning-Making," *Child & Youth Services* 26, no. 2 (2004).

94. Howard K. Bloom, *The Global Brain: The Evolution of the Mass Mind from the Big Bang to the 21st Century* (New York: Wiley, 2000).

95. Ibid., p. 145.

96. William S. Pollack, *Real Boys: Rescuing Our Sons from the Myths of Boyhood*, 1st ed. (New York: Random House, 1998).

97. Ibid.

98. Jamie M. Ostrov, Douglas A. Gentile, and Nicki R. Crick, "Media Exposure, Aggression and Prosocial Behavior during Early Childhood: A Longitudinal Study," *Social Development* 15, no. 4 (2006).

99. Ibid.

100. Ibid.

101. June Feder, Ronald F. Levant, and James Dean, "Boys and Violence: A Gender-Informed Analysis," *Professional Psychology: Research and Practice* 38, no. 4 (2007).

102. Ibid.

103. Ibid.

104. Ibid.

105. Ibid.

106. Kathleen A. Peterson, Sharon Paulson, and Kristen K. Williams, "Relations of Eating Disorder Symptomology with Perceptions of Pressures from Mother, Peers, and Media in Adolescent Girls and Boys," *Sex Roles* 57, no. 9/10 (2007).

107. Charlotte Markey and Patrick Markey, "Relations between Body Image and Dieting Behaviors: An Examination of Gender Differences," *Sex Roles* 53, no. 7 (2005).

108. Cortney M. Moriarty and Kristen Harrison, "Television Exposure and Disordered Eating among Children: A Longitudinal Panel Study," *Journal of Communication* 58, no. 2 (2008).

109. Ibid.

110. Stacey J. T. Hust, Jane D. Brown, and Kelly Ladin L'Engle, "Boys Will Be Boys and Girls Better Be Prepared: An Analysis of the Rare Sexual Health Messages in Young Adolescents' Media," *Mass Communication & Society* 11, no. 1 (2008).

111. Daphna Oyserman, "Identity-Based Motivation and Consumer Behavior," *Journal of Consumer Psychology* 19, no. 3 (2009).

112. Amna Kirmani, "The Self and the Brand," *Journal of Consumer Psychology* 19 no. 3 (2009).

113. Klein, *No Logo: Taking Aim at the Brand Bullies*, p. 129.

CHAPTER 4

1. D. S. Acuff and R. H. Reiher, *Kidnapped: How Irresponsible Marketers Are Stealing the Minds of Your Children* (Chicago: Dearborn Publishing, 2005); Helga Dittmar, "The Cost of Consumers and the 'Cage within': The Impact of the Material 'Good Life' and 'Body Perfect' Ideals on Individuals' Identity and Well-Being," *Psychological Inquiry* 18, no. 1 (2007); Henry A. Giroux, *Stealing Innocence: Youth, Corporate Power, and the Politics of Culture*, 1st ed. (New York: St. Martin's Press, 2000); Tim Kasser et al., "Some Costs of American Corporate Capitalism: A Psychological Exploration of Value and Goal Conflicts," *Psychological Inquiry* 18, no. 1 (2007); Susan Linn, *Consuming Kids: The Hostile Takeover of Childhood* (New York: New Press; distributed by W. W. Norton & Co., 2004); Allison J. Pugh, *Longing and Belonging: Parents, Children, and Consumer Culture* (Berkeley: University of California Press, 2009); Juliet Schor, *Born to Buy* (New York: Scribner, 2004).

2. David Buckingham, *The Material Child: Growing Up in Consumer Culture* (Cambridge, UK: Polity Press, 2011); Martin Lindström, Patricia B. Seybold, and Millward Brown, *Brandchild: Remarkable Insights into the Minds of Today's Global Kids and Their Relationship with Brands*, Rev. pbk. ed. (London: Kogan Page, 2004); James U. McNeal, *On Becoming a Consumer: The Development of Consumer Behavior Patterns in Childhood* (Amsterdam: Elsevier/Butterworth-Heinemann, 2007).

3. Jane M. Healy, *Failure to Connect: How Computers Affect Our Children's Minds—For Better and Worse* (New York: Simon & Schuster, 1998).

4. Acuff and Reiher, *Kidnapped: How Irresponsible Marketers Are Stealing the Minds of Your Children*; Neil Postman, *The Disappearance of Childhood*, 1st Vintage Books ed. (New York: Vintage Books, 1994); Susan Gregory Thomas, *Buy, Buy Baby: How Consumer Culture Manipulates Parents and Harms Young Minds* (Boston: Houghton Mifflin, 2007).

5. AAP, "Policy Statement—Media Violence," *Pediatrics* 124, no. 5 (2009a); "Policy Statement—Impact of Music, Music Lyrics, and Music Videos on Children and Youth," *Pediatrics* 124, no. 5 (2009b); D. Levin and S. Linn, "The Commercialization of Childhood: Understanding the Problem and Finding Solutions," in *Psychology and Consumer Culture: The Struggle for a Good Life in a*

Materialistic World, ed. Tim Kasser and Allen D. Kanner (Washington, D.C.: American Psychological Association, 2004); Brian A. Primack et al., "Degrading and Non-Degrading Sex in Popular Music: A Content Analysis," *Public Health Reports* 123, no. 5 (2008); James D. Sargent et al., "Effect of Seeing Tobacco Use in Films on Trying Smoking among Adolescents: Cross Sectional Study," *BMJ: British Medical Journal* 323, no. 7326 (2001); Mark I. Singer et al., "Viewing Preferences, Symptoms of Psychological Trauma and Violent Behaviors among Children Who Watch Television," *Journal of the American Academy of Child & Adolescent Psychiatry* 37, no. 10 (1998); Keilah A. Worth et al., "Exposure of US Adolescents to Extremely Violent Movies," *Pediatrics* 122, no. 2 (2008); E. Zurbriggen et al., "Report of the APA Task Force on the Sexualization of Girls" (American Psychological Association, 2007).

6. Sherry Turkle, *Alone Together: Why We Expect More from Technology and Less from Each Other* (New York: Basic Books, 2010).

7. Giroux, *Stealing Innocence: Youth, Corporate Power, and the Politics of Culture*.

8. Linn, *Consuming Kids: The Hostile Takeover of Childhood*; Alex Molnar et al., "Schools Inundated in a Marketing-Saturated World," in *Critical Pedagogies of Consumption*, ed. J. A. Sandlin and P. McLaren (2010); Schor, *Born to Buy*; Thomas, *Buy, Buy Baby: How Consumer Culture Manipulates Parents and Harms Young Minds*.

9. David Buckingham, *After the Death of Childhood: Growing Up in the Age of Electronic Media* (Cambridge, UK: Blackwell Publishers, 2000); John Fiske, *Television Culture* (London: Methuen, 1987); McNeal, *On Becoming a Consumer: The Development of Consumer Behavior Patterns in Childhood*.

10. Alison Gopnik, *The Philosophical Baby* (New York: Farra, Straus and Giroux, 2009); Penelope Leach, *Children First: What Our Society Must Do—And Is Not Doing—for Our Children Today* (London: Michael Joseph, 1994).

11. Buckingham, *The Material Child: Growing Up in Consumer Culture*.

12. McNeal, *On Becoming a Consumer: The Development of Consumer Behavior Patterns in Childhood*.

13. Lindström, Seybold, and Millward Brown, *Brandchild: Remarkable Insights into the Minds of Today's Global Kids and Their Relationship with Brands*.

14. McNeal, *On Becoming a Consumer: The Development of Consumer Behavior Patterns in Childhood*, pp. 18–19.

15. Gopnik, *The Philosophical Baby*, p. 4.

16. Buckingham, *The Material Child: Growing Up in Consumer Culture*.

17. Kathy Hirsh-Pasek, Roberta Michnick Golinkoff, and Diane E. Eyer, *Einstein Never Used Flash Cards: How Our Children Really Learn—And Why They Need to Play More and Memorize Less* (Emmaus, Penn.: Rodale by St. Martin's Press, 2003).

18. Leach, *Children First: What Our Society Must Do—And Is Not Doing—for Our Children Today*; Linn, *Consuming Kids: The Hostile Takeover of Childhood*.

19. Buckingham, *The Material Child: Growing Up in Consumer Culture*.

20. Fiske, *Television Culture*, p. 309.

21. Buckingham, *The Material Child: Growing Up in Consumer Culture*.

22. Detlev Zwick, Samuel K. Bonsu, and Aron Darmody, "Putting Consumers to Work: 'Co-Creation' and New Marketing Govern-Mentality," *Journal of Consumer Culture* 8, no. 2 (2008).

23. David Buckingham, *Media Education: Literacy, Learning and Contemporary Culture* (Cambridge, UK: Polity Press; distributed in the United States by Blackwell Publishers, 2003).

24. Martin Lindström, *Buyology: Truth and Lies About Why We Buy*, 1st ed. (New York: Doubleday, 2008), p. 204.

25. Buckingham, *Media Education: Literacy, Learning and Contemporary Culture.*

26. Ellen Seiter, *Sold Separately: Children and Parents in Consumer Culture, Communications, Media, and Culture* (New Brunswick, N.J.: Rutgers University Press, 1993), p. 7.

27. Buckingham, *After the Death of Childhood: Growing Up in the Age of Electronic Media*, p. 76.

28. McNeal, *On Becoming a Consumer: The Development of Consumer Behavior Patterns in Childhood.*

29. Daniel Thomas Cook, "The Disempowering Empowerment of Children's Consumer 'Choice,'" *Society and Business Review* 2, no. 1 (2007).

30. Buckingham, *After the Death of Childhood: Growing Up in the Age of Electronic Media.*

31. Kasser et al., "Some Costs of American Corporate Capitalism: A Psychological Exploration of Value and Goal Conflicts."

32. Zwick, Bonsu, and Darmody, "Putting Consumers to Work: 'Co-Creation' and New Marketing Govern-Mentality," p. 186.

33. Ibid.

34. Joel Bakan, *The Corporation: The Pathological Pursuit of Profit and Power* (New York: Free Press, 2004).

35. E. Seiter, "Children's Desires/Mothers' Dilemmas," in *The Children's Culture Reader*, ed. Henry Jenkins (New York: New York University Press, 1998).

36. Paul E. Willis, *Common Culture: Symbolic Work at Play in the Everyday Cultures of the Young* (Milton Keynes: Open University, 1990), p. 1.

37. Ibid., pp. 36–37.

38. Healy, *Failure to Connect: How Computers Affect Our Children's Minds—for Better and Worse.*

39. Linn, *Consuming Kids: The Hostile Takeover of Childhood.*

40. Healy, *Failure to Connect: How Computers Affect Our Children's Minds—for Better and Worse.*

41. Buckingham, *After the Death of Childhood: Growing Up in the Age of Electronic Media*, p. 148.

42. Joel Bakan, *Childhood under Siege: How Big Business Callously Targets Children* (Toronto: Allen Lane Canada, 2011).

43. Buckingham, *After the Death of Childhood: Growing Up in the Age of Electronic Media.*

44. Ibid.

45. C. Oates, M. Blades, and B. Gunter, "Children and Television Advertising: When Do They Understand Persuasive Intent?" *Journal of Consumer Behaviour* 1, no. 3 (2002).

46. Brian L. Wilcox et al., "Report of the APA Task Force on Advertising and Children" (American Psychological Association, 2004).

47. Buckingham, *Media Education: Literacy, Learning and Contemporary Culture.*

48. Ibid.

49. Buckingham, *Media Education: Literacy, Learning and Contemporary Culture.*

50. B. Wilcox et al., "Report of the APA Task Force on Advertising and Children."

51. Anna Craft, "Childhood in a Digital Age: Creative Challenges for Educational Futures," *London Review of Education* 10, no. 2 (2012).

52. Ibid.

53. Don Tapscott, *Growing Up Digital: The Rise of the Net Generation* (New York: McGraw-Hill, 1998).

54. Healy, *Failure to Connect: How Computers Affect Our Children's Minds—for Better and Worse*, p. 90.

55. Nicholas G. Carr, *The Shallows: What the Internet Is Doing to Our Brains*, 1st ed. (New York: W. W. Norton, 2010).

56. Ibid., pp. 147–148.

57. Sylvia Ann Hewlett and Cornel West, "The War against Parents," in *Childhood Lost*, ed. Sharna Olfman (Westport, Conn.: Praeger, 2005).

58. Ibid., p. 62.

59. Gordon Neufeld and Gabor Mat, *Hold On to Your Kids: Why Parents Matter* (Toronto: A. A. Knopf Canada, 2004).

60. Lindström, Seybold, and Millward Brown, *Brandchild: Remarkable Insights into the Minds of Today's Global Kids and Their Relationship with Brands*.

61. McNeal, *On Becoming a Consumer: The Development of Consumer Behavior Patterns in Childhood*, p. 389.

62. Daniel Thomas Cook, "The Missing Child in Consumption Theory," *Journal of Consumer Culture* 8, no. 2 (2008).

63. Buckingham, *The Material Child: Growing Up in Consumer Culture*, p. 45.

64. Ibid., p. 255.

65. Gopnik, *The Philosophical Baby*.

66. Buckingham, *The Material Child: Growing Up in Consumer Culture*.

67. Oxfam, "Rigged Rules Mean Economic Growth Increasingly 'Winner Takes All' for Rich Elites All over the World" (2014), http://www.oxfam.org/en/pressroom/pressrelease/2014-01-20/rigged-rules-mean-economic-growth-increasingly-winner-takes-all-for-rich-elites.

68. Ibid.

69. Bakan, *Childhood under Siege: How Big Business Callously Targets Children*.

70. Thomas, *Buy, Buy Baby: How Consumer Culture Manipulates Parents and Harms Young Minds*.

71. Cook, "The Disempowering Empowerment of Children's Consumer 'Choice.'"

CHAPTER 5

1. S. Kline, "Limits to the Imagination: Marketing and Children's Culture," in *Cultural Politics in Contemporary America*, ed. Ian H. Angus and Sut Jhally (New York: Routledge, 1989); Susan Linn, *Consuming Kids: The Hostile Takeover of Childhood* (New York: New Press; distributed by W. W. Norton & Co., 2004).

2. Penelope Leach, *Children First: What Our Society Must Do—And Is Not Doing—For Our Children Today* (London: Michael Joseph, 1994).

3. Stephen Kline, *Out of the Garden: Toys, TV, and Children's Culture in the Age of Marketing* (London: Verso, 1995).

4. Frank J. Sulloway, *Born to Rebel: Birth Order, Family Dynamics, and Creative Lives*, 1st ed. (New York: Pantheon Books, 1996).

5. Philip G. Zimbardo, *The Lucifer Effect: Understanding How Good People Turn Evil*, 1st ed. (New York: Random House, 2007).

6. Martin Lindström, *Buyology: Truth and Lies about Why We Buy*, 1st ed. (New York: Doubleday, 2008).

7. Mark D. Pagel, *Wired for Culture: Origins of the Human Social Mind*, 1st ed. (New York: W. W. Norton & Company, 2012).

8. Randal Marlin, *Propaganda and the Ethics of Persuasion* (Peterborough, Ont.: Broadview Press, 2002); Anthony R. Pratkanis and Elliot Aronson, *Age of Propaganda: The Everyday Use and Abuse of Persuasion* (New York: W. H. Freeman, 2001).

9. Marlin, *Propaganda and the Ethics of Persuasion*, p. 22.

10. Robert H. Gass and John S. Seiter, *Persuasion, Social Influence, and Compliance Gaining* (Boston: Allyn and Bacon, 2007), pp. 33–34.

11. R. B. Cialdini and M. R. Trost, "Social Influence: Social Norms, Conformity and Compliance," in *The Handbook of Social Psychology*, ed. Susan T. Fiske, Daniel Todd Gilbert, and Gardner Lindzey (Hoboken, N. J.: John Wiley, 1998).

12. Ibid., p. 152.

13. Robert B. Cialdini, Raymond R. Reno, and Carl A. Kallgren, "A Focus Theory of Normative Conduct: Recycling the Concept of Norms to Reduce Littering in Public Places," *Journal of Personality and Social Psychology* 58, no. 6 (1990); Cialdini and Trost, "Social Influence: Social Norms, Conformity and Compliance."

14. Stephen Coleman, *Popular Delusions: How Social Conformity Molds Society and Politics* (Youngstown, N.Y.: Cambria Press, 2007).

15. Cialdini and Trost, "Social Influence: Social Norms, Conformity and Compliance."

16. Ibid.

17. Cialdini, Reno, and Kallgren, "A Focus Theory of Normative Conduct: Recycling the Concept of Norms to Reduce Littering in Public Places."

18. Coleman, *Popular Delusions: How Social Conformity Molds Society and Politics*.

19. Edward L. Deci and Richard M. Ryan, *Intrinsic Motivation and Self-Determination in Human Behavior*, Perspectives in Social Psychology (New York: Plenum, 1985).

20. Luc G. Pelletier, S. Dion, and Chantal Levesque, "Can Self-Determination Help Protect Women against Socio-Cultural Influences about Body Image and Reduce Their Risk of Experiencing Bulimic Symptoms?," *Journal of Social & Clinical Psychology* 23, no. 1 (2004).

21. Alex Heckert and Druann Maria Heckert, "A New Typology of Deviance: Integrating Normative and Reactivist Definitions of Deviance," *Deviant Behavior* 23, no. 5 (2002).

22. Robert B. Cialdini, *Influence: The Psychology of Persuasion*, Rev. ed. (New York: Morrow, 1993).

23. M. A. Brillinger, "Silence Descends: The Effects of Rising Authoritarianism and Fear on Citizen Engagement" (Master's Thesis, Vancouver: University of British Columbia, 2009).

24. Cialdini, *Influence: The Psychology of Persuasion*, p. 229.

25. Coleman, *Popular Delusions: How Social Conformity Molds Society and Politics*.

26. Ibid.

27. S. E. Asch, "Group Influence: Opinions and Social Pressure," in *Small Groups: Studies in Social Interaction*, ed. A. Paul Hare, Edgar F. Borgatta, and Robert Freed Bales (New York: Knopf, 1965).

28. Ibid., p. 320.

29. Rod Bond and Peter B. Smith, "Culture and Conformity: A Meta-Analysis of Studies Using Asch's (1952b, 1956) Line Judgment Task," *Psychological Bulletin* 119, no. 1 (1996).

30. M. B. Walker and M. G. Andrade, "Conformity in the Asch Task as a Function of Age," *The Journal of Social Psychology* 136, no. 3 (1996).

31. Vernon L. Allen and John M. Levine, "Social Support and Conformity: The Role of Independent Assessment of Reality," *Journal of Experimental Social Psychology* 7, no. 1 (1971).

32. Jennifer D. Campbell and Patricia J. Fairey, "Informational and Normative Routes to Conformity: The Effect of Faction Size as a Function of Norm Extremity and Attention to the Stimulus," *Journal of Personality and Social Psychology* 57, no. 3 (1989).

33. Coleman, *Popular Delusions: How Social Conformity Molds Society and Politics*.

34. Bond and Smith, "Culture and Conformity: A Meta-Analysis of Studies Using Asch's (1952b, 1956) Line Judgment Task."

35. P. Niels Christensen et al., "Social Norms and Identity Relevance: A Motivational Approach to Normative Behavior," *Personality and Social Psychology Bulletin* 30, no. 10 (2004).

36. Bond and Smith, "Culture and Conformity: A Meta-Analysis of Studies Using Asch's (1952b, 1956) Line Judgment Task."

37. Michael Guarino and Pamela Fridrich, "Male and Female Conformity in Eating Behavior," *Psychological Reports* 75, no. 1 (1994).

38. Cialdini, Reno, and Kallgren, "A Focus Theory of Normative Conduct: Recycling the Concept of Norms to Reduce Littering in Public Places."

39. Deborah J. Terry and Michael A. Hogg, "Group Norms and the Attitude-Behavior Relationship: A Role for Group Identification," *Personality and Social Psychology Bulletin* 22, no. 8 (1996).

40. H. Tajfel and J. C. Turner, "An Integrative Theory of Group Conflict," in *The Social Psychology of Intergroup Relations*, ed. William G. Austin and Stephen Worchel (Monterey, Calif.: Brooks/Cole, 1979).

41. Stanley Milgram, *Obedience to Authority: An Experimental View*, Harper Torchbooks (New York: Harper & Row, 1975).

42. Ibid., p. 5.

43. Ibid., p. 6.

44. Ibid., p. 147.

45. Jerry M. Burger, "Replicating Milgram: Would People Still Obey Today?," *American Psychologist* 64, no. 1 (2009).

46. Zimbardo, *The Lucifer Effect: Understanding How Good People Turn Evil*.

47. Ibid., p. 230.

48. Ibid., pp. 445–446.

49. C. Oates, M. Blades, and B. Gunter, "Children and Television Advertising: When Do They Understand Persuasive Intent?," *Journal of Consumer Behaviour* 1, no. 3 (2002).

50. Erica Weintraub Austin, Bruce E. Pinkleton, and Yuki Fujioka, "The Role of Interpretation Processes and Parental Discussion in the Media's Effects on Adolescents' Use of Alcohol," *Pediatrics* 105, no. 2 (2000); Kenneth Fleming, Esther Thorson, and Charles K. Atkin, "Alcohol Advertising Exposure and Perceptions: Links with Alcohol Expectancies and Intentions to Drink or Drinking in Underaged Youth and Young Adults," *Journal of Health Communication* 9, no. 1 (2004); Shannon Q. Hurtz et al., "The Relationship between Exposure to Alcohol Advertising in Stores, Owning Alcohol Promotional Items, and Adolescent Alcohol Use," *Alcohol and Alcoholism* 42, no. 2 (2007); Chen Meng-Jinn et al., "Alcohol Advertising: What Makes It Attractive to Youth?," *Journal of Health Communication* 10, no. 6 (2005).

51. Heather A. Hausenblas et al., "Media Effects of Experimental Presentation of the Ideal Physique on Eating Disorder Symptoms: A Meta-Analysis of Laboratory Studies," *Clinical Psychology Review* 33, no. 1 (2013).

52. Kyongboon Kwon and A. Michele Lease, "Children's Social Identification with a Friendship Group: A Moderating Effect on Intent to Conform to Norms," *Small Group Research* 40, no. 6 (2009): p. 697.

53. Nancy P. Gordon, "Never Smokers, Triers, and Current Smokers: Three Distinct Target Groups for School-Based Antismoking Programs," *Health Education & Behavior* 13, no. 2 (1986).

54. Zeena Harakeh and Wilma A. M. Vollebergh, "The Impact of Active and Passive Peer Influence on Young Adult Smoking: An Experimental Study," *Drug and Alcohol Dependence* 121, no. 3 (2012).

55. Ibid.

56. Hanneke A. Teunissen et al., "Adolescents' Conformity to Their Peers' Pro-Alcohol and Anti-Alcohol Norms: The Power of Popularity," *Alcoholism: Clinical and Experimental Research* 36, no. 7 (2012).

57. Deborah J. C. Meyer and Heather C. Anderson, "Preadolescents and Apparel Purchasing: Conformity to Parents and Peers in the Consumer Socialization Process," *Journal of Social Behavior & Personality* 15, no. 2 (2000).

58. Patrick Colm Hogan, *The Culture of Conformism: Understanding Social Consent* (Durham, N.C.: Duke University Press, 2001).

59. Pierre Bourdieu, *Distinction: A Social Critique of the Judgement of Taste* (Cambridge, Mass.: Harvard University Press, 1984).

60. Hogan, *The Culture of Conformism: Understanding Social Consent*.

61. Tim Kasser, *The High Price of Materialism* (Cambridge, Mass.: MIT Press, 2002).

62. Jim Sidanius and Felicia Pratto, *Social Dominance: An Intergroup Theory of Social Hierarchy and Oppression* (Cambridge, UK; New York: Cambridge University Press, 1999).

63. Hogan, *The Culture of Conformism: Understanding Social Consent*.

64. Ibid.

65. Ibid.

66. Sidanius and Pratto, *Social Dominance: An Intergroup Theory of Social Hierarchy and Oppression*.

67. Ibid., p. 33.

68. Ibid., p. 33.

69. Ibid., p. 227.

70. Ibid., p. 44.

71. James U. McNeal, *On Becoming a Consumer: The Development of Consumer Behavior Patterns in Childhood* (Amsterdam: Elsevier/Butterworth-Heinemann, 2007).

72. Hal Niedzviecki, *Hello, I'm Special: How Individuality Became the New Conformity* (Toronto: Penguin Canada, 2004).

73. Ibid., p. 11.

74. Ibid., p. 73.

75. "Depression," *World Health Organization* (2012), http://www.who.int/mediacentre/factsheets/fs369/en/.

76. Niedzviecki, *Hello, I'm Special: How Individuality Became the New Conformity*, p. 135.

77. P. E. Vernon, "The Nature-Nurture Problem in Creativity," in *Handbook of Creativity*, ed. J. Glover, R. Ronning, and C. R. Reynolds (New York: Plenum, 1989).

78. S. Vosburg and G. Kaufmann, "Mood and Creativity Research: The View from a Conceptual Organizing Perspective," in *Affect, Creative Experience, and Psychological Adjustment*, ed. Sandra Walker Russ (Philadelphia: Brunner/Mazel, 1999).

79. Sandra Walker Russ, *Affect and Creativity: The Role of Affect and Play in the Creative Process*, Personality Assessment (Hillsdale, N.J.: L. Erlbaum Associates, 1993).

80. Ibid., p. 12.

81. Russ, *Affect and Creativity: The Role of Affect and Play in the Creative Process*.

82. Ibid., p. 12.

83. Alice M. Isen, "On the Relationship between Affect and Creative Problem Solving," in *Affect, Creative Experience, and Psychological Adjustment*, ed. Sandra Walker Russ (Philadelphia: Brunner/Mazel, 1999).

84. Ibid.

85. Russ, *Affect and Creativity: The Role of Affect and Play in the Creative Process*.

86. Isen, "On the Relationship between Affect and Creative Problem Solving."

87. Russ, *Affect and Creativity: The Role of Affect and Play in the Creative Process*.

88. Ibid.

89. Isen, "On the Relationship between Affect and Creative Problem Solving."

90. Mark A. Runco, "Tension, Adaptability, and Creativity."

91. Barbaros Guncer and Gunseli Oral, "Relationship between Creativity and Nonconformity to School Discipline as Perceived by Teachers," *Journal of Instructional Psychology* 20, no. 3 (1993).

92. S. Shellenbarger, "A Box? Or a Spaceship? What Makes Kids Creative," *The Wall Street Journal*, December 15, 2010.

93. Gil Richard Musolf, "Social Structure, Human Agency, and Social Policy," *The International Journal of Sociology and Social Policy* 23, no. 6/7 (2003): p. 1.

94. Ibid., p. 3.

95. Zaheer Baber, "Beyond the Structure/Agency Dualism: An Evaluation of Giddens' Theory of Structuration," *Sociological Inquiry* 61, no. 2 (1991).

96. Ibid., p. 223.

97. Stephan Fuchs, "Beyond Agency," *Sociological Theory* 19, no. 1 (2001): p. 39.

98. Sharon Hays, "Structure and Agency and the Sticky Problem of Culture," *Sociological Theory* 12 no. 1 (1994): p. 64.

99. Stephan Fuchs, "Beyond Agency," *Sociology Theory* 19, no. 1 (2001); Sharon Hays, "Structure and Agency and the Sticky Problem of Culture," *Sociological Theory* 12, no. 1 (1994).

100. Hays, "Structure and Agency and the Sticky Problem of Culture."

101. Erich Fromm, *On Disobedience and Other Essays* (New York: Seabury Press, 1981), p. 8.

102. Ibid., p. 21.

103. Ibid., p. 10.

104. Susan Greenfield, *Private Life of the Brain: Emotions, Consciousness, and the Secret of the Self* (New York: John Wiley, 2000); Eric R. Kandel, *In Search of Memory: The Emergence of a New Science of Mind*, 1st ed. (New York: Norton, 2006); Richard M. Restak, *The Naked Brain: How the Emerging Neurosociety Is Changing How We Live, Work, and Love*, 1st ed. (New York: Harmony Books, 2006).

105. M. A. Brillinger, "Brainstorming: How the Brain Science Can Inform Social Justice Groups" (Master's Thesis, Vancouver: University of British Columbia, 2014).

106. Kathleen E. Taylor, *Brainwashing: The Science of Thought Control* (Oxford: Oxford University Press, 2004).

107. Sam Harris, *The Moral Landscape: How Science Can Determine Human Values*, 1st Free Press hardcover ed. (New York: Free Press, 2010), p. 180.

108. Lindström, *Buyology: Truth and Lies about Why We Buy*.

109. Arthur Asa Berger, *Ads, Fads, and Consumer Culture: Advertising's Impact on American Character and Society*, 3rd ed. (Lanham: Rowman & Littlefield Publishers, 2007).

110. Cheri Hanson, "I Can No Longer Remember the Past," *Adbusters Journal of the Mental Environment* 11, no. 2 (2003).

111. Restak, *The Naked Brain: How the Emerging Neurosociety Is Changing How We Live, Work, and Love*.

112. John A. Bargh and Tanya L. Chartrand, "The Unbearable Automaticity of Being," *American Psychologist* 54, no. 7 (1999).

113. David Eagleman, *Incognito: The Secret Lives of the Brain* (Toronto: Viking Canada, 2011).

114. Robert Alan Burton, *On Being Certain: Believing You Are Right Even When You're Not*, 1st ed. (New York: St. Martin's Press, 2008).

115. Coleman, *Popular Delusions: How Social Conformity Molds Society and Politics*.

116. V. S. Ramachandran, *The Tell-Tale Brain: A Neuroscientist's Quest for What Makes Us Human*, 1st ed. (New York: W. W. Norton, 2011).

117. Lindström, *Buyology: Truth and Lies about Why We Buy*.

118. Ibid.

119. Ibid., p. 67.

120. "Smoking and Tobacco Use," Centers for Disease Control and Prevention (2013), http://www.cdc.gov/tobacco/data_statistics/fact_sheets/youth_data/movies/index.htm.

121. Eliezer J. Sternberg, *My Brain Made Me Do It: The Rise of Neuroscience and the Threat to Moral Responsibility* (Amherst, N.Y.: Prometheus Books, 2010), p. 69.

122. Lindström, *Buyology: Truth and Lies about Why We Buy*, p. 138.

123. Ibid.

124. Pratkanis and Aronson, *Age of Propaganda: The Everyday Use and Abuse of Persuasion*, p. 31.

CHAPTER 6

1. Howard K. Bloom, *The Genius of the Beast: A Radical Re-Vision of Capitalism* (Amherst, N.Y.: Prometheus Books, 2010), p. 19.

2. Ibid., p. 149.

3. Milton Friedman, "The Social Responsibility of Business Is to Increase Its Profits," *The New York Times Magazine*, September 13, 1970, http://www.colorado .edu/studentgroups/libertarians/issues/friedman-soc-resp-business.html.

4. Naomi Klein, *No Logo: Taking Aim at the Brand Bullies*, 1st ed. (Toronto: Knopf Canada, 2000).

5. Max Horkheimer and Theodor W. Adorno, *Dialectic of Enlightenment* (London: Allen Lane, 1973).

6. Theodor W. Adorno, *The Culture Industry: Selected Essays on Mass Culture* (London: Routledge, 1990).

7. Ibid.

8. Marshall McLuhan, *Understanding Media: The Extensions of Man*, 1st MIT Press ed. (Cambridge, Mass.: MIT Press, 1994), p. 7.

9. Adorno, *The Culture Industry: Selected Essays on Mass Culture*, p. 142.

10. Ibid., p. 138.

11. Theodor W. Adorno, *Critical Models: Interventions and Catchwords* (New York: Columbia University Press, 2005), p. 66.

12. Zizi Papacharissi and Andrew L. Mendelson, "An Exploratory Study of Reality Appeal: Uses and Gratifications of Reality TV Shows," *Journal of Broadcasting & Electronic Media* 51, no. 2 (2007).

13. Theodor W. Adorno, "On the Fetish-Character in Music and the Regression of Listening," in *The Essential Frankfurt School Reader*, ed. Andrew Arato and Eike Gerhardt (Oxford: Basil Blackwell, 1978).

14. Adorno, *The Culture Industry: Selected Essays on Mass Culture*.

15. Ibid., p. 33.

16. Horkheimer and Adorno, *Dialectic of Enlightenment*.

17. Ibid., p. 126.

18. Ibid., p. 131.

19. Ibid., p. 154.

20. Hal Niedzviecki, *Hello, I'm Special: How Individuality Became the New Conformity* (Toronto: Penguin Canada, 2004).

21. Ibid., p. 80.

22. Ibid., p. 79.

23. Ibid., p. 79.

24. Horkheimer and Adorno, *Dialectic of Enlightenment*, p. 125.

25. Ibid., p. 158.

26. Ibid., p. 124.

27. Ibid., p. 133.

28. Ibid., p. 142

29. Adorno, *The Culture Industry: Selected Essays on Mass Culture*, p. 85.

30. Ibid., p. 89.

31. Adorno, "On the Fetish-Character in Music and the Regression of Listening," p. 280.

32. *The Culture Industry: Selected Essays on Mass Culture*, p. 79.

33. Herbert Marcuse, *One Dimensional Man; Studies in the Ideology of Advanced Industrial Society* (Boston: Beacon Press, 1964).

34. Ibid., p. 3.

35. Ibid., pp. 4–5.

36. Ibid., pp. 112.

37. Ibid., p. 9.

38. Ibid., p. 14.

39. Ibid., p. 9.

40. Stuart Ewen, *Captains of Consciousness: Advertising and the Social Roots of the Consumer Culture* (New York: McGraw-Hill, 1976).

41. Ibid., p. 27.

42. Ibid., p. 30.

43. Ibid., p. 35.

44. Ibid., p. 37.

45. Ibid., p. 42.

46. Ibid., p. 46.

47. Ibid., p. 47.

48. Ibid., p. 54.

49. Ibid., p. 75.

50. Ibid., p. 83.

51. Ibid., p. 91.

52. Ibid., p. 92.

53. Ibid., p. 102.

54. Ibid., p. 136.

55. Ibid., p. 171.

56. Ibid., p. 184.

57. Ibid., pp. 202–203.

58. Gilles Deleuze, "Postscript on the Societies of Control," *October* 59 Winter (1992): p. 4.

59. Joel Bakan, *The Corporation: The Pathological Pursuit of Profit and Power* (New York: Free Press, 2004).

60. Horkheimer and Adorno, *Dialectic of Enlightenment*, pp. 166–167.

61. Ibid., pp. 133–134.

62. Benjamin R. Barber, *Consumed: How Markets Corrupt Children, Infantilize Adults, and Swallow Citizens Whole*, 1st ed. (New York: W. W. Norton & Co., 2007).

63. Ibid., p. 33.

64. Ibid., p. 87.

65. Ibid., p. 91.

66. Ibid., p. 99.

67. Ibid., p. 91.

68. Ibid., p. 108.

69. Ibid., p. 112.

70. Ibid., pp. 128–129.

71. Ibid., p. 167.

72. Ibid., p. 194.

73. Ibid., p. 213.

74. Ibid., p. 220.

75. Ibid., p. 247.

76. Bakan, *The Corporation: The Pathological Pursuit of Profit and Power*, p. 2.

77. Noam Chomsky, *Media Control: The Spectacular Achievements of Propaganda*, 2nd ed., An Open Media Book (New York: Seven Stories Press, 2002).

78. Sheldon S. Wolin, *Democracy Incorporated: Managed Democracy and the Specter of Inverted Totalitarianism* (Princeton, N.J.: Princeton University Press, 2008).

79. Ibid., p. xxi.

80. Ibid., p. xxii.

81. Ibid., p. xxiii.

82. Ibid., p. 7.

83. Michael Moore, *The Official Fahrenheit 9/11 Reader*, 1st Simon & Schuster Paperbacks ed. (New York: Simon & Schuster Paperbacks, 2004).

84. Wolin, *Democracy Incorporated: Managed Democracy and the Specter of Inverted Totalitarianism*, p. 44.

85. Ibid., p. 46.

86. Ibid., p. 54.

87. Bakan, *The Corporation: The Pathological Pursuit of Profit and Power*.

88. Wolin, *Democracy Incorporated: Managed Democracy and the Specter of Inverted Totalitarianism*, p. 57.

89. Ibid., pp. 139–140.

90. Michael Moore et al., *Capitalism: A Love Story* (Montreal: Alliance Vivafilm, 2009).

91. Chris Hedges, *Empire of Illusion: The End of Literacy and the Triumph of Spectacle* (New York: Nation Books, 2009), p. 138.

92. Kono Matsu, "The Cult You're In," *Adbusters Journal of the Mental Environment* 6, no. 2 (1998).

93. Horkheimer and Adorno, *Dialectic of Enlightenment*, p. 167.

94. Jason Hickel and Arsalan Khan, "The Culture of Capitalism and the Crisis of Critique," *Anthropological Quarterly* 85 (2012); Fernando Perez and Luigi Esposito, "The Global Addiction and Human Rights: Insatiable Consumerism, Neoliberalism, and Harm Reduction," *Perspectives on Global Development & Technology* 9, no. 1/2 (2010).

95. S. Kline, "Limits to the Imagination: Marketing and Children's Culture," in *Cultural Politics in Contemporary America*, ed. Ian H. Angus and Sut Jhally (New York: Routledge, 1989), p. 299.

96. Ibid., p. 315.

CHAPTER 7

1. Juliet M. Corbin and Anselm L. Strauss, *Basics of Qualitative Research: Techniques and Procedures for Developing Grounded Theory*, 3rd ed. (Thousand Oaks, Calif.: Sage Publications, 2008).

2. John W. Creswell, *Qualitative Inquiry & Research Design: Choosing among Five Approaches*, 2nd ed. (Thousand Oaks, Calif.: Sage Publications, 2007).

3. J. L. Kincheloe and P. McLaren, "Rethinking Critical Theory and Qualitative Research," in *The Sage Handbook of Qualitative Research*, ed. Norman Denzin and Yvonna Lincoln (Thousand Oaks, Calif.: Sage Publications, 2005).

4. A. Fontana and J. H. Frey, "The Interview from Neutral Stance to Political Involvement," in *The Sage Handbook of Qualitative Research*, ed. Norman K. Denzin and Yvonna S. Lincoln (Thousand Oaks, Calif.: Sage Publications, 2005).

5. Steinar Kvale, *Interviews: An Introduction to Qualitative Research Interviewing* (Thousand Oaks, Calif.: Sage Publications, 1996).

6. L. Crociani-Windland, "How to Live and Learn: Learning, Duration, and the Virtual," in *Researching beneath the Surface: Psycho-Social Research Methods in Practice*, ed. Simon Clarke and Paul Hoggett (London: Karnac, 2009), p. 69.

7. Michael Quinn Patton, *Qualitative Research and Evaluation Methods*, 3rd ed. (Thousand Oaks, Calif.: Sage Publications, 2002).

8. Yvonna S. Lincoln and Egon G. Guba, *Naturalistic Inquiry* (Beverly Hills, Calif.: Sage Publications, 1985).

9. Corbin and Strauss, *Basics of Qualitative Research: Techniques and Procedures for Developing Grounded Theory*.

10. K. Charmaz, "Grounded Theory in the 21st Century: Applications for Advancing Social Justice Studies," in *The Sage Handbook of Qualitative Research*, ed. Norman K. Denzin and Yvonna S. Lincoln (Thousand Oaks, Calif.: Sage Publications, 2005).

11. Corbin and Strauss, *Basics of Qualitative Research: Techniques and Procedures for Developing Grounded Theory*.

12. Ibid.

13. Norman Fairclough, *Analysing Discourse: Textual Analysis for Social Research* (London: Routledge, 2003).

14. Ibid., p. 205

15. Ibid.

16. Lincoln and Guba, *Naturalistic Inquiry*.

17. Egon G. Guba and Yvonna S. Lincoln, "Paradigmatic Controversies, Contradictions, and Emerging Confluences," in *The Sage Handbook of Qualitative Research*, ed. Norman K. Denzin and Yvonna S. Lincoln (Thousand Oaks, Calif.: Sage Publications, 2005), p. 208.

18. Ibid.

19. Ibid.

20. Lincoln and Guba, *Naturalistic Inquiry*, p. 124.

21. William A. Firestone, "Alternative Arguments for Generalizing from Data as Applied to Qualitative Research," *Educational Researcher* 22, no. 4 (1993).

22. Lincoln and Guba, *Naturalistic Inquiry*.

23. Ibid., p. 300.

24. Ibid.

25. Guba and Lincoln, "Paradigmatic Controversies, Contradictions, and Emerging Confluences."

26. Maureen Jane Angen, "Evaluating Interpretive Inquiry: Reviewing the Validity Debate and Opening the Dialogue," *Quality Health Research* 10, no. 3 (2000): p. 387.

27. Ibid.

CHAPTER 8

1. Jim Sidanius and Felicia Pratto, *Social Dominance: An Intergroup Theory of Social Hierarchy and Oppression* (Cambridge, UK: Cambridge University Press, 1999).

2. R. Williams, "Marxist Cultural Theory," in *Keyworks in Cultural Studies*, ed. Meenakshi Gigi Durham and Douglas Kellner (Malden, MA: Blackwell, 2006).

3. Howard K. Bloom, *The God Problem: How a Godless Cosmos Creates* (Amherst, N.Y.: Prometheus Books), p. 170.

4. Jane Pilcher, "No Logo? Children's Consumption of Fashion," *Childhood* 18, no. 1 (2011).

5. Helga Dittmar, "Are You What You Have?," *The Psychologist* 17, no. 4 (2004).

6. Lan Nguyen Chaplin and Deborah Roedder John, "The Development of Self-Brand Connections in Children and Adolescents," *Journal of Consumer Research* 32, no. 1 (2005): p. 119.

7. Rachel Russell and Melissa Tyler, "Branding and Bricolage: Gender, Consumption and Transition," *Childhood* 12, no. 2 (2005).

8. Edward L. Deci and Richard M. Ryan, *Intrinsic Motivation and Self-Determination in Human Behavior*, Perspectives in Social Psychology (New York: Plenum, 1985).

9. Jennifer Smith Maguire and Kim Stanway, "Looking Good," *European Journal of Cultural Studies* 11, no. 1 (2008).

10. Hillevi Ganetz, "Youth, Culture and Modernity," in *Youth Culture in Late Modernity*, ed. Johan Fornäs and Göran Bolin (London: Sage Publications, 1995).

11. Helga Dittmar, Emma Halliwell, and Suzanne Ive, "Does Barbie Make Girls Want to Be Thin? The Effect of Experimental Exposure to Images of Dolls on the Body Image of 5- to 8-Year-Old Girls," *Developmental Psychology* 42, no. 2 (2006); Helga Dittmar and Sarah Howard, "Professional Hazards? The Impact of Models' Body Size on Advertising Effectiveness and Women's Body-Focused Anxiety in Professions That Do and Do Not Emphasize the Cultural Ideal of Thinness," *British Journal of Social Psychology* 43, no. 4 (2004).

12. Ganetz, "Youth, Culture and Modernity."

13. Dawn Currie, *Girl Talk: Adolescent Magazines and Their Readers* (Toronto: University of Toronto Press, 1999).

14. Michael Billig, "Commodity Fetishism and Repression," *Theory & Psychology* 9, no. 3 (1999).

15. Richard Kahn, "Producing Crisis: Green Consumerism as an Ecopedagogical Issue," in *Critical Pedagogies of Consumption*, ed. J.A. Sandlin and P. McLaren (Los Angeles: Routledge, 2010).

16. "2011 Teens and Money Survey," *Charles Schwab & Co. Inc.* (2011), http://www.aboutschwab.com/images/press/teensmoneyfactsheet.pdf.

17. Sharon Boden, "Dedicated Followers of Fashion? The Influence of Popular Culture on Children's Social Identities," *Media, Culture & Society* 28, no. 2 (2006).

18. Michel Boivin et al., "Early Childhood Development" (The Royal Society of Canada & The Canadian Academy of Health Sciences Expert Panel, 2012), p. 2.

19. Robert Alan Burton, *On Being Certain: Believing You Are Right Even When You're Not*, 1st ed. (New York: St. Martin's Press, 2008); David Eagleman, *Incognito: The Secret Lives of the Brain* (Toronto: Viking Canada, 2011); Kathleen E. Taylor, *Brainwashing: The Science of Thought Control* (Oxford: Oxford University Press, 2004).

20. Michael Shermer, *The Believing Brain* (New York: Times Books/Henry Holt & Co., 2011).

21. Susan Linn, *Consuming Kids: The Hostile Takeover of Childhood* (New York: New Press; distributed by W. W. Norton & Co., 2004).

22. Robert Chernomas and Ian Hudson, *Social Murder: And Other Shortcomings of Conservative Economics* (Winnipeg: Arbeiter Ring Pub., 2007); Naomi Klein, *This Changes Everything: Capitalism vs. the Climate* (London: Allen Lane, 2014); Kalle Lasn et al., *Meme Wars: The Creative Destruction of Neoclassical Economics*, A Seven Stories Press first edition. (New York: Seven Stories Press, 2012); Yves Smith,

Econned: How Unenlightened Self Interest Undermined Democracy and Corrupted Capitalism, 1st ed. (New York: Palgrave Macmillan, 2010).

23. James E. Hansen, *Storms of My Grandchildren: The Truth about the Coming Climate Catastrophe and Our Last Chance to Save Humanity*, Pbk. ed. (New York: Bloomsbury, 2009); Bill McKibben, *Earth: Making a Life on a Tough New Planet*, 1st ed. (New York: Times Books, 2010).

24. Klein, *This Changes Everything: Capitalism vs. The Climate*.

25. Ibid., p. 89.

26. Chrystia Freeland, *Plutocrats: The Rise of the New Global Super-Rich and the Fall of Everyone Else* (2012).

27. Chris Hedges, "Zero Point of Systemic Collapse," *Adbusters* (2010).

28. Paul Hawken, *Blessed Unrest: How the Largest Movement in the World Came into Being, and Why No One Saw It Coming* (New York: Viking, 2007).

29. Sam Harris, *Free Will*, 1st Free Press trade pbk. ed. (New York: Free Press, 2012).

30. Jerry Mander, "Privatization of Consciousness," *Monthly Review* 64 (2012): p. 5.

31. Susan Greenfield, *Private Life of the Brain: Emotions, Consciousness and the Secret of the Self* (New York: John Wiley, 2000), p. 57.

32. Shermer, *The Believing Brain*.

33. Susan Greenfield, *Id: The Quest for Identity in the 21st Century* (London: Sceptre, 2008), p. 10.

34. Howard K. Bloom, *The Global Brain: The Evolution of the Mass Mind from the Big Bang to the 21st Century* (New York: Wiley, 2000).

35. Ibid., p. 42.

36. Tim Kasser et al., "Target Article: Some Costs of American Corporate Capitalism: A Psychological Exploration of Value and Goal Conflicts," *Psychological Inquiry* 18, no. 1 (2007).

37. Ibid., p. 8.

38. Tim Kasser et al., "Some Costs of American Corporate Capitalism: A Psychological Exploration of Value and Goal Conflicts," *Psychological Inquiry* 18, no. 1 (2007).

39. Ibid.

Index

About the Author

Jennifer Hill has a PhD in interdisciplinary studies from the University of British Columbia Okanagan. She has worked with adults and children in a variety of settings over a period of 20 years as both a consultant and therapist. Currently, she is self-employed and is planning to deliver lectures and workshops on consumer culture. Dr. Hill cofounded the media awareness nonprofit "Who Minds the Child?" at whomindsthechild.org. She published her first book, *Sad without Tears*, in 2009. She resides in British Columbia, Canada, with her husband.

About the Series Editor
and Advisors

SERIES EDITOR

Sharna Olfman, PhD, is a clinical psychologist and professor of psychology in the Department of Humanities at Point Park University. Her books include *The Science and Pseudoscience of Children's Mental Health* (2015), *Drugging Our Children* (2012), *The Sexualization of Childhood* (2008), *Bipolar Children* (2007), *Child Honoring: How To Turn This World Around* (coedited with Raffi Cavoukian, 2006), *Childhood Lost . . . How American Culture Is Failing Our Kids* (2005), and *All Work and No Play . . . How Educational Reforms Are Harming Our Preschoolers* (2004). She has written and lectured internationally on the subjects of children's mental health and parenting. She was the founder and director of the annual Childhood and Society Symposium, a multidisciplinary think tank on childhood advocacy from 2001 to 2008.

ADVISORS

Joan Almon is coordinator of the U.S. branch of the Alliance for Childhood, and co-chair of the Waldorf Early Childhood Association of North America. She is internationally renowned as consultant to Waldorf educators and training programs, and she is the author of numerous articles on Waldorf education.

Jane M. Healy has appeared on most major media in the United States and is frequently consulted regarding the effects of new technologies on the developing brain. She holds a PhD in educational psychology from Case Western University and has done postdoctoral work in developmental neuropsychology. Formerly on the faculties of Cleveland State University and John Carroll University, she is internationally recognized as a lecturer and a consultant with many years experience as a classroom teacher, reading/learning specialist, and elementary administrator. She is author of numerous articles, as well as the books *Endangered Minds: Why Our Children Don't Think and What We Can Do about It* (1999), *How to Have an Intelligent and Creative Conversation with Your Kids* (1994), *Your Child's Growing Mind: A Guide to Learning and Brain Development from Birth to Adolescence* (1994), and *Failure to Connect: How Computers Affect Our Children's Minds—For Better or Worse* (1998).

Stuart Shanker, PhD Oxon, is a distinguished professor of philosophy and psychology at York University in Toronto. He is, with Stanley Greenspan, co-director of the Council of Human Development and associate chair for Canada of the Interdisciplinary Council of Learning and Developmental Disorders. He has won numerous awards and currently holds grants from the Unicorn Foundation, the Templeton Foundation, and Cure Autism Now. His books include *The First Idea: How Symbols, Language, and Intelligence Evolved from Our Primate Ancestors to Modern Humans* (2004), *Toward a Psychology of Global Interdependency* (2002), and *Wittgenstein's Remarks on the Foundations of Animal Intelligence* (1998).

Meredith F. Small, PhD, is a writer and professor of anthropology at Cornell University. Trained as a primate behaviorist, she now writes about all areas of anthropology, natural history, and health. Besides numerous publications in academic journals, Dr. Small contributes regularly to *Discover* and *New Scientist*, and she is a commentator on National Public Radio's "All Things Considered." She is the author of five books, including *What's Love Got to Do with it? The Evolution of Human Mating (1996); Our Babies, Ourselves: How Biology and Culture Shape the Way We Parent (1999);* and *Kids: How Biology and Culture Shape the Way We Parent (2001, paperback 2002).*